EDGE *of*
BLUE HEAVEN

EDGE *of* BLUE HEAVEN

A journey through Mongolia

Benedict Allen

PHOTOGRAPHS BY ADRIAN ARBIB
AND BENEDICT ALLEN

To Suzie, negotiating your own mountains, steppes and deserts

This book is published to accompany the BBC television series
Edge of Blue Heaven broadcast in 1998
Executive Producer: Bob Long
Producer: Salim Salam

Published by BBC Worldwide Limited,
Woodlands, 80 Wood Lane, London W12 0TT

First published 1998

ISBN: 0 563 38375 5

Commissioning Editor: Anna Ottewill
Copy Editor: Emma Shackleton
Designer: Isobel Gillan
Cartographer: Olive Pearson

Photographs by Benedict Allen on pages:
2/3, 10, 15, 18/19, 26, 30/31, 34, 38, 42, 43, 47, 50/51, 54, 70/71, 74,
75, 110/111, 127, 130, 134, 138/139, 143, 146, 147, 150, 159, 162/163,
179, 182, 183, 191, 198/199, 206/207, 214, 218/219, 223, 226, 234,
235, 242

All other photographs by Adrian Arbib

Photograph on page 2 and 3: Desert steppe on the Gobi margins
of south-west Mongolia.

Set in Granjon
Printed in Great Britain by Cambus Litho Limited, East Kilbride
Bound in Great Britain by Hunter and Foulis, Edinburgh
Colour separations by Radstock Reproductions Limited,
Midsomer Norton
Jacket printed by Lawrence Allen Limited,
Weston-super-Mare

CONTENTS

Map of Mongolia • 6

Preface • 8

chapter one
KILLING WEATHER • 11

chapter two
MAKE HASTE SLOWLY • 27

chapter three
PEOPLE OF THE EAGLE AND BEYOND • 39

chapter four
DEALINGS WITH NOMADS • 59

chapter five
THE GUARDIAN CROW • 79

chapter six
THE THREE GERS • 95

chapter seven
'THE FLIES, THE FLIES' • 119

chapter eight
RUNNING REPAIRS • 135

chapter nine
KERMIT FADING • 155

chapter ten
SPIRITS OF THE LIMITLESS FIELDS • 171

chapter eleven
MUTINY • 187

chapter twelve
THROUGH AMBER LIGHT • 215

A Short History of Mongolia • 239

Select Bibliography • 248

Acknowledgements • 250

Index • 253

MONGOLIA

PREFACE

Why Mongolia? To start from first principles, to me exploration isn't about many of the sort of things we've come to expect: conquering nature, planting flags or even about science, if that only means extending our Western understanding of the world. In other words, it's not about going where no-one's gone before in order to leave your mark. It's about the opposite of that, about making yourself vulnerable, opening yourself up to whatever's there and letting the place leave its mark on you.

In short, the word explorer has been misappropriated – or, if not misappropriated, at least mislaid. It's become associated with the past, not the present, and with people who might be described as conquerors as much as discoverers. But, whether we are Iban hunters of Borneo or Zurich bankers, we are all explorers. Our desire to see what's around the next corner is there from birth. And, perhaps, simply because I was from a family of travellers, and have always been particularly restless, I seem to have a bit more of this desire than is usual – I don't need much of an excuse to pack my bags.

And where more alluring to explore than a country which from out of nowhere set about and almost succeeded in conquering every major power in the world, and accidentally brought along the bubonic plague with their armies and ended up killing one in three of our ancestors? Later, having had a nasty dose of the Black Death themselves, the Chinese felt inclined to build the Great Wall, the world's largest man-made structure, to keep them out.

The Mongols touched everyone then, and they are touching us now. To us Europeans, the Mongol word 'horde' is, even after all these centuries, the very definition of a rampaging force. In Turkish, the word has come to signify 'army' and in the Indian subcontinent has given rise to 'Urdu', the name of what was once just the army language. It was in India too that the word 'Mongol' was adopted by their distant descendants, the Moguls, to suggest formidable strength.

Here are some diary extracts leading to my decision to visit the Mongols of today:

Drizzle over Shepherd's Bush. I walked down the road to the cashpoint machine and queued behind a couple of girls, one of whom was trying to extract some cash from it. The machine snatched her card and kept it. 'I don't believe it,' she muttered to her girlfriend. 'Might as well be in Outer Mongolia,' They wandered forlornly away.

Eventually, no cash for me either, I was on my way to Hammersmith library. I was still thinking of Outer Mongolia, this land of (allegedly) no cash point machines. Like Timbuktoo, the place defines for us what we mean by remote or out of touch. Horsemen, nomads of the steppe, Genghis Khan... It is a faraway place, never-never land. I found myself wondering whether the real Outer Mongolia has cashpoint facilities?

I looked up the word Mongolia in a few encyclopedias but there's an almost total absence of source material in English. I discovered that about half the population still live in 'gers', felt tents, which we think of as yurts, the Russian name, and that almost everyone has relatives in them. So, oddly enough, Mongols do actually exist out there in the grassland steppe just as they do in our imagination. Furthermore, 'Chinggis Khan' still crops up in conversation out there, and on banknotes and vodka bottles.

Almost eight centuries after his death, the medieval warlord is still a symbol of unity and hope as, with the break up of the Soviet Union, the country obtained formal independence in 1990 and is now beginning to come out from behind Russia's iron curtain.

I would love to go there right now. Never mind cashpoint facilities, the last time Mongols emerged from nowhere they brought the Islamic powers to their knees, conquered China and came within a hair's breadth of destroying Europe. Which direction are they going in now?

Rang the Mongolian Embassy in Kensington. The man answering sounded suspicious. 'Yes?' I told him I was an author and film maker and was hoping I might get permission to travel alone through their beautiful and very special country. 'Oh well,' the voice said sadly. He seemed to be about to hang up. I pressed on. 'Can you offer any advice?'

'I'm afraid you will have to request officially,' he said, sounding rather sorry for me. I had vision of soul-destroying Soviet-bequeathed bureaucracy – applications submitted in triplicate, then re-submitted after a month's wait because the first lot were mislaid. The voice added, now kindly, like a teacher offering a hint: 'It might help to ask in person.'

'Travel all the way to Mongolia to ask permission to go there?' I chuckled amicably. 'It won't really come to that, will it?'

There was an awkward silence.

chapter one

KILLING WEATHER

*For the moment, the only sheet anchor that
binds together the entire population is the ever-powerful
figure of their once-great Genghis Khan.*

Robert Marshall on the departure of the Soviet overlords from present-day Mongolia,
STORM FROM THE EAST, *1993*

ON A PLANE TO MONGOLIA: Soon we'll be coming into land, and I'm not sure I want to. It's winter down there and all I've seen so far of Mongolia is a 100-kilometre snowdrift. Not a tree even trying. People are actually living in those conditions! It's all so blatantly aggressive – not the slow debilitating abundance of rain forest, nor the stark hot desert, which at least offer hope at dusk and dawn. Nothing but cold – the infamous Mongolian winter. 'Killing weather', the Russian passenger sitting next to me called it – he hadn't even started on his vodka then.

10th December

The weather will improve. I'm only here to ask permission to come back again in February, to begin building my expedition. But where do I begin? I mean, Mongolia is an island cut off by the Altai mountains, the wastes of Siberia and the Gobi Desert, not to mention two superpowers, Russia and China. The Mongolians are not, it seems, an easy people for us outsiders to understand – and I don't just mean because of their exasperating language. Jeremy, the Aeroflot rep. at Heathrow, had been sent to Ulaanbaatar to train staff at MIAT, the national airline. 'Six weeks of unadulterated misery,' he exclaimed. 'It was a rout. Talked among themselves, disputing and conferring. They were nomads, not airport staff,' he concluded with a sad little sigh. 'Nothing I could do.'

I am reliant on one local contact, someone called 'Ogi' who's a friend of Nara, a Mongolian student I tracked down in Notting Hill Gate, back in London. She promised me that Ogi would be at the airport

*Left: To the west
of Lake Khövsgöl,
two gers (yurts in
Russian), the felt
tents which are
home to half the
population of
Mongolia.*

without fail. I rather hope so because in Mongolia, apparently, you 'don't so often have taxis,' you just flag down a passing car – I'm picturing myself standing around in 'killing weather' flagging down passing cars and asking them in sign language for a ride to a centrally positioned, clean but cheapish hotel. I decided I'd better start building up contacts straightaway. I asked my Russian neighbour – for he seemed to have sobered up – what he was going to be doing in Mongolia.

'I …' the Russian managed, 'repair runway.'

'You repair runway?' I asked, suspicious. 'What's wrong with it?'

But he was looking longingly over his shoulder, beyond an assortment of clean-cut Mongolians in out-moded suits, to a drinking party of Czechs and Ukrainians, who'd assembled in the back of the aircraft, turning it into a smoky saloon bar. Representatives of the entire former Soviet Union seem to be on this aeroplane to help Mongolia with construction projects. In fact, it looks like there are also consultants from Japan, North America, South Korea, and just about every G7 nation.

I had another try with my Mongolian language cassette course – ordered from the United States at great expense. I've already devoted hours to it, and even the English translation isn't grammatically correct. The course sounds home-made, a sleepy American professor whose voice is frail and sometimes lets out a squeak. And in the background there are all sorts of strange thumpings – a despairing neighbour in the flat upstairs?

LATER: We started our final approach. Down below, I could see the first 'gers', the felt tents, and they were packed around by snow. Just discernible were little figures trying to dig themselves out.

'At least it isn't a blizzard,' I told myself. 'That is, not technically.' As I watched, visibility declined sharply.

Then we were touching down and the Aeroflot airhostess announced in Russian, and with a degree of resignation, that we had arrived. She then said something about the outside temperature.

My Russian neighbour opened his eyes. 'Eighteen,' he said in English. 'Much satisfaction.' He smiled, contentedly. After a moment I realised he meant minus 18 degrees.

'Thank God,' a British consultant added, wrestling with his overhead locker. 'Looks like Mongolia's enjoying a warm spell.'

No-one hurried off the plane … The G7 nationals gathered their briefcases with practised aplomb and the men from the former Soviet

Union knocked back the last vodka and tried to orientate themselves. Delay as everyone dressed up for outside, then the walk out across the runway. I was reminded of a cracked glacier I once crossed with crampons in northern Iceland. My ears were burning – everyone else had somehow produced a hat from somewhere. We made it indoors, and I peered at the crowd of locals pressing on the glass door: Mongols, people that school children across Europe hold in awe, even now. This lot were impatient to be reunited with relatives – a bee swarm of hectic bodies, all in fur and wool. Some were wearing the leather boots with curled toes that Genghis Khan himself might have favoured, while others were in the Mongol del, the tunic you see in depictions of the Golden Horde – a natty robe fixed with silver buttons at the right shoulder, a silken sash wound around the waist. I saw a man answering to the description of 'Ogi' – cheery round face, glasses. He was there looking out for me among the overcoats and furs. I manoeuvred my luggage trolley towards him through the throng – a smell of mutton.

'Well, this is Mongolia!' he said, commandeering a car and sweeping me into it. 'So, what are your immediate plans?'

I said that I was afraid I had no plans for the moment other than to talk to the Ministry of External Relations. 'I have an appointment for 9.30 tomorrow.'

He nodded, knowingly.

A lorry trundled by, its engine protected by a shaggy cowskin. There was a jeep by the roadside, a bonfire under it to ease off the ice. An escapee cow wearing a coat was being prodded homeward. I told Ogi, who it turns out, works for a British company which analyses mineral samples, that when the summer comes, my plan is to travel by horse and camel through the three major divisions of Mongolia. To set out from the mountainous forests adjacent to Siberia in the north, accumulating skills as I head down through the steppe – the level, treeless plains – so that I'll be ready to cross the third zone, the Gobi Desert.

'I don't think it will be all that easy,' he said simply, as a horse ridden, it looked like, by a toddler, cantered across the road. 'Even for a Mongolian.'

That was rather what I was starting to think. But at least I did now have one ally out here – Ogi. He was the first building block of my expedition – not a great chatterer, but amiable. He'd be patient with me, I thought.

Ulaanbaatar was ahead of us, crouching under a neat cloud of blue pollution. A Soviet power station was puffing out steam inconsiderately over the capital, which consisted of skyscrapers and dull residential flats that looked like prison blocks. In addition, creeping up the northern hills like creamy toadstools, the Mongolian tents, the gers, each protected by a wooden fence.

'So, this will be my Headquarters,' I thought, looking for signs of the office life that you would expect to find in any of the world's capital cities apart from Mogadishu. I said, 'Public telephones?'

'Eight, I think.'

'What about post offices?'

'One. That's where the eight telephones are.'

Conversation continued like this for a while: 'Fruit and vegetables scarce in the winter… milk available only in the morning …' By now it seemed a bit pointless to ask if Mongolians used cashpoint machines.

'Streets aren't signposted,' Ogi went on. 'Nor are towns, often.'

But there was more to this place than met the eye. Ogi turned out to have a mobile phone dug deep inside his coat, which chirruped from time to time. He asked if I was 'regularly on the internet' – I wasn't – or if I at least had an e-mail address – I haven't. Affluent Mongolians, it seems, have found a way of circumventing the Russian system. The rest of the country, I suspected, wouldn't be left far behind.

We drew up at a housing block. In front, taking up the full pavement, was an ice-slide, lovingly maintained by children. Ogi took me into a dark stairwell and upstairs to the flat he'd kindly arranged. He unlocked an outer door, then an inner, heavy door padded for insulation. We were met by a blast of heat. It had been minus 18 degrees in the stairway, here it felt like plus 35. 'There's nothing we can do about that,' Ogi said, as we dumped down my bags. 'If I open a window you'll wake up covered in snow.' I suggested turning off a radiator or two. It wasn't that simple. The central heating was a triumph of the socialist era – no taps, and every radiator plumbed to a central plant. It had been ordained that Ulaanbaatar's heating would be turned off on 15th May – whether at that time there was a heatwave or Siberian chill. No wonder the Soviet Union collapsed – it was the heating bill.

However, the flat was tidy and cosy, and central, and I also had my own phone. I couldn't have asked for more.

Ogi took me round the corner to get some basic supplies. 'That means shop,' he said, pointing to a word in the Russian, i.e. Cyrillic, script scrawled like graffiti over a narrow doorway in the apartment wall. Sure enough, a youth came out carrying a cow leg over his shoulder. Inside, I found myself peering with polite and quiet children at four shelves. They displayed two more chunks of cow, a hundred or so bottles of vodka, a thousand or so loo rolls and two potatoes and five, maybe six, carrots. The serving lady didn't seem keen to part with any of them.

'She's a relict of the Russian times,' Ogi said, as if referring to a statue.

'But this is all changing fast.' He took me outside to a street kiosk, the new spirit of free enterprise. We bought some Czech biscuits, tea and three small sweet, frost-bitten apples.

And now I'm back in my flat, sitting here with my diary, trying to make sense of my day: a capital city without telephone boxes, a shop with a thousand loo rolls and a red and blue national flag which expresses the Mongolian land and spirit – proudly incorporating a medieval geometric design, the soyombo – but which flies over a city that is an exported chunk of Moscow.

I do understand one thing: in Mongolia, almost nothing is as it first seems to outsiders. The 'Mongolian' on the language tape is even more

Below:
Ulaanbaatar at minus 33 degrees Celsius. The capital city is like a piece of Moscow transplanted to the steppe, but this is still largely a place of nomads and, beyond the drab apartment blocks, traditional tents form the suburbs.

incomprehensible than normal and is probably from Inner Mongolia, to the south – what is now part of China. The shoeshine boys, whom you can't help but feel sorry for, actually earn $40 per month – more than teachers. There's not one supermarket in the capital, but shoppers proudly carry plastic bags marked 'Sainsbury's' – bags rejected by the UK.

Evening: I keep falling asleep with the headphones on, still listening to my Mongolian tape, still unable to speak a word.

11th December

Woke this morning at 9.30, half an hour late for my appointment with the Ministry of External Relations – the meeting I'd travelled across Europe and Asia to attend. I couldn't run to the ministry – the ice. Arrived breathless, bursting through formal main doors and found myself in an austere and splendid hall, with an oil painting of a horseman dwarfed by precipitous purple mountains. A policeman at the reception desk was looking me up and down so I proffered the bit of paper on which Ogi had thoughtfully written Mr Gansukh's name in Cyrillic script.

Mr Gansukh came up – cheerful, fresh face – looking at his watch. 'You know, up until recently, we were closed.'

'Oh, I thought I was late.'

'I mean Mongolia,' Mr Gansukh said. 'Up until recently, we were closed.' Over the course of our conversation I began to realise that Mr Gansukh was sympathetic to my project, but had been asked by the Old Guard to get me to talk it over again. No-one had ever been allowed to film for months on end, wandering alone so far off into Mongolia. So I talked over my previous books and films, and how I was so grateful to Mongolia for giving me this chance. Everything seemed to be going well.

'Good,' Mr Gansukh said, suddenly standing up.

'I have permission?'

'I mean to say, good, now I feel completely ready to discuss the matter with the Ministry of Education, the former Ministry of Enlightenment, and security police, formerly the KGB.'

'KGB?'

'You can please return on Monday, when I have completed a visit to my mother in the countryside.'

'And then?'

'And then, everything will be ready for discussion.'

It seems that we haven't even begun.

As I walked back home, for the first time a stranger said 'hello' – a small boy who giggled into his scarf afterwards. Otherwise, passing the young and old I got nothing. They just bumped into me, their vision obscured by hats and coat collars.

3 P.M.: Now I've made a cup of tea, and tried out the telly. There are two channels: Eagle TV, a digest of American culture produced by American missionaries, and Mongolian Television. This gave a round-up of views from snow-bound herders across the nation, then an item about a Mongol wrestling match – muscled, square-shaped men locked together, walked like crabs, with their feet encased by large leather boots, and did victory dances at the end of each bout, their arms slowly flapping outstretched as eagle wings. It was splendid, but, as usual, perplexing and round them an audience of men who looked like the politburo on a day out.

3.30 P.M.: Outside, women and men are trying to break up the packed ice. Ragamuffin children are picking at a skip of rubbish – they've already taken the lightbulbs from the stairway. They live wherever they can, sometimes even popping up from manholes. The Russians have gone, and with it social support. The Mongolians are left with the physical remnants – school buildings, hospitals – and, if the other passers-by are anything to go by, the habit of drinking vodka.

I'm still hoping to go back to England next week with some sort of understanding of what on earth is going on out here. All I can do for the moment is hang on, trying to breath slowly and deeply, like someone with a stress disorder.

4 P.M.: Ogi came round and asked what I had achieved so far. I told him that I had achieved nothing at all so far, and that I just wanted to get out into the countryside I'll be journeying through, be out under these famous, huge blue skies. I'd heard that you can hear your breath freeze and then cascade as ice crystals to the ground, but all I've seen so far is this strange dull city, and it's making me wonder why I ever wanted to come to Mongolia. Quite honestly, I was beginning to understand why the urban Mongolians drink. To cheer me up Ogi talked about the Mongol horses, hundreds of thousands of them out there in minus 30 or 40 degrees, able to make do without so much as a horse blanket or sugar lump between them. In the Gobi Desert, camels take the place of horses and also take on the duties of dogs as well. 'They say that they automatically herd sheep a little,' he told me, 'but they also guard homes while the owner is away.' Recently a man had gone to visit his neighbour

and been sat on by his friend's camel. He probably tried to talk the camel out of it, but the camel was proud, the camel was defiant: he wouldn't let him go for seven days. By then it was too late: he was a block of ice.

The moral of the story? I'm not sure. But I get the feeling the urban Mongolians bring up the subject of the countryside when life in the apartment blocks is getting too much. It acts like a sanctuary, a balm to the nomadic spirit, which is oppressed here in Ulaanbaatar but still alive.

Right: *The images foreigners bring from Mongolia tend to be of summer when conditions for travel are favourable. But summer is only three months long, and this is perhaps a more typical scene – the long, fierce winter which is never far from the herder's mind.*

According to an article I read back in the UK the jobless young, disillusioned by the capital city, are returning to the countryside, and that this is good news for Mongolia. The truth is that, yes indeed, the young are going back to the provinces, but they have lost their shepherding skills and it's leading to overgrazing. NOTHING is as it seems at first to the foreigner. Another example? Look around you and you see apparent poverty – yet in Mongolia there's a higher incidence of

gonorrhoea than dysentery. And so I find myself stalking Mongolia. It's an elusive creature, and, like an amoeba which changes form, it keeps re-inventing itself, no Westerner quite seems to have a grasp of it.

Tonight, I'll go along to the Emon, one of the new bars that has sprung up. It's in the interests of research – well, partly. There's also Matisse, Motor Rock, Hollywood, Top Ten, but the Emon has, the British embassy warned, 'a reputation'. It's why I'm going there. I'd like to see a colour other than grey in this exported Russian city.

EVENING: I walked into the bar – empty disco floor. It was 10 p.m. – too early.

Sat alone in the corner, sipping beer sheepishly, thinking over what the British consul had said … 'Word of advice. If your feet touch someone else's, even while dancing, shake their hands. It shows you meant no disrespect. Don't worry, it'll be instinctive after a while.'

Girls in high heels took the orders. Around were dotted Mongolians, the young urban elite of Mongolia, some of them perhaps Ogi's acquaintances. They wore dapper cashmere scarves and years before had been dispatched abroad by the Communist government. It was the same for students throughout the Soviet Union: Cuba for dentists, Czechoslovakia, Hungary and Germany for engineering, Leningrad and Moscow for musicians. Many also came to Mongolia, though I'm not sure what they'd have learnt in Ulaanbaatar.

Consultants came in in dribs and drabs and looked relieved to see another Westerner here – one of their own. They made their way over to me.

'Bit thin on the ground tonight. In winter the professional girls fly south to Korea, like migrating birds. Come back in the tourist season, such as it is: four to every man.'

The Mongolians were muttering, and it was about us. Consultants are regarded as suspect – as bad as missionaries. They are both imperialists. Having got rid of the Russians, and probably now seen off the Chinese, they are facing a new threat: us lot. Through our bank loans, we are steering Mongolia just the way we want it. Besides, the consultants drive in Landcruisers, rather than freezing in Russian jeeps like everyone else, and now word is going around that four varieties of melon were dished up for the recent World Bank conference. Whatever the truth about their luxury life, the foreigners here don't look well on it. Like me they've come out tonight to let their hair down and make sense of the confusions which have beset their day.

A British consultant, out here repairing the airport runway, politely showed the bar girl how to pour beer into a glass without it frothing. He let her do the next glass herself, and she did it just the same as before, but quicker. We watched in dismay as the froth rose up, out of the glass, and flowed across the table.

'God these people are proud,' the consultant said with admiration, as she triumphantly strutted away in her black heels.

The music was from the Bee Gees, Beatles, Smoky Robinson – just right for the Mongolians who'd known the bars of Eastern Europe and also the consultants, who were in their early forties and didn't want, or couldn't manage, anything too strenuous.

Though Mongolia does have its own urban music scene – groups such as 'Blue Sky' – there was a collective sigh of appreciation as the first bars of dated foreign hits came through the loudspeakers, instead. Suzy Quatro was my pin-up girl once – in her leathers, her giant guitar swinging from her hips – but I was then aged ten. Now she's arrived in Mongolia and is worshipped afresh, almost thirty years late. The youngest Mongolians sat in one corner, excited by this sound of the future, the outside world, while the expats and older Mongolians slouched in other corners, reminiscing.

Meanwhile, in conversation with fellow Europeans it became apparent that the consultants, who have millions of dollars to spend on their ten-day trip while I have only five hundred, have learned no more about the modern Mongolian than I:

A stout German, unpicking a 'professional girl''s hand from his lapel: 'Zer Mongol sees himself as zee most European of zer Asians. But are zey really? ZAT is zer question.'

British consultant: 'They are a confused people, still scarred by the Stalinist purges. They do not know what they are.'

Dutch consultant: 'They have a veneer of Russia, and how deep it runs we in the West are waiting to see. Certainly, each and every Mongol has Genghis Khan in the back of their minds and they are waiting for another Genghis to lead them to greatness again.'

They are fumbling about with theories as am I, trying to understand what's going on as Mongolians adjust to the demands of the outside world. The girls, at least, were well practised at the market economy. They were draped around some of the best-maintained stomachs in Europe, working on regaining some money for Mongolia. In the light of the current invasion of Mongolia by us, it seemed almost patriotic.

I made my excuses and headed to the loo. It had a single door, revealing peeing men every time someone entered or left. After, as I stood by the bar, a clutch of VSO workers came up. 'There you are!'

'You've been looking for me?'

'We tend to keep an eye on each other,' explained Jenny. A teacher for two years, she was something of a veteran in Mongolia. 'Are you familiar with the situation here? When the Mongolians get drunk they sometimes become very anti-foreigner. Men have not infrequently been beaten up in the loo.'

I could quite see why a Mongolian would sock a consultant who probably had $200 per day in expenses and definitely a seventeen-year-old Mongolian girl around his neck. But, as usual in Mongolia, it seemed the true story was more complicated. Jenny was referring to an incident involving not a wealthy consultant but an impoverished young VSO worker, and it was not jealousy over a girl but over a Mongolian's hat, which the VSO worker had moved off a seat and onto the ground.

'He was hospitalised,' Jenny said, with impressive brevity.

'Out here,' another VSO worker chipped in, 'you don't ever step over someone's hat, or treat it with disrespect. Without a hat, you can die. Like boots, they are a piece of your body.'

Smoky Robinson stopped abruptly: time for the 'fashion show'. A girl strutted up to the platform, into the white light, wearing what might be a rent-open cosmonaut suit. Silver material glittered from her limbs – less and less of it as she gyrated. Finally, she was topless, examining her breasts and rubbing her cosmonaut panties up and down a pole. Then, unexpectedly, the spotlight abruptly switched off. The consultants let out a unanimous sigh of frustration.

Soon I was walking home, Bee Gees fading into the night. 'My God,' I thought, as I swerved the drunks. 'Who are these people, the Mongolians?' A man walking by spat, laboriously, and the spit froze into a mini-slab as it spread on the pavement. And I might have given up on Mongolia, there and then, but there was a ray of hope: the Mongolians themselves. The city people of Indonesia, New Guinea, Brazil, Britain and all around the world dismiss their countryside brethren as slow, as backward, but not one Mongolian had talked disrespectfully of the ordinary herders, the country people who live out there in tents. They are seen as equals or superiors – the people who exist much as they did at the foundation of Mongolia under Genghis Khan – as if they are the true spirit of Mongolia, keeping it alive, despite all that the Russians and we have done.

Today I broke out of Ulaanbaatar – at last. David Pearson, who's from 14th December TACIS, a European aid group, took one look at me last night and said, 'You, Benedict, need to get out. We all do, once in a while.' So he picked me up in his four-wheel drive this morning and drove me, with VSO friends, out through the hills to where the roads were lost to snow, then on to where the snow itself had been spun aside by the screaming wind. We stopped at a river, a fixed ribbon of ice that bulged like blown glass at the outer edges of bends. A nuthatch ascended a birch. A Eurasian jay swooped over the larches. An azure-winged magpie alighted on a cow carcass, locked in the ice and held deep frozen. It was safe for the time being, entombed as it will be for another four months, until the spring when the waters run again and the cow will be released, as if from someone's deep freeze, for the awaiting magpie.

'I need not go further than here,' I thought. Why traipse all through Mongolia? But in this country, though the sky waits over you, the land ushers you on. It is extraordinary, perhaps a function of the crisp Mongolian air, empty of moisture, which offers views to places on the farest horizon, and skies that stretch beyond that horizon.

We couldn't stay long. It was minus 26 and dropping fast. We stopped for a quick cup of tea and I watched the tea bag freeze into a block as it was lifted from the steaming hot water. And beyond that little tea bag, for the first time since my arrival, I sensed something very beautiful in this mixed-up, elusive country in the middle of nowhere. In the biting air, beneath the blue sky of heaven, sitting on a cliff crag high above the gers which may be packed up and gone in an hour or a month, I sensed a loss of time. I'm not sure why. I suppose it was the thought of the animals curled up beneath the snow beneath my feet – the red fox, badgers, polecats, root voles. Animals that are mostly sheltering now, like me, planning to launch out in the summer. And at last I remembered why, back in Shepherd's Bush, in the drizzle of West London, I so wanted to journey through Mongolia.

Back to the Ministry of External Relations. The bright-eyed, young face 16th December of Mr Gansukh: 'The people at the top,' he pointed to the high ceiling, 'say that they want to know they are not responsible. My boss Mr Tsolmon said, "what happens if he is eaten?"'

Eaten by what? Mr Gansukh didn't say. I guess he meant by wolves.

'In the majority, Mongolia is well inhabited. But you finally want to walk through the Gobi. We Mongolians do not do this alone. It is like a rule for us.'

I did not feel very happy about tackling something that even the Mongolians – of all people – wouldn't feel able to do.

Mr Gansukh continued. 'Mr Tsolmon says I must say certain things to you: next year is a difficult year for us. Fires all over our nation have spoiled the grazeland, and a very snowful winter there was. If there is a warm day, much snow melting there will be, and then if freeze there is, the snow will be made solid, and the cows and sheeps cannot eat the grasses. Horses have sharp feet, like knives, and they are smart. But cows and sheeps are not, and it means terrible losses.'

In the end I promised to write a letter accepting all responsibility. When I come back in February once again 'everything will be ready for discussion.'

15th January

U.K.: Laurens van der Post on the radio – *Desert Island Discs*. He died a month ago, but I listened with all the intensity of someone sitting at a deathbed. He seemed like someone passing on his last thoughts. Sue Lawley asked, 'How would you like to be remembered?'

He said words to the effect: 'As someone who loved life, and loved people.'

The one book he'd take to the desert island – he sounded genuinely relieved to hear that he would also get Shakespeare and the Bible – was *The Golden Bough*. A book full of magic, dreams, quests.

Laurens was a gentle man, who had touched me. Full of grace, when I sought his advice – the errors I've made, what contribution I can make in the future.

'I published too young, too naively,' I told him, when he invited me for tea. 'I went across the Amazon – nearly died.' Told him how, eventually, I managed to put the gist of it down on paper and get it published: an adventure story which veiled an angry cry against the whiteman. The result? Hopeless.

'What happened to the book? It's out of print long ago, I suppose.'

'Not a bit of it,' I said. 'Sells like hot cakes. It's called *Mad White Giant*. Children love the tales of jungles and Indians, adults find it suitably light bedside reading – even scientists buy it, often because they assume it's all exaggerated, just a yarn, and therefore no threat to them. Only 10 per cent get the point and many of them are literary eccentrics or else the fresh lot of Angry Young Men. Tried the idea *again* an Amazon video diary on the telly – same result!'

'But that is the joy of our craft!' Laurens said. 'Write and write, and learn as you write.'

I have all my stores ready: boots, hats, socks and coats that can cope with minus 40 (Gobi winter), and boots, hats and socks that can deal with plus 40 (Gobi summer). And, sitting in a Notting Hill café with Nara, the Mongolian student, I've also been working hard – though to little avail – with the Mongolian language. Tomorrow I'll be flying in again – a strange feeling of desolation – to that land spread with snow, and plains so wide and unchanging that you think you must be circling over the same countryside. But you are not. You are covering mile upon mile of empty ground, only 2.5 million people down there in a country the size of western Europe. I am clinging to words from Laurens, two or so years ago: a Zulu saying, 'Make haste slowly'. He saw a frustration in me then, but it was as nothing compared to what it's like now, up against strange and vast Mongolia.

Whatever I do out there, I'll be tailed by the ubiquitous Genghis Khan. It's infuriating. I want to explore MODERN Mongolia. But, like all the other travellers before me, I find I'm under his shadow. I sit having Mongolian lessons with poor old Nara and she says that it was Genghis Khan who helped adopt the script of the Uighurs – western neighbours he subjugated – for the Mongolian language. When I investigated weather conditions a Cambridge scientist illustrated just how bleak the Gobi is by saying 'after all, remember that this is the place where an enemy of Genghis dumped his friend – it was a death penalty'. Even having an injection for rabies: 'Little known fact about Genghis Khan,' the nurse said, lifting my sleeve and inserting the needle, 'he was afraid of dogs.' So, it seems I'm stuck with him – the thundering army, the terror in the eyes of those to be destroyed by him, the might of this man and nation from nowhere. 'I am the punishment of God,' he said, as he set about levelling Bukhara, a pillar of the Islamic world. 'If you had not committed great sins, he would not have sent a punishment like me.' After the slaughter of the garrison, the surrounding plain seemed to be 'a tray filled with blood'. Then the mosque was converted into a stables, the population was cleared from the city to ease the hectic business of looting, 30 000 skill-less men were put to the sword, while the others, with women and children, were trotted off to Mongolia as slaves.

And why do I bother to write down all this? Because, far from being dead and buried over 770 years ago, he still has a hold on the modern Mongolians' heart. The Mongols have not forgotten, nor have the Britons.

chapter two

MAKE HASTE SLOWLY

'I am a Mongol; we know about the cold' he said.

For Mongols, coping with the cold was an everyday event

that didn't require a lot of talk and thought.

Anthropologists Melvyn C. Goldstein and Cynthia M. Beall,

THE CHANGING WORLD OF MONGOLIA'S NOMADS, *1994*

MONGOLIA: Arrived to a sunny, fine day (minus 16), the Mongolian's sacred blue sky clear – just as it always is, the Mongolians say with satisfaction, for start of the lunar New Year. Winter is traditionally calculated as eighty-one days long (rather optimistically, I feel) and this is Tsagaan Sar, the White Month, the start of the year, the Year of the Cow. The Ministry told me to report to Mr Gansukh on arrival for my permits, but the whole building was shut up. Celebrations are continuing … Anyway, according to an old hand here, a Scotsman called Wilfred McKie, it's best not to embark on any venture today. It's Tuesday, which is inauspicious. So I'm spending a day indoors, looking out across the concrete flats, each with their stencilled number, out to the blue skies stretching to the infinite. I'm listening to the tape made by Nara, back in the Notting Hill café, of basic Mongolian phrases. But I find myself attending not to Nara, but to the background sounds, noises from home. There's the clacking of teacups, an Oasis song on the radio, and the waiter shouting, 'SHUT THE F-ING DOOR!'

Another thought, from Britain. Funny about Laurens van der Post. During our chat about *Mad White Giant*, he listened patiently, letting me explain about its weaknesses, why its message had largely failed with the establishment. Yet, as I was leaving, I spotted it in his bookshelves – rather oddly, next to a volume on Kafka. Surely, he must have known my book all the time. Like a sort of tribal elder, he knew there was nothing to do but listen and then pronounce the verdict – I should make haste slowly.

11th February

Left: *An* ovoo, *or shrine. Cairn-like stacks of stones or wood, they are heaped with offerings such as silk scarves and the hair of favoured horses. Positioned on peaks and roadsides, they pre-date Buddhism, but as shamanism shares the same tenant of harmony with the land, they have become dedicated equally to Buddha and more traditional spirits of the mountains and rivers nearby.*

First, a recce expedition: I badly need to make two friends out there – one in the extreme mountainous north, where I'll launch from the border with Siberia, and the other in the extreme west, the Altai mountain chain, which I'll be riding on to, before turning south towards the Gobi. I also need to know where to find water in the Gobi, but that's hopeless for now. Wells are opened by herders as and when necessary, and, as usual in Mongolia, wherever people are now they won't be there then. So for now I'll concentrate on at least finding those two friends. My main worry: the Mongolians think of travelling in terms of days, but I'll be travelling for five months and if I am late starting in Siberia, or delayed en route to the Gobi, then the Mongolian winter will be here again, my breath will freeze, my animals stop.

Wilfred McKie is working for the World Bank Transport Rehabilitation Project. He is a large, bespectacled man who swings his chair round from his paperwork, spreads his legs and tells his theories about the inexplicable Mongol. 'Remember,' he will say, 'Mongolia is not an underdeveloped country, it just has an underdeveloped economy.' He lends encouragement while his secretaries, Tsolomon and Sergelen, offer their thoughts.

Wilfred is a strategist and his army training is helping me organise everything to achieve the journey in the five-month window, June to October. He has equipment lists and thoughts on all potential problems, even Mongol tea, which I've yet to taste. 'Think of it as soup,' he said mysteriously, 'then you can't go far wrong.'

For the recce trip, I will need a translator, two jeeps – one to rescue the other if it gets stuck in snow – two drivers and food for three weeks. Wilfred goes over to the wallmap once again, arcing his arm over thousands of kilometres, prescribing the route we will attempt. We work out that by the time we have got things organised, it'll be inauspicious Tuesday again.

Tsolomon and Sergelen began murmuring. 'People don't even have haircuts on Tuesdays,' Sergelen said.

Wilfred has found me a translator, Ermek. Educated in the city's Russian schools, he is a computer operator and has thick blue glasses, small, intelligent eyes and a kind, earnest face. He is only in his twenties, but talks like someone older than me. Just like his computers, he is extremely logical and, though very polite about it, wants to define my every thought. 'Can you explain for me your exact long-term intentions?'

I explain for him my exact long-term intentions.

'Is this crossing through the Gobi really even possible?'

The long and the short of it is, I don't know. Finding water will be a big problem. Because of the proximity to the Chinese border, the only maps the military allow are 1:1,000,000. Hills scarcely buckle the contours at this scale, and locating the wells becomes almost arbitrary.

'Our job now is to make friends at the journey's starting point in the north, the Siberian border, and at the halfway point in western Mongolia. There's no point in even trying to make friends in the Gobi. The Mongolians evacuate the true desert in the summer, and when they return in the autumn, when I'll be going through, they won't be up-to-date as to which wells and springs are dry.

'I see,' he says, extremely dissatisfied.

I ordered a pair of winter boots, with Ermek's help. The cobbler drew an outline of my feet, sighing in disbelief. He was unused to foreigners, he said. He huffed and puffed at all this extra work. 'Mongolian men are always size 42,' Ermek explained.

Wilfred has found two drivers. Bold is a circus strongman and seemed almost square-shaped to me at first. Bronzed from the wind, he wears enormous leather boots and a baseball cap. He doesn't speak English and everything is said through his brother, Bakbold, who has small false incisors, like a rodent's.

After we negotiated pay, we broached the tricky subject of leaving on a Tuesday. Bakbold dismissed the problem: 'You know, we were brought up under Lenin.' He paused to think about this, and frowned. 'Though it seems that much else Lenin taught us is disproven …'

'What about Baatar, the second driver?'

'Probably he'll just do a quick trip to the temple,' Bakbold said. 'It is standard procedure.'

'They treat it as a cheap insurance policy,' Ermek added, a touch cynically. For he is also one of Lenin's protégés.

I picked up my special winter boots. The cobbler must have lost his nerve because, to be on the safe side, he made the boots so long, so outrageously voluminous, they are suitable only for a circus act.

17th February

Did leave today, a Tuesday, and regretted it immediately. Thanks to my clown boots I fell on the ice on the dark stairway and dislocated my shoulder.

18th February

'Make haste slowly,' I kept repeating to myself, walking about in the street, waiting for the sub-zero temperature to stop the swelling and

Overleaf: *Near Dayan Nuur, in the Altai. Wood shelters have replaced gers as winter quarters in the windswept mountains. A Mongolian's strategy for survival in winter is based on finding water – either from snow, or river ice – and rationing out the standing vegetation over eight months, until pastures are renewed again.*

numb the pain. 'Make haste slowly.' But the sooner I am recalling words of wisdom from a Mongolian, rather than a South African, the stronger I'll feel here.

I've brought along stacks of warm clothing and food. The others have only blocks of cooked meat, hunting knives (stuck in their boots) and thick winter del tunics. They keep the long sleeves down, to cover their hands, and half the men haven't even brought gloves. With me in the first jeep are Ermek, and the chief driver Bold. Following behind in the other jeep are Baatar, the second driver, and, today being inauspicious, his older brother Enkhbold to look after him – his mother had insisted.

We drove out, planning to head west along the northern edge of the Gobi towards the Altai range and Ermek's people, the Kazakhs. The Kazakhs are Muslims and are the largest minority group. They have a reputation, among the Mongols, as sharp traders. They simply do not mix with the Mongols, yet the two peoples have found a way of getting by together, now they've got rid of the Russians, and they are still united in their mutual suspicion of their other great neighbour, the Chinese. Among Ermek's distant relatives is a Kazakh shepherd called Dundoi. My hope is that this will be the friend and ally I need, at my halfway point towards the Gobi.

Bold drove and drove, his baseball cap down to block out the snow's reflection. The roads, when visible, were the most whimsical I have ever seen. Roads serve to connect people, and in Mongolia many of those people keep moving.

Outside now, snowlands, landscapes as if blown flat. The snow itself is light, the crystals small, filling creases in the land like sand. They are so small it's as if they have been rounded by the hills and lakes and marshes they've tumbled over, perhaps all the way from Siberia. Every now and again, we see gers. In ones, twos and threes they are dotted over the steppe, as they are over most of Mongolia, a network of support for every other Mongolian – and, in the future, I hope for me. Every district outside the capital is remote, but only in the Gobi and near the Siberian border are there areas with no people. The gers are not only hubs of life for people but also for herds of sheep and goats, desperate bands now out on the hills. Mongolia also boasts the *sums*, scattered settlements introduced in the socialist era partly to get the nomads to settle down, but this is still a land almost entirely without fences, a common three times the size of France.

'Our progress is quite sizeable,' Ermek said, from time to time. But there was no evidence other than the mileometer.

Out in the wind, a horseman mustered his cattle, sweeping them up from the snow in which they were embedded. A girl trotted her horse along an escarpment, a lamb in her lap. A motorbike ahead of us was carrying sacks of rocks to shore up winter defences. He swerved and we knocked him off; blood streamed from his head. He just got back on again and rode off. This is the story of Mongolia – winter, the longest season of the year, the story of everyday heroics.

Though it might have seemed a bright, sunny day with people riding about as if enjoying a glorious park, on the other side of the windscreen it was minus 27. When I stepped outside for a moment I didn't bother with gloves and the skin of three fingertips froze, and died.

We began looking for somewhere to stay the night, and eventually steered to a lone ger with smoke billowing from the black metal chimney protruding from the apex. A horse stood outside, pawing at the snow like a dog unearthing a bone. It looked at us, then turned back to the snow, biting a mouthful and chewing it for a drink.

A dog lifted itself out of a snow heap and began baying at us. A child leapt out through the door of the ger and grabbed its collar. The dog became more and more livid. This animal really wanted to get its teeth into our legs. I began to see why Genghis Khan had a thing about dogs.

'This is a true Mongol dog,' Ermek said. 'They are an especial old breed and very interesting.'

However, he didn't find the dog interesting enough to hang around. We darted to the door, while we were still unwounded.

I followed inside, wondering why Ermek hadn't even knocked. He walked around the left side of the interior, the portion devoted to visitors. On the right half, a family group looked up at us, wondering what the weather had brought in this time.

If you marched straight into someone's home anywhere else in the world you'd get bewildered glances. In London you'd be removed by the police. In New York you might be shot. Here we were beckoned round to the left, the male side, under the protection of Tengger, the great sky god. Ladies would have come over the threshold and been invited to turn right, the east side, under the safe-keeping of the sun. We were ushered to the far end, the place of honour, the *khoimor*, or altar. Here there were red wooden chests decorated with hand-painted geometric whites and blues and yellows. Perched on them were family photos in collapsible picture frames and a photo of the Dalai Lama, who had a broad grin on his face, and a postcard of a golden, cross-legged Lord Buddha – just the sort of images which were forbidden in

Above: In upland areas, where there are few camels, yaks play their part moving gers and family possessions. Each ger might keep half a dozen yaks for their daily needs; unlike sheep, which are milked only in summer, they can provide milk for nine or ten months a year.

communist times, when all ornaments had to be approved by the Party. We settled ourselves, facing our hosts, and said greetings to an old man who was himself just in from the cold – there was ice melting on his moustache. The woman, in a kingfisher-blue del, was already busy putting the tea on, knocking leaves from a solid brick, and a little girl in a magenta satin del, her cheeks red in a confined lotus flower blotch, was piling cow dung into the stove.

'Soon they will understand that we'd like to stay the night as well,' Ermek said simply. Living in a towerblock donated by the former Soviet leader Brezhnev, he takes pride in displaying his countryside credentials. The old man, a Khalkha Mongol, by far the largest ethnic group among the Mongolians, knelt with a great creaking of joints in front of Bold, another Mongol and the oldest man of our party, and offered his snuff bottle. It was more than kindness, it was a ritual of welcome, done with great deliberation: the bottle proffered in the right hand, left hand supporting it at the elbow. Bold squared up to him, letting out a sigh of satisfaction as he knelt, and summoned up his own bottle. The two men gently exchanged them in their palms. Boldt, with a practised eye, admired the agate stone vessel, with its red coral top, then took a pinch of snuff and with the same decorum returned the bottle.

The girl in the magenta del, now finished with her stove duties, talked in whispers to three little siblings. Indoors, they never stare, they never fight, they never run. It is as if they live within their own worlds, creating their own space in the confines of the ger. Were they children or grandchildren? None of the faces gave a reliable indication of age – they all were scorched dark by the wind.

Now the tea was being proffered in bowls. A generous knob of fat spiralling in mine; oily bubbles spun in its wake and – oh dear – in the murky depths was a sunken knot of gristle. But I remembered Wilfred's advice: think of it as soup.

'It's mutton soup, it's mutton soup,' I told myself as I sipped at the salty liquid. He was right. Just as long as I remembered it was soup, it was fine.

'Ooooo!' the lady suddenly gasped. She snatched my bowl away and fished around for the gristle, apologetically shaking her head. 'Uuchlaarai!'.

'She's very, very sorry,' Ermek explained as she handed me a fresh bowl. 'It's got some sheep in it!'

'I noticed. Isn't it meant to have sheep in it?'

Below: *The ger is always aligned in the same direction with the door facing south and the altar opposite it (left of the photo). It is a perfect expression of democracy and civility, with the eastern half (shown here) reserved for the family who directly face visitors, for whom the west side is reserved.*

'Generally, that's at breakfast,' said Ermek. 'When you might like to warm up your sheep by pouring tea on it.'

'I might,' I thought, 'but unlikely.'

While Ermek tried to explain to the family why we are travelling so far in winter, the girl with the magenta del went outside on a brief errand, taking her fur coat out of the cupboard, and neatly packing it away afterwards. By bedtime, she had done this a total of five times. Order is essential to the nomad: camels willing, they could be away from here in the time it takes to change a set of car tyres.

The old man was anxious to get me talking, so as to study me better. 'He has the golden hair of a camel,' he whispered to his wife.

The questions he asked via Ermek placed me in time and space: how old am I? where am I from? where am I going to? But my answers only caused culture shock.

'He says you actually look like twenty-six not thirty-six,' Ermek translated. 'And he does not know of "England."'

'Try Britain?'

'I have. And the "United Kingdom" and "Europe" and the "EC". And he cannot see why anyone wants to go anywhere so far inside Mongolia just now.'

Ermek handed over a package of gifts we had prepared: cigarettes, soap, sugar, sweets. The woman accepted them gravely, with both hands, and with great aplomb touched the bundle to her forehead. 'And the foreigner is twenty-six, you say …'

'No,' Ermek said, 'as I told you, THIRTY-six.'

'Ah yes, thirty-six.' She nodded as before, agreeably, but clearly couldn't bring herself to believe it. 'And you say he's Russian…'

'English!'

There was some silence, then some conferring.

'So he's twenty-six …' the woman began again.

'THIRTY-SIX!'

'And from where?' she said, trying to trick us into giving the right answer this time. 'Moscow?'

Conversation didn't move on for another fifteen minutes. 'For heaven's sake, let's change the subject,' I thought. I told Ermek to tell them that I'd heard a Japanese story that Genghis Khan was not after all Mongolian but Japanese. What did they think?

Suddenly the mood changed. It was as though we were back in medieval times, the Mongols were once more on the rampage. It was scarcely believable.

'They cannot take HIM away from us!' Bold said. He stuck a single, rude finger in the air.

'It's like a plot!' the old man chipped in.

'The Japanese are already turning Mongolia into a golf course!' said Baatar.

'We're just a recreation ground, that's all,' said Enkhbold.

'It's a disgrace,' said the woman, 'DISGRACE!'

'For heaven's sake,' I said. 'Tell them it's only a story going round. They shouldn't get all hot and bothered.'

But Ermek wasn't listening. 'I am so angry. I will think of reasons why it cannot be true in the morning, but now I am too angry.'

Time to change the subject once again. I turned to admire the family photos. There were grannies and grandpas standing grimly facing the camera, and young men posing heroically with prized possessions – favourite camels, horses, motorbikes – and girls posing in Sükhbaatar Square, as thrilled as foreign tourists to be actually standing there though they're in their own capital city.

Eventually, when everyone had calmed down again, we cleared a space and lay down to sleep, the Mongolians none the wiser about the outside world, and the outside world not much the wiser about the Mongolians.

chapter three

PEOPLE *of the* EAGLE *and* BEYOND

'Nature is our manager.' A Mongolian shepherd,

interviewed about his husbandry skills.

Melvyn C. Goldstein and Cynthia M. Beall,

THE CHANGING WORLD OF MONGOLIA'S NOMADS, *1994*

19th February

On my way again, and with a renewed respect for Mongol tea. I now realise that, containing salt, it's perfect rehydration liquid, like the sachets you buy in European chemists for diarrhoea. Furthermore, late last night the tea became a massage ointment: the old gent ladled in more salt and performed a miracle on my shoulder, his technique honed from a thousand riding mishaps. And this morning, just as Ermek promised, the tea was added to last night's mutton left-overs, and, less miraculously, supper became breakfast.

20th February

We continued west towards the Altai mountains across southern Mongolia, stopping at gers whenever we were in need of a warming cup of tea, or just to find out where we were. Each time we stopped, another piece of the expedition plan fell into place. Or didn't.

The key to the journey will be the Mongolians, this half of the population which is thinly spread across the country. They are a resource that I can and must take advantage of. But the Mongolians, while seeing hospitality as their code of life, are also very self-sufficient. They can get by without me, just as they can – as nomads – get by without international loans. I must acquire skills from them to be self-sufficient myself. That means, getting to know the Mongol horse, the animal I see tethered outside the gers – their nostrils steaming away, icicles from their whiskers. The way the horses eye you, they seem half wild, which is exactly what they are, left to their own devices in winter. Heaven knows what they are like by the time the spring comes and they are rounded up for work.

Left: *Dundoi, by a hün chuluu, or stone man. Erected at grave sites by Turkish tribes (6th–8th century) the characters are probably revered figures of an ancestor cult.*

PEOPLE OF THE EAGLE AND BEYOND

39

'You have ridden such a horse, of course,' Ermek said to me, unpicking an icicle from a horse's whiskers.

'Oh yes,' I said. It seemed unnecessary to cloud his confidence at this stage by saying it was in the Andes, and the horse tried to destroy me. Furthermore, that the horse partly succeeded, breaking three of my ribs.

Another thing: I've learned that loading the camels in Mongolia is a two-man operation: one man to hold the saddle padding to either side of the camel, the other to affix it around the humps. When that's done, the luggage is strapped onto the padding, both men straining with opposite ends of a rope to achieve the right tension across it. I think that anyway I'll take a horseman with me to help me manage the caravan I'll need until the Gobi. How I'll manage the loading system after that, is as yet a mystery.

21st February

Now we are approaching Govi-Altai *aimag*, or district, in the south-west of Mongolia, grinding through plains of stones and twiggy shrubs, the northern edge of the Gobi. 'You cannot hope to cross the desert alone,' the herdsmen we meet continue to say ...

'Don't worry Ermek, we'll find a way,' I continue to say.

'Good,' he says, doubtfully. I'm not even sure if I deserve this loyalty.

Very few gers now, but occasional domestic camels. In their thick winter coats, the camels wrench determinedly at tussocks, sometimes chewing soil for the roots. Are they as strong as the Arabian camel? The Bactrian looks stumpy legged, and those that we see are so generously adorned with winter fur it's difficult to know what the rest of their physiognomy is like. They work hard, eating what they can find even though their reserves, two humps of fat, are still large. They have three more months to last out.

I will depend on such camels one day, but I am finding it hard to get a true gauge as to their capabilities. I suspect that to Genghis Khan – that man again – they were as vital as his renowned horses. The famous horses were the spearhead of the operation, but the camels, gathered up from the Gobi, were, with oxen, the mainstay. They bore tents, catapults, water, food, the wounded, and all that goes into running a war machine and keeping that spearhead sharp.

The Mongolians say that their camels can, in fact, go forty-five days without water but they mean standing about, grazing. I still haven't met anyone who has travelled more than a week with loaded camels. The true extent of their stamina will only become apparent when I am relying on them myself.

Our fifth day of driving and now, approaching the Altai range, we have veered north to Khovd *aimag*. Here the snow has sometimes gone altogether; sometimes it lies only in thin veils. Twists of yellow brown dust dance across the plains, the first winds of spring. We negotiate mile wide fans of debris from the violent spring floods of last year. For a while longer, we ourselves are safe from these. The rivers are held tight, cracked from invisible forces, and we can drive straight over them, even over marshes and lakes.

After one such lake, the water frozen into a blue glass, we came across a family on the move. A string of four camels was wading through snow with a family's entire house and contents on their backs. The only other assets of the family were tailing behind: the livestock. They were led by the horses, which wheeled through the snow, spinning it from their hooves. Then, slower, a thicket of cows and yaks, heads down, doing their best, felt jackets fitted to the young, but some nonetheless trailing, hardly caring now that they couldn't keep up. Another lot of camels trotted loose behind, looking around whimsically to left and right for the next meal possibility. Two men on Russian motorbikes escorted them like police outriders, trying to keep some order. Finally, far away on a hill blown bare of snow, a herd of sheep and goats flowed like an army of white ants.

Through to the Altai mountains, at Mongolia's western border, nearing Dundoi, Ermek's Kazakh relative. We drove up into the range, and came across a cow herd being moved round to the south-facing slopes, where the snow is beginning to clear. Too cold to melt, it's evaporating, absorbed by the dry air. This is the first glimmer of the end of the winter, the end of the struggle, but for some it's too late. There were calves lying about back downslope, their throats slit. This was not an act of brutality but mercy. They couldn't make it further. Now they lie like the mutilated of a battle. I wonder why their owners bothered to stop in the freezing winds, dismount and kill their cattle. Death would have followed in hours anyway. It seems the Mongolian winter breeds an unexpected tenderness as well as toughness – man and animal sharing the same battle.

We meandered up a valley bowl, cut through a few solid rivulets, gradually rising to an escarpment. We stopped to ask where Dundoi's family is presently located, and found ourselves invited into a family's winter quarters. Such homes, log cabins sealed with mud, are even more remarkable than the gers because just like them, these houses can be moved.

As we've done thirty times in gers since leaving the capital, we sat around the stove trying to heat up our fingers, while we listened for directions. The house was bare except for felt rugs tacked to the walls and a bridal bed, hung with simple ruby tapestries and also an amulet of owl feathers, the dark banding of which is said to be like scribbled notation from the Koran. Beside us was a baby in a cot, strapped tight down. She had a potty fixed to the underside of the apparatus, and seems utterly content with her lot, which is just as well. She'll be like this in the daytime for a year, released only for feeding and to be washed according to a fixed procedure: bathe in oily tea one night, water another, black tea another.

Dundoi's home was higher up the valley, a cabin secreted in a nook below the ridge. We arrived an hour later. Dogs were secured and we were beckoned indoors. Kazakh men were already gathered around the stove, in the middle of a long discussion over tea and cigarettes. 'The next move around the mountain is about to happen,' Ermek said. 'They are deciding who has the good jobs.'

I peeked in the next-door room: felt rugs on the floor, embroidered tapestries on the walls, pictures in fold-up frames, suitcases stacked, just as they are all year, ready to go.

I was introduced to Dundoi, who is large, has a fearsome presence and booming voice, but kindly eyes. Ermek said, 'He wants me to tell you he has been in these hills for seven generations.' '*Duloo!*' Seven, Dundoi repeated, and dragged me off to see a photo of himself at my age, an upright citizen in a military uniform sprayed with medals. 'Best livestock keeper – provisional category – for FIVE years in a row!' 'FIVE!' he repeated, proudly.

Below: *Dundoi, in fox-skin hat, hacking out blocks of ice to store as drinking water.*

Ermek continued, 'And he insists I tell you that he was so good, he was awarded with a tour of the Soviet Union. Russia, Poland, Czechoslovakia. In one hotel, he even saw an African. It was marvellous!'

We sat around the stove having tea and warming up. Dundoi has eight children, most of them girls, so he gets his nephews along to help, when he's on the move. The family and herds do a round trip of 200 kilometres every year. The cabin is left behind, moving only for an occasional change in winter pastures. This cabin has been over the mountain three times. Then, only the chimney remains.

Apart from the kitchen, it didn't seem much warmer indoors than out. It was certainly below zero – there was ice on this side of the window. It had been there a while, dusty and opaque, like old melted candle wax. I went for a little look around. The sun was shining and there was no wind. Dundoi came with me to fend off the dogs. My curiosity was drawn to an outhouse, from which came cheeping noises, the sound of an overgrown budgerigar. I hoped it would be a golden eagle, the bird with which the Kazakhs hunt foxes, even wolves.

Dundoi opened the door. It was his larder, or more accurately, bearing in mind the temperature, deep freeze. From racks hung bits of horse: heads, legs, feet, guts, stomachs. 'Khool', Dundoi explained. Food. On the floor were blocks of ice – the family's emergency water supply. And in the corner, the 'overgrown budgerigar'. Dundoi carried him indoors, so Ermek could help explain about him. 'His name is Little Yellow,' Ermek said. 'And he is worth more than even the very best race horse. $4000 – or so he claims.'

'He ought to be insured!' I said, having a good chuckle.

'He is,' said Ermek.

Little Yellow is the best in the province, according to Dundoi at least. He was taken from his nest, up in the cliffs one early July. That's when the eagles are not too weak, but not big enough to fly the nest. Actually Little Yellow is small for a golden eagle, but that gives him more speed. If he fails in his first attempt to grab a fox, he can quickly rise and drop again. He wears a cluster of owl feathers on his back – it can't help his efforts to fly, but at least brings luck. He could kill – or at the very least pin down – a wolf, and golden eagles have been known together to take on the king of all mountains, the snow leopard.

25th February

I wake in the morning with a smoker's cough – the dung in the stove.

I find my skin is becoming oily: my back and neck is clothed with thick dampness, a sweat that doesn't freeze; the mutton grease I eat all day has permeated through. According to my calculations, a family would eat maybe twenty sheep and goats a year, mainly in the winter, when there are no dairy products. That means you'd need a flock of a hundred to keep you from going under. Dundoi agreed with my maths. 'And I have 650 animals,' he said, with satisfaction.

26th February

Half a dozen men rode up to the cabin this morning, moustaches grey with frost. They were a hunting party, and each carried an eagle on their right arm, the weight supported by a wooden prop from the saddle.

Dundoi produced three more horses, and before I knew it I was being lent a Kazakh winter coat – black corduroy, lined with an ibex, that is, wild goat, skin. It was as thick as roof cladding and reached down to my knees. It was also extremely heavy and Ermek had to help me ease it on, as one might a suit of armour.

Time to try out a Mongol horse. I climbed on, extremely warily, and was about to ask for a few tips when the rest of the hunting party turned to the hills and trotted off. My horse wasn't going to be left behind and he followed. Off we went and soon the others were already halfway up the hill ahead. I began to look around for an easy route. My horse ignored me, picking his way like a true professional straight ahead up a scree slope with which I would have had difficulty on foot. He stopped only to munch snow as he climbed.

I was so caught up in the wonder of this creature – his ancestors had, after all, carried the Mongol armies all the way to the Danube – that for a while I forgot we were on a hunt. We rode over hills, waiting on the crests, looking out over the slopes, waiting in silence for the clink of a pebble dislodged by a fox. Sometimes we dismounted to listen some paces away from the fidgeting horses and Dundoi then explained a little more. He hunted with male eagles, which were fattened in the summer and kept hungry in winter, the hunting season – the best time because foxes left tracks in the snow and the pelts were thick. Eagle hunting ran in the family – his father took fifty foxes a year. 'Good money!'

The eagle is a powerful and dramatic killer, but what was remarkable to me out here was the co-operation between these three animal species – man with his brain, the horse with his legs, the eagle with his eyes.

In the end we returned empty handed – 'Not even one hare!' Dundoi said. 'Terrible!' But for me it was enough to be out under the bare blue sky, with Little Yellow and the other eagles awaiting their chance, heads twisting, eyes alert to the movement of every vole, hamster and ermine within 100 metres.

I have what I came for. Dundoi will be a good ally for me if I ever need his support out here on my way through in the summer. I have promised to seek him out then, even if things are going well. Now I have a friend out here, someone to turn to en route to the Gobi.

We left towards the far north in the morning, driving our two jeeps back down into the valley and stopping to go to the loo near a frozen stream – an exquisite snake of silver glass. Nearer the ice I heard a chiming sound, a thousand miniature bells. I stopped and listened harder. Somewhere under the plates, a trickle of water. It wasn't much, but it was a beginning. The thaw was underway.

We hadn't gone much further when we learnt that to proceed much beyond Ölgii, capital of this *aimag*, was impossible. A snow drift the size of England stood in the way.

ÖLGII: have sent back Bold, Baatar and Enkhbold. There is no other choice other than waiting three months for the snow to melt. Ermek and I will fly on to Mörön, capital of Khövsgöl *aimag*, and then take a jeep or two north to where Mongolia bulges into Siberia. Up there are a Tuvan people who might also help me. They are the sole occupants of the border country and have the knowledge to guide me through there later, at my journey's start. They are the Dukha, known to the Mongolians as 'Tsaatan', literally 'reindeer herders'. They move more often than even the Mongols, and there are only twenty-three families – I might not even find them.

We've left Mörön and have driven a day north towards the Tsaatan with a 'country boy' – as Ermek described him – called Khurmit. His hair is long and he has brought not a single piece of luggage, just a knife in his riding boots and his cheap green del which, like the plaid of olden day Scottish highlanders, serves as a blanket as well as clothing. He doesn't talk much, but has enormous charm and girls we meet in the gers scattered along the way find him fascinating. He also finds them fascinating. And though he doesn't speak a word of English, he portrays himself to them as some sort of BBC correspondent, manhandling the cameras as an actor does his props. As we drive north, 'Kermit', as we call him, relishes the photos he somehow acquires from girls. 'Oooooooor!' he giggles, rubbing his leathery thumb over their features. 'This one has good bones,' Ermek translates, 'but her neck is wide, like the neck of a fattened horse, a horse say in late summer.'

'But what about THIS one?'

'Her face is indeed good, but in fact she is too tall for a Mongol.'
'And this one?'
'She has beautiful red lipstick, but the lips underneath are old and grey.'

We drove across lakes to bypass this crumpled, folded landscape which is dusted by snow, and followed the lowlands between the ranges of Ulaan Tayga and Khordil Saridag, to the west of Lake Khövsgöl, a trap of cold air where temperatures can dip to minus 50.

6th March

Through larch forests, and down to the far northern settlement of Tsagaan Nuur, beside a lake mirroring the blue sheen of the heavens. The settlement is made from timber, every house a stout cabin, the snow banked up against the buildings. It looks just like a Siberian outpost, which is exactly what it is. Another attempt to get the locals to settle, and like the communal chimney-stack, which the socialists also inflicted on the population, only partially successful.

Left: *Uugantsetseg leading a reindeer. Though nowadays no tents and few items of clothing are made from reindeer skin, the Tsaatan are still heavily dependant on their furs and antlers as a source of income, and almost totally rely on them as transport and food throughout the year.*

The Tsaatan being so inaccessible – even Kermit had never visited them – we picked up Sainbayar, a friend of his who once was married to one. Sainbayar said we were lucky, as it happened there were two families just now within reach through the snow. However, like all the Tsaatan they are self-sufficient and suspicious of outsiders. We must be careful not to upset them. He steered us through fir forest, then ran ahead, stamping the snow to locate pockets of it which seemed at times to be bottomless.

Ahead, wood smoke, a dog yapping, and two tents like North American tepees. Beside the tents, half a dozen reindeer stood around, like amiable but gormless dogs, tied with ropes made from their own hair. Others, further off in the forest, were searching for lichens to eat, shovelling the snow away with their black hooves. An old woman came out, her left hand leaning on the shoulder of a little girl who was a convenient, walking-stick height.

Ermek waited for Sainbayar to lead the way and even Sainbayar waited to be invited into one of the tents. We sat on reindeer skins, warming our hands, dark canvas stretched over our heads, and all was rather quiet, though the children and parents from next door had crowded in to look us over. Unlike the Mongols they didn't automatically begin making tea, but sat for a moment wondering what to make of us. The children watched, tongues playing with their chewing gum, made, it emerges, from tree resin. I noticed a shrine at the back: a curtain of miniature rag dolls, cotton ribbons hanging from them in blues, whites, greys.

'The colours of heaven,' Ermek said. 'These are the spirits of our great Blue Sky.' Other than the shrine, the interior is undecorated, just the canvas and poles. From these hang strips of reindeer meat and also the snowy pelt of an ermine.

The old lady, called Tsend, politely said in Russian that we were welcome, but we weren't all that convinced and Ermek and Kermit were still looking hopefully around for signs of either mutton or a tea pot. Then Sainbayar explained who we were and what I was doing – enough to get even a hermit talking – and Tsend in turn told us that the little girl is a seven-year-old grandchild called Uugantsetseg, 'Beginning Flower'. The other girls are called Munke, short for Munkhtsetseg, 'Forever Flower', who is twenty-four, and wears a satin del with the sheen of a Blue Morpho butterfly, and Enke, short for Enkhtuya, who is thirteen. She was adopted from a family with rather too many daughters: she's loud, quite a handful.

It's clear that the eldest girl, Munke, is the powerhouse here, continually on the move, maintaining the kitchen stove and firewood supply. She was at last getting tea underway: she lit the stove and dispatched the quiet little grandchild to collect snow to melt for water. Enke was instructed to scour the cooking pan with pine twigs, and had to be told off, because she did it with maximum noise, wanting to claim back some attention.

We settled down, Ermek, who went to Russian schools for eighteen years, asking if they could please speak Mongolian. 'Their Russian is breaking my ears!' he whispered. Ermek told them that we'll be back in the spring at the start of my journey, north in the mountains, and maybe we'll see them again. We don't push our luck by so soon asking for their help on my return for the expedition, but they are clearly interested by the idea that we'll meet again. People make it up this far north once, but not twice. We were suddenly potential friends, people who have made a commitment (of some uncertain kind) to their place.

After a while I went outside. With nowhere to stand up or lie down, I found the tent small. Besides, Kermit took up so much room, assembling and disassembling my tripod.

Uugantsetseg was among the trees, stuffing snow into a sack with a piece of bark. It was colder by this time and many reindeer were curled up tightly on the ground, their thick coats sealing out the cold, legs folded in tight, a white frill of rump hair stopping a draught up the rear end.

The air was very still and, except for the woodpeckers clacking on the trees and the crystal tinkle of dry snow slipping from branches, all was quiet. A chipmunk rattled along a fallen pine. Walking up slope, the human, dog and reindeer tracks gave way to those of a score of animals I have not yet seen or heard. Martens, ermines and numerous small rodents have laced their way all over the forest floor, higher up the slope small deer, and criss-crossing them the runs of wolves. There were forage ways, animals on the scent or on the search, and elsewhere more regular passage ways, animals on patrol. At this time of year the bears are said to be hungry and irritable. Last month a man stumbled on a bear and fought it off by stabbing it in the eye with a penknife. Even so, the man was the only one who ended up critically injured.

Back down to the two tents, and Batmanh, a young man from next door, came up to the reindeer I was stroking… Next thing, he swiftly punched the deer in the face, knocking him unconscious. As the deer dropped silently from my hands, he placed a knife in his heart. 'Sorry,' I find myself saying. The reindeer's end, though mercifully quick, seemed treacherous. I felt I had a part in that treachery.

Overleaf: Tsaatan tents are made from a canvas material which is wrapped around three pine poles that have been lashed together with an extra few laid against them for support. This simple but effective construction can be dismantled in moments so that the reindeer can transport the canvas and the Tsaatans' handful of possessions. The poles, which can always be replaced from the forest, are left behind.

Indoors again, and Munke was now sieving the melted snow for pine needles. Ermek, not the world's most outdoor man, was worrying about having to survive out here on reindeer meat, which lacks the fat of mutton. 'Is it very cold at night?'

Tsend said, 'Yes, we have to be taken outside into the sun to thaw.' She laughed suddenly.

'No, seriously …' Ermek said. This recce trip was starting to wear him down. Munke gave Ermek more disheartening news: 'Sometimes we wake up and there's a big pile of snow in the middle of the tent. We don't mind. As to why no-one closes the hole, we don't know. It is just the way it is.'

Uugantsetseg sat studying us, head to one side, gazing. She rarely spoke. Enke – hot headed, demanding – insisted on reading to her mother. It's some sort of campaign to get herself allowed back to boarding school. Reading is a passport to school and school is a glimpse of the outside world. Tsend was sympathetic, but stared impassively away. I suddenly realised that she's almost blind.

Munke, who was cooking up more tea to keep us warm, asked Ermek to tell her some more stories. 'Munke says you are all city guys,' he explained. 'You have interesting lives. We just sit in the trees, looking at the blue sky.'

So Ermek told her about his life in Ulaanbaatar. She wasn't impressed. 'I have been to Ulaanbaatar to get a prize for herding reindeers,' she says. 'It was not so very good.'

That's for sure.

Ermek tried again. He isn't a man for dancing in the Top Ten club, he's a man for sitting at computer modems. So exotic highlights for him are the things you can now buy in the market: 'bananas and oranges, even in winter!'

'We don't like them, even in summer.' Munke said.

'Yes we do!' Enke said, furious that Munke was ruining a chance that we'll bring novelties from Ulaanbaatar. 'We eat everything.'

Gradually Tsend also warmed to our company, asking about Britain and telling us she was born across the Russian border in Siberia proper. Those were the days when everything was from the reindeer – skins for the tents, skins for shoes, clothes, food. She was born in the winter, a terrible time when Stalin was killing. 'Her mother gave birth to her,' Ermek said, 'and the next day was running.' Many children were left behind. Finally, Tsend and family were over the border and in Mongolia.

LATER: We are sitting in the candle light, Kermit trying to fix the microphone clips he's broken so far. I am writing up my notes, Ermek is hugging the stove. Uugantsetseg has a bad ear-ache and Tsend has heated up a bone marrow, and just now gently poured the oil into her ear. Immediately Uugantsetseg is quiet and before we have rearranged ourselves to sleep she is snoring.

EARLY MORNING: Munke already awake, melting snow for our tea.

Ermek wonders when food will be provided. He is always waiting for more calories: 'It is as if we are living off starters!'

'Did you sleep?'

'Oh yes,' said Ermek, putting on a brave face. 'There is no problem at all. And it is healthy to be in countryside air.' He looks terrible.

Munke asked Ermek if I'd had a strong dream because I slept far too near the shrine. Actually I didn't sleep at all in the cold; this morning I discovered that there was an iceblock under my makeshift pillow. She is now purifying both the shrine and me, burning pine needles to cleanse the air.

I'm not surprised to learn that Tsend is a shaman [that is, a priest trained to visit the spiritual dimension of our world and intercede with the spirits and supernatural forces which govern us]. Sainbayar said it's something that runs in her family: her mother, eighty-nine years old, was a shaman before her. There are few shamans now, but the religion preceded Lamaism [the Buddhist teachings of Tibet] which was formally represented at the court of Khubilai Khan, the grandson of Genghis, and gradually took hold. But Mongols still seek favours from the traditional spirit world. They stop to pay homage at the roadside shrines or *ovoos* – cairns decked with small bank notes, skulls and hair of departed horses and vodka bottles – while the famed blue silk scarves of the colour of heaven accompany every Mongolian blessing, every Mongolian gift.

LATER: Tsend was loath to talk about her profession, but we waited until no other adults were present, then Ermek broached the subject and we discovered that she has a crow spirit which acts as her spiritual guide through the vagaries of the Other World. This bird is her trusted friend, offering its wisdom, its eyes and its senses, leading her through encounters with the good, bad and simply mischievous spirits she'll meet out there. Ermek also managed to get her to explain the solar eclipse, due on 9 March. 'We say that the sun is eaten by a sort of monster,' Tsend

explained. He is called 'Rag', we gathered, or was she saying 'Nag'? He has a human top half, serpent bottom half, and no rear end. Hence when the monster swallows the sun, the sun has to be ejected from the stomach. Humans have to help by making noise: dogs must also be made to bark, so as to create – as Ermek put it – 'maximum effect'.

Just then, Gana, a son who's been trading reindeer skins and antlers down in the valley, came riding up on a reindeer, leading two more behind. He swung off the little saddle and into the tent. The reindeer looked around, panting – so did his two companions – Gana had ridden them in relay, jumping from one to another along the way, as each tired.

Like Tsend, Gana wasn't very enthusiastic about visitors at first, and lay spread-eagled on his back, budging us out of the way. However, he couldn't take his eyes off Kermit's Kazakh knife and after Kermit had been convinced to part with it Gana actually asked us to visit his family when we return. He lives right up on the border, exactly where I'm hoping to start the journey, among the mountains and taiga forest. 'You could bring some boots for me, as well!' he suggested. 'The Russian ones.'

'One pair size 42 boots,' wrote Ermek.

'How would we find our way there?' I asked. 'It must be two days ride, through mountains.'

'It is a mere two days ride, if it doesn't snow,' Gana pronounced. 'Munke will guide you.'

Will she? We all turned to Munke.

'Will I get some boots as well?' Munke asked. 'The Russian ones?'

Ermek amended his notebook. 'One size 38 boots.' It seems that women's feet also come in only one size.

Suddenly, we have what we need: our second lot of friends, these ones right up in the mountains of Siberia.

I noticed Uugantsetseg, standing silently watching me. She wanted something, and eventually Munke prised it out of her. 'She says, will you bring some oranges and bananas for her to look at when you come back? So many other people have seen them.'

We agreed to make a shopping list tomorrow and settled down to sleep. I lie awake for a moment wondering about Munke. She's twenty-four. Even for a student in Ulaanbaatar that's getting old not to be married. When a boy wants to propose marriage to a Tsaatan girl he offers a sable fur skin and a sky blue silk sash to her parents. Who would not offer a sable skin for someone as hardworking as Munke? Maybe it's

Left: *Tsend, an almost blind Tsaatan shaman, with Uugantsetseg beside her. Traditionally a shaman might intercede with many spirits, even the great Sky God, Tengger (the Father), or the Earth God, Etugen (the Mother). The Earth determined the shape of things, but the Sky the fate of things, and was continuously watching man's conduct towards nature.*

just too convenient for Tsend to keep her on here. Whatever, Munke seems happy for now. She looks up to the apex of the tent, into the cosmos. 'We can count twenty-four large stars though the hole,' she simply observes, 'and a hundred thousand small ones.'

8th March

We get the feeling we are not wanted here much longer. I suspect it is tomorrow's eclipse – Tsend doesn't want us to see her ritual, her flight with a crow spirit into the Other World. But I have anyway found out all I need. I can get up to Gana, in the far mountains with Munke's help, and I can easily find Munke because Tsend is blind and they won't be moving far from here. I've also decided to employ Kermit to ride with me down to the Gobi. I need a horseman to manage what I now judge will amount to a caravan – three horses and three baggage camels. In some ways, Kermit is perfect. I don't want an urban Mongolian, a product of that most un-Mongolian institution, Ulaanbaatar, but nor do I want a countryman, who might suddenly want to return to family duties as winter begins to blow. Of course Kermit, presently dismembering my only remaining torch, is a little bit too fond of my gadgets. But he'll be fine, unless something or someone along the route also takes his fancy.

He's very pleased to be coming on the journey, especially because I'm filming it. 'I will be shown all around the world,' he said. His eyes went glassy for a second, as he let his imagination run. 'And all I have to do is ride horses around?'

Ermek said sharply, 'Kermit, the whole of Mongolia, not just you, will be shown on the telly. The honour of our country is at stake. This project must succeed. You must not let Mongolia down.'

Ermek turned to me. 'Sadly, I think we have chosen someone who is like a kid.'

We will be leaving early tomorrow and Munke has drawn up a shopping list, as children might for Father Christmas – which is fair enough, as the legend of Santa Claus probably originated from their cousins the sami who live west through the snows, hoping – as do we all – for a kindly visitor, presumably like them dressed in a red coat and with reindeer.

9th March

We left in the early morning, Tsend calling after us in the dark that she'll gather some herbs for Ermek's hair – he has something of a thinning problem.

Two hours later we were waiting for daylight with the jeep on the hillside. Then, none of the usual soft reds of early dawn. Instead, a copper light, which brightened to tarnished silver, foggy, gunmetal greys. When the sun appeared, it was already running with the moon. They ascended linked together, the air stilling, the woods behind us quieting, as the moon moved over to mask the sun. What light there was now shone strangely off the iced valley below, trembling light refracted from a frozen river meander. A sense of decay, of strange interferences of the natural process – the world taking a breath, hesitating, unsure if it will carry on. A horse down in the valley was stock still. A guard dog quietened on its rope. Only one sound in the universe, a lone crow, the bird that was Tsend's spiritual guide. Under the circumstances – the dog stilled, the horse stilled, us humans stilled, the planet Earth stilled – it was hard not to believe that crow was there to watch us.

PEOPLE OF THE EAGLE AND BEYOND

chapter four

DEALINGS *with* NOMADS

There is a legend saying the Mongol was born on the horseback,

lives on the horse and dies on the back of the horse.

Guidebook of The Natural History Museum, Ulaanbaatar

Back in 'U.B.' – as the expats call it. Still more than two months to go before the communal pipes, with their heavy rust load, stop again for another brief Mongolian summer.

Today, spring is in temporary retreat. Passers-by once more have their heads down, and are kicking through snow – there's 10 centimetres worth already. Everyone moves quickly and children, who yesterday were playing hopscotch on the pavements, are now gone, as if blown away.

A meeting with Mr Avirmed, Head of the Gobi National Park. A crucial moment: this man will know, if anyone does, how to go about crossing the desert alone. A great honour that he came to my flat, especially as I need permission from him even to set foot in his portion of the Gobi. He's a substantially built man who looks rather serious, a demeanour I mistook at first for gruffness.

Left: Riding Ulaan. With me riding him, his centre of gravity must have been at his head height yet, typical of his breed, he took me up cliffs and through marshes without slipping in all the 1,000 kilometres we were together.

'Mr Allen looks like a camel,' he told Ermek in the hallway. It didn't seem to be an insult, just an observation that I somehow fitted the requirements of the desert. As I put on the tea, Ermek said he thought that I could take it I had permission.

Mr Avirmed spread my maps on the floor and set about neatly pencilling a route through the Gobi. 'Finished,' he announced quietly after a while, chucking the pencil down. 'Tell Mr Allen that probably no-one has done this route on camel – it's certainly not an old caravan route – and if they had done it they would have gone accompanied. And even then, where would they have found water along the way?'

The correct answer appeared to be 'nowhere'. All in all, there didn't seem to be very much point in Mr Avirmed having spent half an hour carefully drawing his little line across all my maps.

'I'm not saying these things to stop Mr Allen going there,' Mr Avirmed said kindly to Ermek, 'but just to inform him.'

Ermek said, 'So there is no way he can survive along the route that you've kindly drawn?'

'I wouldn't say it's definitely impossible, but it might be. And I don't know what else to suggest. Much further south and there is no hope of water, and further north you will be out of the true desert, the proper Gobi, and into what we call 'desert steppe'. Anyway, please tell Mr Allen that I am sorry. I haven't been very helpful.'

'No, you have, you have!' I said, trying to take my mind off my expedition plans, now reduced by Mr Avirmed to nonsense. All that can be said is that I at least know all about camels.

'Another matter to mention,' Mr Avirmed said, getting up to go. 'Mongolian camels. Mr Allen should know his team very well before he takes them from their home. Otherwise, they will pine away.' This sounded slightly quaint, not what you expect from a scientist. But I'd already noticed that country Mongolians talked this way, as if every creature has its homeland. Horses mustn't be taken from their pasture, camels from their scrub. Even Kermit had his habitat. 'Your companion comes from Khövsgöl?' Mr Avirmed asked. 'Well, he belongs in the mountains and cold. He will grow weak as you both ride away from his fatherland.'

We escorted Mr Avirmed to the door. 'Oh yes, and you must take along a guard dog,' he said, just as I hoped I'd finished with bad news for the day. 'You know, against drunks.'

'Won't it attack other dogs, when I arrive at the gers?' I asked Ermek, as we closed the door behind him.

'Absolutely!' Ermek said. He told me that Kermit had already offered one of his dogs, a Mongol dog, the sort G.K. was afraid of. They are burly, black and with yellow spots above the eyes. I remember this mutt of Kermit's, sitting in the courtyard, tied to its weighty chain. It was all too typical of its breed.

Ermek added, 'Kermit says he is a very honest dog. If you give him sweet things, he will be your friend.'

'I'm more worried about people who aren't his friend. Every person and every dog along the route will be mauled. Besides, people won't invite me to stay if my dog has just killed theirs. At least, I wouldn't.'

'But on the other hand you get 100 per cent security.'

There was no point in discussing the subject further, not while I didn't have a way to cross the desert. But Ermek had already set his analytical, megabyte brain onto the problem.

'The army!' he said, excitedly. He could hardly keep back his plan. 'They must do patrols. They'll definitely have wells out there.'

'Brilliant!'

Ermek beamed. 'I just need to convince them you are harmless.'

17th April

Spring is here, time is ticking away. News from the army HQ about using their wells is promising. Ermek and I just have to keep our nerve. We have a starting date – 1st June. According to my calculations, I'll get down from Siberia, and down through the Mongolian steppes by the end of the summer, crossing the Gobi from the Altai in the west in the autumn, when it's cool. Too early, and I'll roast. Too late, and I'll freeze.

Ermek on the phone. 'I have spoken to Kermit in Mörön and he said he has some equipment requirements.'

I braced myself for these 'equipment requirements'. Though he didn't have much experience of town life, Kermit, aspiring cameraman and filmstar, would surely have expensive tastes.

'He asks for two things. A cowboy hat and also a pair of sunglasses like Elvis Presley wore. But I think he means James Dean.'

'Do they have these things in Mongolia?'

'Oh yes, in the market. There is quite a demand.'

18th April

My flat is roasting – still twenty-seven days to last out until 15th May, when the heating goes off. Today my new teacher, Ganchimeg, set me a language test. She sat in the kitchen while I paced back and forward, mouthing Mongolian words, wondering what can be done about the pollution. As usual, the cause is not what one would think, in this case the billowing Soviet power stations, but the romantic-looking gers, which around Ulaanbaatar are forced to rely on coal.

In front of the State Circus, an old woman went by, pushing a pram. Inside the pram, soft drinks for sale. Two Mormons in the street, seemed to be waiting for a bus. White shirts, black name tags, swigging Chinese coke. Where were they going? What were they doing? I went back to look at them from time to time. Buses came and went. They seemed stranded with nowhere to start spreading their empire - another conundrum: Mongols hate the imperialist missionaries, yet share their family values. The invading American junk culture, however, they seem to adore.

My neighbour has a visitor. She's out on her balcony flicking milk to the sky, blessing her day as if she's back home in the steppe, not on the fourth floor of a housing block. I already miss the unhindered hospitality of the people of open spaces, and the open spaces themselves, now being unwrapped from the snow, like food from clingfilm in the freezer.

19th April

Ermek and I are assembling the riding equipment. I've found only one Westerner who dared claim he was comfortable in a Mongol saddle. He was 5 ½ feet tall, square and chunky, like a Mongolian. However, I must try to understand this saddle and so I'm asking Kermit to fly down from Mörön to help build one that's my size. We also need to buy the camels. Kermit will ride them up to Mörön, in Khövsgöl, the start of the mountains. We surely can't be expected to worry about Mr Avirmed's warning that Mongol camels get 'homesick'.

Right: *Young monks at Gandan Khiid monastry, Ulaanbaatar. Buddhism is resurgent after years of communist repression, and a new twenty-six-metre copper statue of the Buddha has been erected and gilded to replace the one dissected and removed to Russia in the purges, when priests were killed and more than 700 monasteries destroyed.*

Kermit has arrived. However, he is not quite the same Kermit. In place of his del, he is wearing a fake leather jacket, and in place of his riding boots, he wears plastic slip-ons. His hair is greased and cropped around the side like a Teddy Boy and he stinks of perfume. He was wearing sunglasses and had difficulty seeing his way along the hall.

'What's happened to him?' I whispered to Ermek. 'He looks like a Miami Beach pimp.'

'He's not so used to Ulaanbaatar,' Ermek said, sympathetically. 'All country boys look like this at first.' He added, slightly less sympathetically, 'He's run out of money, but he wonders if you can give him some of his wages to buy one of those stupid false ties on elastic.'

'Has Benedict bought my cowboy hat and new sunglasses yet?' Kermit asked, feeling his way to a seat. I put on the kettle, and we got out the maps and Ermek briefed him about the intended route to the Gobi. Then we went off to the market to buy bits and pieces for a Mongol saddle.

After the sparse countryside, the market was extraordinary: Mongolians in a group of more than a thousand, entrepreneurs offering carpets, boots, whole gers, other men and women ambling about proffering a stirrup, a milk churn, a spare tyre, a dented cigarette lighter. The sight was both pitiful and uplifting – the optimism of man, even on the brink.

Once Kermit had upgraded his sunglasses to the James Dean version and we had acquired the cowboy hat, we were free to go about looking for the components of a saddle. Kermit led the way, smoothly fending off substandard stirrup irons, blithely accepting a perfect wood base. Eventually we had the full kit, even those brutish metal studs designed by Genghis to combat laziness in horsemen.

Aeroplane to Altai, in the western Gobi: Ermek has placed Kermit next to me so that I can practise my Mongolian. As the plane meandered around the runway, Kermit settles down to teach me. He does not know that I've been through five teachers already.

Later: In Altai we seconded a jeep and, after dithering around a market while Kermit looked for more trifles, headed off. The Gobi plains had now lost their dusting of snow, and there was a tinge of green new shoots among the browns and greys of the exhausted pastures.

'You know, the Gobi is good for children's eyesight,' Ermek said, as mile upon mile of plain stretched out ahead, reaching like a calmed sea to the sky. 'The land stretches the eyes, until you don't need spectacles like mine.'

Beyond Sharag *sum*, we began calling in at gers, having to accept a cup of tea from each before we could ask who had camels for sale. Finally, a youth filled our jeep with his in-laws and led us across the flatlands to his wife's sister's best friend's place. As we neared their ger some of the camels stopped in the road, and the biggest one stared at us indignantly, expecting us to get out of the way.

Finally, having outmanoeuvred the camels, we drew up to the ger and sat ourselves down for a cup of tea. I noticed that, spring having advanced across the Gobi before the rest of Mongolia, nearly everyone here was in warm weather clothes, which seems to mean baseball hats, track suits in florid blues and yellows, arms and legs decorated with white 'go-faster' stripes. Now that winter is receding, it's beginning to look as if the entire country is going to an amateur athletics meeting.

Ganbat, the camel owner, started up his motorbike and took a boy called Enkhjin away to herd the camels nearer – they'd mysteriously slunk away. Enkhjin – ten years old but looks six – is expected to lasso one of these big male camels, mount it bareback and ride it back to the ger bringing with him the rest of the herd. Off he went, barefooted on the back of the motorbike, to begin the task. He thinks nothing of it.

I went outside to watch the camels approach. I was stopped by a sweet smell, a scent that was utterly new to me in Mongolia. Then I realised it was simply the smell of fresh water.

The camels came, a rippling dark line that gradually separated from the silver mirage. They thumped towards us, maybe thirty chocolate-brown males, heavy coated and magnificent, their necks draped with thick fur, humps tufted, shaking and waving as they ran. There was no hesitation as they came towards a ditch – straight across, smashing through the water. They swerved around an abandoned bicycle, up a shingle slope and down. There was a fearlessness about them which I haven't seen in the Arabian dromedary. Yet all thirty of these animals were being controlled by Enkhjin, as he rode deep within a dark sea of fur.

Kermit had been briefed to act as the buyer; he walked slowly from the ger, and cast a disinterested eye over the camels. 'These specimens are what you are trying so hard to sell?'

'Actually, we are rather reluctant to sell them at all,' Ganbat retorted. Sadly, it seemed that Kermit – man of cameras, shirts and ties though he'd like to be – had here met his match.

While the little boy kept the herd tight, directing his camel in the Mongol fashion – one hand on a single lead running to the camel's wooden nose peg – Kermit looked over the herd. They looked back –

thirty pairs of dark eyes peeking from behind thirty thick fringes. The one giant camel had dug his way into the centre of the herd so as not to be chosen, and was now looking out across the lesser camels to his beloved Gobi plain.

Ganbat and his brother swung cowhide lassoes around the camels' heads, effortlessly roping in a few at random for us to look over. The big camel was the obvious first choice; it was just a question of trying to winkle him out from the others – mane billowing like smoke, head artfully dodging lasso. 'You won't regret the choice,' Ganbat gasped, half an hour later, still struggling manfully. 'He outlasted my bicycle two years ago.'

Finally, the Top Camel was captured and tied up to the ger. He paced about, wondering what to do next. We still had two more camels to choose. Kermit picked out one which was as happy to come along as a faithful spaniel. Our third choice was Enkhjin's camel, almost certainly used by him because it had a calm temperament.

We were done. Time for another cup of tea, and Kermit was just settling down with Ganbat to sort out the money when his wife, Munkhnaran, 'Forever sun', realised that it was Tuesday. Inauspicious! The deal will have to wait until tomorrow.

In the last light Kermit is practising with a home-made gun – a 2.2 rifle with sawn-off barrel. He has insisted I buy it for tomorrow's launch north to Khövsgöl. 'We must be careful. The wolves are enemies of humans.' I'm certain there are weak calves and other, far more tempting prey around. But it's another reminder that, though there used to be trading caravans, Mongolians rarely travel long distances through desert alone; no-one is very clear about what perils, if any, really do await in the Gobi.

Overleaf: The camels would be heading north, up to these mountains in Khövsgöl. Even at their eventual departure again with the horses in early June, when this photo was taken, winter was still lingering.

22nd April

Ermek warned me that the handing over of the camels had to be done with great ceremony. Sure enough, Kermit dressed up in his new James Dean sunglasses, Ganbat and co. in their best baseball hats, and an old lady from nowhere in a gleaming gold del. She stood ready to present us with blue silk scarves and a bowl of milk, as a blessing.

Already the Top Camel was getting bored and began a sulky roar, so we thought we'd better get on with it. First, we needed to buy our own lead reins, but even this simple act became complicated. Mongolians say that if a camel is led away by the previous owner's rope, it'll one day walk all the way back home. So, while the Top Camel huffed and puffed, Ganbat's brother bought three new reins from Ganbat, and then sold

them on to Kermit, who undid Ganbat's original reins. This was followed by exchanges of snuff, countings of money and, as the reins were finally placed in Kermit's hands, the old lady stepped forward and presented a blessing: the milk and three silk scarves, each the holy blue of heaven. We touched each scarf in turn to our forehead, then each sipped some milk. There was only one thing left: the ritual handing over of Polaroid photos. Ganbat, his brother, wife, cousins, trickled up one after another to be photographed, while the Top Camel stood furiously bubbling away, a fountain of rabid spittle descending about us.

Now it's midday, and as Kermit has a three-week trek ahead of him he wants to leave right away. He'll travel north to the brink of the mountains where he'll leave the camels and head a little further north still to start the expedition with me in Tsaatan country. I'll accompany him long enough to settle the Top Camel and get Kermit safely out of the Gobi. Ermek and the driver will meet us each night, taking me away after about three days, so that we can prepare supplies to take north.

I'm calling the Top Camel 'T.C.' for now – working Mongol horses and camels don't have names, they have handy descriptions instead, for example, 'red maned-with-white-splodge-on-front-left-fetlock'. T.C. does not want to leave. Every time Kermit tries to mount him he springs up, hoping to throw him off. This would be my idea of murder – an irascible camel with a brain. But it's Kermit's idea of heaven: a companion who wants to play. I'll ride the second, placid, camel. The third, a young and willing red-maned camel, can carry our luggage at the rear.

<table>
<tr><td>23rd April</td><td>The first few hours went fine. The camels thought they were on a day's excursion, perhaps popping in to see a neighbouring ger. Kermit rode in front on T.C. – a bear rug taking huge strides slowly, the black thigh fur shaking with each heavy step. He gnashes his teeth as he walks, and bubbles furiously, creating a fine white foam in his cauldron mouth. 'No. 2', my camel, followed reluctantly, his neck ruff flowing. I led the third camel, who I've come to call 'Freddie'. Freddie is pale cheeked, eyes large and wondering – perhaps he wonders, like me, when T.C. will try his first escape bid.</td></tr>
</table>

We cut across a brown valley, a billionaire's gravel drive, the sun low but the wind warm – a roasting heat, like that of a fan oven. Our exposed skin became red, as if from a distant nuclear blast. The air is so dry and clean, objects we see on the horizon are actually tens of miles away and seem never to come nearer – they are always out of reach. That is why I want to return to travel through the Gobi Desert. The landscape seems to be only half obtainable – all the rest is a creation of magic.

Suddenly there was no sun, only grey sky and cold wind, horizons diffused in the gravels, and for a while I couldn't fix on anything with my compass. The speed of change was alarming, but the least of what I can expect on my return to the Gobi.

On from our rendezvous point with Ermek and still we weren't out of the same valley, flat and black, like burnt toast. As we did finally ascend out of it, the camels looked back in desperation. They kept doing this, craning round for that last glimpse of home. Then, ahead, I came across a human skull – a cranium, rocking around in the wind, blowing among the blades of grass. Is there a calamitous story here? A lone traveller caught out? Or an altogether more peaceful end. Traditionally, the dead were not buried but left out in remote hills for the buzzards and crows to take away, piece by piece, into the heavens. The practice was discouraged in communist times but maybe an old buffer somehow got one last dying wish, that his remains would be reclaimed by heaven as in the days gone by. I left the skull to its peace. Whatever the reason for its presence here, Mongolians do not feel comfortable talking of the dead, or even of misfortunes, and Kermit rode right on by, whistling – a refrain that's already driving me to distraction. I'm to have his company every day and night through the summer – and I have a nasty feeling he has no more songs in his repertoire.

Across a plain of stones as jagged as railway chippings. Nothing out here, it seemed, but us – and the occasional lizard or gecko panicking at the onset of large feet. The air we breathe is dust laden, perturbed by the winds. Freddie trots along behind. He is doing his best. He must have a very sweet temperament because he's not a strong camel. He is happy as long as he is with T.C., who seems to be something of a hero to him.

Though Kermit speaks no English and I speak lamentable Mongolian, we both understand only too well that T.C. can make or break my expedition. I wonder what is beneath all that camel hair? Sometimes, when the wind parts his coat, I see a huge, solid backside and this morning he bounded up a steep scree slope with the excess energy of a puppy. But he is still seething. He wants to go home and keeps stopping to remind Kermit of that. With T.C. on my side, how can I fail to cross the Gobi? But he is not yet on my side.

On approaching Taishir *sum*, the settlement where I'll leave Kermit, we took the camels to where Ermek was staying, a ger on the edge of town. The ger stood within a fence enclosure patrolled by guard dogs which were vicious even by Mongolia's high standards. T.C. made short work of them, flushing them out into the darkness.

Right: *West of Lake Khövsgöl. Mongols do little walking. Each family owns a string of horses and keeps one permanently saddled beside the ger ready for errands, replacing him after a week so he can graze and fatten up again.*

We had tea, while talking over the potential problems lying ahead for Kermit. As usual, his manner was easy, and he played with his new sawn-off rifle, as we counted out rations of sugar and cigarettes for him. Ermek went through it all with Kermit and rather to my alarm I saw Ermek was having to work hard to drum any sense of the importance

of his task into him. 'These camels are expensive! $100 each! This project must succeed for the honour of Mongolia! Do you understand? You might be seen on telly!'

'Be seen on telly,' Kermit repeated, something deep in him suddenly satisfied.

Am I really going to rely on this man? I can already tell he is going to frustrate me, with all his dreams, but I also admire him for his ease with animals, his ease with life. I suspect these qualities are held by all rural Mongolians to a degree and I must get into their psyche, become a little bit Mongolian myself to get along out here.

It was only as we were getting up to leave that Kermit glanced over the maps for himself. He rapidly began asking questions. So unperturbed by the world until now, Kermit suddenly was just a little bit overawed by the responsibility placed on his shoulders. Ermek said, 'Kermit is wondering, Supposing the big camel refuses to stand up? Should he abandon it?' We stayed on a bit to reassure Kermit. There were people living all the way north of here; they'd help him out. He should just do his best. But as we left he still looked alone.

9th May ULAANBATAAR: Ermek and I are getting on with other major tasks. I have stepped up my lessons in Mongolian and we have ordered a tent from some matronly ladies who are taking to the enterprise with gusto, insisting on emblazoning it with motifs that Genghis Khan might have favoured.

Everywhere I go, it's Genghis Khan this, Genghis Khan that. I've given up trying to escape, and am going to Kharkhorin *sum*, beside the site of his ancient capital Karakorum, to face up to him. I must find strength in modern Mongolia, in time, and I do at least have friends in Tsend and Dundoi. We shall see. But for now it's either be inspired by Laurens van der Post, or by G.K., like any Mongolian searching for inspiration.

10th May I have already written on and on about the paradoxes of this country – have I mentioned that in Mongolia, where car tyres are routinely stitched back together again with cowhide, the driving test comes after weeks of lessons and is an intellectual task that would challenge a member of Mensa? Here's another: G.K., having forged a nation out of the disparate nomadic tribes, was forced to administer his new-found empire from a fixed capital, Karakorum. His son Ogedei Khan was to complete the structure, his grandson Khubilai, who ruled North China from Shangdu ('Xanadu'), and later as Great Khan from near Beijing, was to go further, building hospitals, art galleries, medical academies and even conceivably Coleridge's 'stately pleasure dome'. In two generations, the Khans had changed from destroyers to builders. Khubilai even introduced paper money to control inflation.

I'm walking with my notebook about the late-16th-century temple complex of Erdene Zuu, the first centre of Lamaism, built from the ruins of Karakorum, and ruined itself after the collapse of the Mongol empire, then the Stalinist purges of the 1930s. Cattle are being ushered out of the complex, and monks are blowing conch shells to proclaim the start of a religious ceremony. The sky is dull white – the spring fires. It is a uniform, sullied mask and robs the air of all colour, sucking on the buildings, the chipped paint of the stupas. However in this temple, as in temples across Mongolia, there is a sense of spring, of growth. Wood scaffolding is ascending, the green tiles of the temple have the polished look of young leaves. Buddhism is flourishing again, out in the sunlight after seventy odd years in the Communist shadow.

I've entered a small, side temple that is reserved for the Dalai Lama. It has a low ceiling of wood panels, red timber posts, a wood floor spread with carpets. The golden Buddha's serenely extended hand is draped with the blue silk scarves of his visitors; around him are *thangka*, Buddhist scenes painted on cloth. There are also figurines, wood chests defended by gilded lions and cymbals on both sides magnifying in gold the sparse light. And all this, every object, is movable, stacked as in a ger. Ready to move on. It is as if the Communists have perhaps only nipped out and they may be back any moment.

In search of something left from the Great Khans though, I've now walked out of the temple, into the surrounding plains. Here, a giant granite tortoise, one of several that once acted as bases on which to stand royal proclamations. He is craning up, inquisitive, lonely among the frazzled brown grasses.

One of the first Europeans to bring back a detailed account of the Mongol court was a French monk, William of Rubruck, from his journey of 1253–55. His tales were shocking: not because the Mongols were such blood-thirsty monsters but because they weren't. Yet these were the people who had in only the previous decade been about to crush Europe. They turned back only because news had come through of the death here of their Khan, Ogedei, Genghis's successor. The Islamic world was to be saved in the same way, this time by the untimely death of Mongke, the Khan when William visited.

Right: *Kermit receiving a blue scarf, a symbol of the sacred sky, after buying the camels; T.C. is bubbling furiously behind. Transactions are made with decorum and ritual, a mark of the importance of mutual co-operation which enables the Mongolians to thrive in this barren land.*

What Rubruck saw was a place which encouraged religious debate. This was the hub of the continent, the most powerful city in the world; there was continual traffic of ambassadors from all over the great empire. Rubruck described a silver fountain shaped like a tree, created by a Frenchman captured in Hungary. At a signal blown from the trumpet of a mechanical silver angel, which rose up the tree to the top branches, out flowed a choice of alcoholic beverages – distilled mares' milk, wine, mead or Chinese rice wine. Catering for the capital was a daily logistical feat: 500 carts made their deliveries of food and drink. The milk supply was the product of 3000 mares.

And here the Mongols are, seven centuries on, all the wealth gone, and in tents again, living off the land as they were at the birth of Genghis, on the Onon River.

Far right: *The herd of male Bactrian camels from which the selection for my team was made. They are still wearing their winter coats which are harvested, then spun into yarn by women as the summer comes on.*

In the end the opulence, the trappings we count as civilisation, counted for little. They had all this and the empire which, under Khubilai, the last Great Khan, stretched from Korea to the Danube, but the Mongols didn't leave their nomadic roots behind. For, despite the rooms, the finery, Khubilai's courtiers actually preferred to live in gers, which they pitched in the gardens.

The lesson I draw from this settlement is how deep-seated is Mongolia's nomadic culture. Even the modern capital, Ulaanbaatar, has moved twenty-five times. And in this tight relationship with the land, not Genghis Khan, there must surely be enough for me to learn to cross the Gobi Desert alone.

Ermek went to the military people to ask them about water sources in the Gobi. They know all about my project from the security police, still known as the KGB, though they've changed their name twice. They've acknowledged that they do indeed have various wells, but the co-ordinates are secret. Ermek is going to have further talks with them, and has asked for a budget for 'lunch meetings' – a phrase he has evidently picked up working for European consultants.

12th May

Ermek rang to say that Kermit has safely delivered all three of my camels to Mörön as planned. The camels will wait there in the lowlands with a shepherd. We will collect them once we have launched from the Siberian border, down through the mountains.

13th May

Shortly Ermek and I will fly up to join Kermit. Adrian [Arbib, the photographer] is also joining us from the UK to record the start. It's time to buy last supplies …

I've always made a point of living off local food on expeditions, but true nomads do not plant vegetable plots and I suspect that the old men of Mongolia are bow-legged not just from horseriding but also rickets. So I have three family-size bottles of vitamin tablets from the UK and the British embassy staff are digging through their emergency supplies to create some muesli for me.

19th May   All the supplies were packed and put into the jeep for transport north. This includes the tent, complete with Genghis Khan logos, and £400-worth of veterinary medicine. As I watched the jeep leave, a violent drunk in a long black leather coat accosted the driver, Ermek's uncle, who, unhappily for the drunk, turned out to be a circus acrobat.

'This is why you need a dog,' Ermek said. 'You are not an acrobat.' Unfortunately Kermit's family have migrated for the summer, taking his family brute with them. Kermit has told us he'll try to pick one up on the actual journey.

21st May   By aeroplane with Adrian and Ermek to the provincial capital Mörön, where we've met up with Kermit and the jeep. Final supplies at the local market. While the camels, positioned somewhere nearby, fatten up, we shall continue north into the mountains to get our horses, find Tsend and start the journey.

Spring is very late. As we set off it became obvious that only now is the grass coming through, and what grasses there are have been mown flat as a putting green by horse teeth. The grasses are yellow, there is more death in them, it seems, than life. We knew that the horses we'd buy would be thin.

Kermit took us up a side valley to a family he knows. Forests swept down from crests, ending not in fences, as they might in Britain, but petering out among the grasses which spread like lawns to meet them. There was a horse herd nearby – hips protruding, manes of long, swinging tousled hair.

The head of the ger came out to greet us. He wore a maroon del, Russian cavalry boots and a fake Reebok bobble hat. With him were two girls, apparently sisters. Both were very pleased to see Kermit. He wasn't sure which one he favoured, though Ermek said his girlfriend was meant to be the one in the purple silk del. Her red cheeks were brighter than her lips and rose to meet a fringe of raven black. The only ornament on her body was a thin silver ring on her left index finger, yet standing there before Kermit, she shone as if adorned with precious metals. Her sister was shorter, in a blue silk del, eyes harder but more alert; her hands were blue with the cold, though she wasn't aware of it. The two girls exchanged glances. The girl in the purple del seized the initiative by putting on a scarf, swinging up onto a tethered horse, and galloping away to round up the herd for us. It was a glorious sight: a teenager the master of forty horses, her scarf catching the reflected light of the snow, the breath of the horses as they steamed towards us. She guided them into a stockade, the hooves rumbling on the frozen ground. These animals had been fending for themselves for six months and showed no desire to be recaptured now that the spring pastures are coming through. They shoved, kicked and bit each other, trying not to be chosen. The lasso fell on a dark chestnut with black, stormy eyes; resentfully, it lunged with its back legs at other horses.

Kermit elected to buy this beast of a creature, I suppose for its strong spirit, and also a grey horse which was docile but by no means dopey. The others were simply not strong enough; Kermit will look elsewhere for our third horse and bring them all along to Tsend's ger, where we'll prepare for the ride north.

Kermit dressed up for the ritual of buying, brushing down his del, buffing up his cowboy hat. The Beast stamped impatiently, his black nostrils flaring. This is an angry horse, but also a beautiful one: his tail hangs all the way to the ground, his eyelashes and mane are dark, his body like a polished wood ornament, slightly burnt. The grey stood quietly, rubbing his pink nose on a wood post; like the owner, he had already put as much distance as he could between himself and The Beast.

Though Kermit and the horse owner grandly enacted the handing-over ritual, there was more ceremony in the taking of the Polaroids, than in the buying of the horses. Kermit used up a whole film on the young sister, who looked doomed to have her eyes scratched out, once we were gone.

chapter five

THE GUARDIAN CROW

Genghis Khan quickly overcame his awe of the shamans

when it was a question of the survival of his supremacy.

Paul Ratchnevsky,

GENGHIS KHAN: HIS LIFE AND LEGACY, *1991*

Alpine peaks, wolf and bear kingdoms, snow plastered by wind into the grooves of the rock slopes. There are eagles up there, as free as the clouds that gather and rise with them. Passed yaks dragging bundles of ger wall lattices. Onward to Tsagaan Nuur. Last time snow was blowing horizontal across us and it looked like a Gulag outpost. Now, in the spring, there is a more open, more deceptive sky, and under it that most beautiful sight, a lone horseman traversing the land. He does so at a gallop, and though standing in his stirrups as one must when using the unforgiving Mongol saddle at speed, he seems at ease. He is part of something great, at one with horse and world.

We found Tsend not in the forest, but lodging in a ger a little nearer, right by the lakeside. 'The snow went away and we had no water to drink,' Munke explained, as she hurried to put the tea on. Enke, the adopted daughter, is away in the north but Uugantsetseg is here, still staring in wonder. She squirmed away when Tsend pushed her forward. 'She insisted that reindeer skins were especially prepared for you,' Tsend said, gesturing at the skin rugs.

There's no doubt they are eager to see us again. Soon, they began boiling up some fish, a typical Tsaatan summer food. Ermek was brave about it, but boiled trout, grayling and perch, is just not boiled sheep: 'It is unacceptable,' he said, bluntly, and went to the jeep to dig out some pot noodles. Tsend said, sprinkling salt onto a fish head, that Gana, her son, again happens to be trading down in the settlement and can guide us up to the extreme north.

29th May

Left: *Riding off with Kermit and The Beast. The spring grazing of Khövsgöl was already severely restricted due to drought in the north.*

Ermek and I went outside to try pitching my tent for the first time. It is circular, a miniature circus big top, and with its Mongol motifs looks like something ancient, from the Battle of Agincourt – Genghis Khan's army surplus. There is a 2-metre centre pole, the rest of the canvas is supported by six outer poles. It had been made by a committee of tent manufacturers, and it now seems it has to be put up by committee. As we struggled a wind came from nowhere and every passing horseman came over to lend a hand. Even then it collapsed and Tsend disgraced everyone later by resurrecting it alone, steered by Ugantsetseg around the guy ropes.

AT DUSK, Munke took Ermek outside for a quiet word. Ermek came back in, smiling. 'We are very lucky, I think.' It seems that, while we were away, Tsend somehow felt that on my return here she should contact the spirit world, whatever powers govern us, and ask their advice about my long journey. After her secrecy over the solar eclipse ritual, it's more than I dared hope. And if this really does happen, it'll be something extraordinary. Tsend did a ritual once for a Japanese film crew, who'd offered $10 000 and appealed to her against her better judgement. The result? 'Terrible. Seven of the best reindeer died.' She will never do it again for foreigners with cameras. In our case it was the spirits, not us, who requested.

30th May

Kermit arrived as I was down by the lake, watching the terns. He had three horses, as promised: the dark chestnut called (by me) 'The Beast', which I noticed lunged at Kermit when he came over to greet me; the docile grey, which looked skinnier than last time; and the new, third horse, who was nervous and stubborn, an unhappy combination but at least he's fit. Kermit will try to change him on our way south. Meanwhile I do wonder about the dark horse. When I went for my quiet evening walk through his grazing patch, he tried to run me down. It was only because he was wearing hobbles that I escaped at all. Then he stood there, daring me to try again, nostrils tubular, two blowtorches of fury. He'll get me one day, I suppose.

I went back into the ger, and found that the air was thick with a sweet smell of pine resin. An altar had been unveiled at the far end, the head, northern end of the ger. It was simply an empty shelf, but above hung the curtain of little spirit figures that I'd seen last time, like a rainbow, each representing a fragment of the sky.

Ermek had already made preparations for the ritual. He said I should put my hat on as a sign of respect, and go forward and gently place a bottle of 'Chinggis Khan' vodka – rustled up beforehand from Kermit's secret stash – on the altar together with a white sheet Ermek had purloined off his uncle the driver, and a bag of sweets from our supplies.

'What now?'

'It seems, we now wait for the stars to come out.'

We sat about, all of us expectant. Only Kermit was uninterested, but whether these matters were above him or below him, he knew this was important to me, and set about helping with the camera, whimsically tweaking it this way and that.

Then the stars must have come out because Tsend began dressing in a cloak of ribbons, and a young man appeared and tuned a large handdrum over the stove. Munke then lifted a head-dress of black crow feathers onto Tsend, fitting it as if back to front, ribbons from the head-dress obscuring her face like strands of unkempt hair. This is the garb of the classic shaman: for the Other World which she enters is one which steers but also reflects ours; it is a back-to-front, mirror existence which can reveal our own world, if you have the power to enter this other one.

Slowly, Tsend began beating the drum. We watched intently, Kermit now like us, drawn in by the theatre. As the rhythm gathered, she began spinning. Then singing, quite softly at first. Then the beat slowed, became heavy, portentous. Two men positioned themselves at Tsend's feet, to stop this blind woman from falling back onto the stove, but already I had the feeling this was no longer the dear little old lady. When I glimpsed her face it was strangely calm, eyes closed, the wrinkles gone. She was changed: younger and stronger and no longer with us, in her mind carried away to this Other World, supported by her spiritual guide, her crow.

This was not trickery, there was no doubt in my mind that she had gone from us, perhaps into a corner of her consciousness, perhaps indeed into a spiritual domain, the land of the forces which govern us and keep our planet in equilibrium. Out there she would encounter spirits, perhaps ultimately even the great god of the sky, Tengger. Like the land of Odin and the Norse gods and the realm of Zeus for the Greeks, the immortals of the spirit world may grant favours to whoever seek them there and ask, as Tsend was doing, for guidance. Some spirits are good in nature, some bad and some mischievous. None can be treated lightly. And all play their part in ensuring us mortals maintain harmony with the heavens and also our earth, the spiritual and material, not exploiting either. There's no room for Western notions of Progress here. Sometimes Tsend stopped spinning, and

Right: *Waiting, as Tsend begins her ritual for my journey. Wearing a hat indoors, especially for such formal occasions, is considered respectful in Mongolia, where hats are a prerequisite for survival and almost part of the body.*

Far right: *At the end of her journey to the spirits, Tsend, supported here by daughter Munke, collapsed back into our world. Tsend had been dressed in a back-to-front headdress, ribbons obscuring her face, to enter the spirit world – often seen as a mirror version of her own.*

waited, hand out, demanding a gift to placate or please a spirit. Munke listened intently by her ear, ready to proffer a drink from the wooden bowl, or a smoke from the wooden pipe. Then, thump, thump, she was spinning again, spiralling, spiralling, becoming more frenetic. Such was her speed, little bells, apparently sewn like the ribbons onto her back, now began rattling, jingling. She moaned, she wailed. Then, all of a sudden she was sobbing, and collapsed back towards the fire, gasping for breath. She was caught by the two kneeling men. Munke rubbed her throat, massaging it. There were concerned glances – this was someone past her prime!

Munke told Ermek to hurry up and place more sweets on the altar. At this, the travelling shaman recovered herself, then laughed hysterically – the present had done the trick. Then spiralling, spinning, on and on. She made her way, sometimes a hand came out for more vodka, sometimes for a smoke from the wooden pipe. The portrait of Genghis Khan, on the bottle of vodka, flickered as the shadow of the dancing figure crossed it – just as it did us, like the flapping wings of a black crow.

'Two hours and 40 minutes,' whispered Ermek, as the dance calmed, drawing like the heavy breathing of the dying to a close. Munke again stood by her, waiting for instructions. 'She wants us to put on the tea,' Ermek said.

Tsend was helped off with her cloak, and then laid by Munke on the floor. She was now in pain, rubbing the wrist which had beat the drum all time. Other than this, no sign that this visit to the other world had happened. She was just the blind old lady again.

After breakfast – delicious salted fish for me and Adrian, pot noodles for Ermek and Kermit – we chose a quiet moment, and at last were able to ask for a diagnosis of last night's activities. Tsend sat on her bed and I found myself down on one knee, in that grave, respectful way that Mongol men exchange snuff in greeting. It wasn't that I particularly fully believed or even fully understood her religion, but I was in awe of her, this visually handicapped, straight-backed, old woman. Last night she was a cackling dervish half her age, and that transformation alone commanded respect.

She talked quietly with Ermek for a while, and I found myself more- and more intrigued. Ermek finally spoke up. 'Okay. There's not really all that much to say.'

'Come off it! You were talking for ages.'

'Oh yes. That was about my hair problem. She has made a treatment of herbs for me.' He brandished a neat little packet, made of newspaper.

'But what did she say about my journey?'

'Only that you will be all right. Nothing will harm you. Though you should avoid dairy products.'

This was sensible advice for any traveller, though Mongolians are studious in offering only boiled milk and brucellosis is uncommon. Ermek handed me another neat little package. 'This is to keep you safe.'

'I thought you said we'd be safe anyway.'

'I have to mention that you must also be careful not to visit three gers on your travels.'

'Which three are those?'

'Any.'

'What, all groups of three gers? Does she know I'm on a five-month journey? That I'm reliant on the hospitality and guidance of all the gers scattered between here and the other end of the Gobi?' Besides, in Mongolia you don't just ride right by someone's home, ignoring the occupiers. It's like sticking two fingers in the air at a stranger: you simply don't behave like that.

'If you do visit the three gers, she says a bad spirit of the dead may attack you or your animals,' Ermek replied.

I went outside with Ermek to have a quick, quiet chat about this. 'Do you believe in this?'

'As you know, in theory I'm an atheist. I was schooled with Russians. I was taught that God is not available.'

'What about the spirits, are they available?'

'You know, this old woman really makes me think all over again.'

Ermek took off his thick blue glasses, rubbed them with his shirt, plonked them back on his small nose. We looked out over the lake, a man out there on a raft was hauling in trout. They were so large – stocks of fish are not exactly overexploited by the mutton-loving Mongols – the raft is already half underwater. 'What can I advise?' Ermek went on, 'I can only tell you she says a spirit of a dead person lives in the three gers.' Ermek shrugged. I could see that he was still wondering how this blind lady had had such an effect on us. 'Maybe, just TRY and avoid groups of three?'

I suppose I'd better, out of respect for her. But what do I do if a little old man pops out of a ger, and invites Kermit and me for tea? I can't very well say, 'Sorry mate! I have reason to believe there's a dead spirit here.'

Even without the Curse of the Three Gers we have a problem. The Mongolians say that the grazing around here is the worst in living memory, and some of them have lived seventy-five years. It's best if Ermek rides with us north up to the border to the true starting point for my journey. Then soon after we've launched back south from there towards the camels – waiting, I hope, in the lowlands – Kermit will go on ahead and move them so that we intercept them at the Mörön River. This'll mean a more westerly route, away from the heavily grazed lakesides, down through the hills. The jeep will wait there with the tent and most of the major supplies. For now, we will find food and shelter from gers we come across along the way.

'Make haste slowly ….'

LATER: Kermit put a Russian saddle on my grey horse – I'm not ready for the prominent studs adorning the Mongol one – and off we went, led by Gana and still accompanied by Ermek and Adrian, through low, forest-capped hills towards the Siberian border. The country was easy for a while, and it was a chance to get to know the three horses: the grey, which seems reasonably content; the dud, which we must swap somehow; and the dark horse, ridden by Kermit, which seems to be frothing at the mouth.

Kermit loves The Beast for its fighting spirit, just as he loved T.C. for joining in battle with him. He cantered to and fro, giggling as the horse tried to wipe him off in the trees. Ermek would tut, from time to time. 'As I have said before, sadly, Kermit behaves like a kid.'

Yes, I thought, and he's tiring his horse … Before long, though, we came to a river, which we had to cross by ferry – a semi-submerged raft powered by the ferryman and any willing passengers, who had to yank at the cable. Our horses were very good about this. They stood in the

Right: *The Tsaatan move once a month as their reindeer deplete the local lichen and have to move on through the taiga forest.*

1st June

powered by the ferryman and any willing passengers, who had to yank at the cable. Our horses were very good about this. They stood in the shallows, as Kermit came to them in turn, hoicking one front foot aboard with the lead rein, encouraging them to make the leap up onto the wet planks – which they did, perhaps because to a Mongol horse riding a raft is no challenge at all after facing winter.

The hills grew steeper, and the larch forests descended the slopes as if growing in confidence. Then we could go no further – freezing rain swept in, and we were forced to shelter in a lone ger.

We wound into a fir-lined valley, with snowy bare slopes ahead as we rose higher and higher up the northernmost valleys of Mongolia's most northerly river, the Tengis. Soon we were among trees in true taiga forest: crystal air, lichens, untrodden mosses, alpine flora – gentians, anemones. I bent in the grass and smelt the smell of home, a tendered herb garden – wild chives.

Up round a broad, snow-streaked mountain. Up and up. Now around us Siberian pine. A capercaillie in the shrubbery; a white ptarmigan silent and still, its plumage with the same ruddy freckles of the lichen boulders.

Then the horses on foot down a steep slope of mud and rock. Soft, emerald pine needles were budding from winter-blackened branches. Lichens were spread on rocks like ancient, flaked paint, some of them unhindered out here by our world's industrial pollution – as large as cabbage leaves. The trees fell away and we were in a broad, high valley. Smoke was drifting from the apexes of the Tsaatan tents, girls with long plaited hair gathering wood, reindeer scratching at the lichens. We drew up at Gana's tent. His wife, also called Gana, was milking the reindeer into a bucket of birch bark; the mothers were honking loudly, impatient to be left with their young.

Inside Gana's tent, a baby was dangling from the ceiling poles, tied securely into a wood cot, a plank of bark. Reindeer meat hanging about him in strips. At the back a simple shrine of coloured ribbons, a central doll with smart black fur cuffs.

2nd June

Gana says his family moves house ten or twelve times a year, such is the slow rate of growth in a place with a two-and-a-half-month summer and not a generous spring or autumn either. The tents are easy to dismantle – the canvas is set on three poles tied at cross angles, with other poles laid on top – when it's time to move, the poles are left where

As we warmed ourselves around his fire, I asked Gana what he wants most in life. This is not a romantic existence, there are no hospitals, nor is there money for shoes. What's more, Gana is in a position to know exactly what he's missing. He was in the army and has a prized photo of himself in uniform, a spread of medals down his short chest. I had good reason to expect a shopping list.

He decided on an answer. Ermek listened, translated. 'I want just to keep the family well and happy.' Then he hesitated. He's tempted, I thought: 'Given the cash, what he'd really like is a Sony Walkman. A chainsaw.' Gana thought a bit more, then reached his decision. 'I have one girl and one boy. I want one more of each, really.'

3rd June

Snow has been blowing through the valley, more and more steadily. I climbed to a ridge to look out over Siberia – the border is 15 kilometres away – and to be with the last of winter's diminishing ice. I slipped and strode on the shales. The snow came heavier – this is summer in Siberia.

Now I am up here, writing in my notebook. Ermek, down in the valley, thinks I'm mad. 'You'll get sick. You have a tough journey ahead. Tomorrow is the BIG DAY.' But I feel alive up here, looking out over the forests. Down below, older reindeer are grazing, the young are bounding through thickets, wolves are somewhere up here with me, also forest lemmings, wolverines, lynx, sable. But all are invisible and silent, perhaps sleeping.

This is the start of my journey. From northernmost Mongolia, the edge of Siberia, I'm heading down into the steppes and then into the Gobi Desert. I can take encouragement from one extraordinary man, who emerged from Mongolia. Not, for once, Genghis Khan, but his right-hand man. His name was Subedei, some people say a Tsaatan himself and some people say the greatest military strategist the world has ever seen. Alexander the Great's achievements were squandered by his generals, Napoleon met his Waterloo, but the empire Subedei helped create was four times the size of Alexander's before Genghis died and passed it on to further generations to expand. Subedei was to go on to win a total of sixty-five pitched battles. In the poetic medieval record, The Secret History of the Mongols, Subedei is quoted as telling Genghis, as they set out to unify Mongolia at the very start of their careers: 'Becoming a rat I shall gather with others.' This is what I have to do in my own little way, gather skills as I go along. Then I'll be ready to walk alone through the Desert, rather worryingly the largest arid expanse in Asia.

Gana stood quietly with his wife as they watched us slowly ride out through the shallow snows, into the trees which are now ghostly, ill-defined shadows.

We zigzagged up out of the valley, the unshod feet scratching, clacking. My horse veered from the trail, too sensible to wrestle with the mud, preferring instead to barge through scrub. Freezing sleet fell as we traversed the crest and descended. A great grey owl cut silently across our path.

Already I am so fond of the bony, grey horse – his pink lip, his facial hair. He's patient with me. He's tolerant of my ignorance, trying his best, like a good boy scout. In England this white horse would be known as a 'grey', and, in the same convoluted logic of horsemen, in Mongolia he would be known as 'Ulaan', which means red. Meanwhile, Kermit continues to charge back and forward on The Beast across my path, hitting out with a *tashuur*, the whip, like a wooden truncheon, carried by every horseman. The Mongolians handle their horses as we in the West might treat a hire car, using them until exhausted, then returning them. They are not given names and never fed by hand. It's a business relationship. And when it's finished, a replacement is plucked from the pool. I have to keep reminding myself that this is survival: you cannot be sentimental out here. Or rather, that's the young Mongolian's view. I've noticed older men tick off Kermit and other youths for their cavalier attitude towards using the whip, and the more leathery and seasoned herdsmen definitely develop a soft spot for favourite and faithful horses which have suffered many winters beside them. Over a cup of tea they get quite dewy eyed recalling particularly valiant, though still nameless, steeds.

Tonight we are reliant, as we will be until we have our tent and other supplies, on the hospitality of gers along the way. We must get away from the poor grazing as quickly as possible. Tomorrow, onward south-west towards the camels.

I rode on with Ermek, Kermit and Adrian disappearing for a while to swap our dud horse, and returning with a chestnut. This horse seems moderately fit and we now have our three proper mounts. Much to Kermit's astonishment, I made an effort to let him get to know me. The chestnut was wary at first, but I talked to him, letting him get used to my smell. He seems to be beginning to trust me. 'Your friend!' Kermit said. He thinks it's very funny to get to know a horse, but also pointless, and maybe stupid.

Overleaf: *Horses, masters of the Mongolian steppe, are herded here by reindeer. The hope of these small Tsaatan bands, which only narrowly evaded communist attempts to settle them, is to be allowed to be reunited with reindeer herders living across the Russian border in Siberia, where they came from.*

THE GUARDIAN CROW

Through glades of Siberian larch, moving with a herd of yaks. The shadow of a black kite passed over us. As we came up, a baby yak slipped smoothly from her mother's womb. I jumped off my horse and watched as the mother licked her calf, occasionally biffing away an interfering heifer. I waited the two minutes it took for the calf to be able to stand. Each lick of its mother's tongue was strong enough to knock it off its feet. I hope I'm never too old to find magic in such a moment. We trotted on, up through the firs, Scotch pine, then aspen. A lone, red-billed chough on an ungrazed rise; beside it, edelweiss growing brightly.

13th June

For five days I have continued south-south-west with Ermek. Kermit and Adrian have gone on to Mörön to move the camels to our rendezvous point. Ermek knows little about the countryside and is like a boy scout, insisting on checking compasses, checking maps. We rode up through the valley where we bought The Beast and Ulaan. Now there is only a brown patch of grass where the ger once stood, but that didn't stop the horses dilly-dallying and looking around for their herd. We crossed ice, which plugged a river, and zigzagged up into a larch forest, then down, through air sweetened by tree buds, now spilling out tender new leaves.

Onward, asking directions from herders we encountered: a boy taking a ride on a billy goat, a woman stoning her dog to keep it out of range of us. Down into a stony valley bed, inching out of the mountains, towards the steppes of Mongolia. Beside a meltwater stream a duck – I think a ruddy shelduck – plunged out of the sky, into my path, and began a little dance for me, whirling on the spot, spreading one wing. It was mimicking a wound, drawing me away from its young; I stopped, hobbled The Beast, and looked around for the chicks. I found eight or nine being tossed in the river current. I turned back to The Beast, and found he wouldn't let me on again.

Now we are in a ger near Mörön River, our supposed rendezvous point with Kermit. We have been waiting here for two days and no sign. It is no-one's fault. Where do you arrange to meet someone in a country of nomads? Roads shift, houses move. The maps look great at first sight, studied works of art. Then you start to notice that the only permanent habitations, the Russian *sums*, are in brackets. This is a map for nomads. The shepherds we consult get off their horses, sit cross-legged on the ground and read the names of mountains, and ponder fondly on blue lines which represent lakes and rivers which are not there either, just yet. Sometimes they enjoy pinpointing which families are in which valleys, knowing where, like the rivers, their herds flow.

We have now moved a further day south, then west, to ask around about Kermit and the three camels. Here, rock crags jut out from pine slopes and the grazing is as exhausted as further north. Any families arriving now will have to move on again, hunting pastures which will normally have had another few months of recuperation. Ahead somewhere, the steppes and the enormous skies that seem to reach to heaven.

We are staying in a small ger, the owner of which has a red face and watery eyes. That means he's either been drinking or has been out in the wind. He had heard of a man with three camels about a day's ride away and, given a bit of financial inducement, has now ridden off there himself to spare our horses.

I've now come with Ermek to where the horses are grazing, tethered on a long rope to a stake in the ground. Even The Beast looks tired. Surely, a lot of this is Kermit's fault? He drove the animal hard, cantering back and forward up the mountains to the Tsaatan.

It's not just Kermit. I know little about horses, and this is THE country of horsemen, but I do know about camels, and I can see that the young men place loads unevenly, horse girth straps are sometimes tightened around the guts, the horses' mouths have dermatitis because of ill-fitting iron bits and all domesticated animals are routinely thumped to keep them going. Again, I think this treatment is the recklessness of youth – the same thing that, back in Britain, results in higher insurance premiums for younger car drivers. But this all means we might have trouble on our hands. The young Mongolian herder, in this case Kermit, is used to having a herd at his disposal, a place where the horse can recuperate while you pick out another mount. We have no such horse herd.

THE THREE GERS

In Mongolia it is not accepted to knock at the door of a yurt...

The guest is supposed to shout loudly, 'Hold the dog!' even if there is no dog,

for what he actually means is to let the host know that he is coming.

Advice to foreigners, Ya Yunden, G. Zorig and Ch Erdene, THIS IS MONGOLIA, *circa 1990*

15th June

The jeep, driven by Ermek's acrobat uncle, has turned up with Adrian, guided by the ger owner on horseback. Ermek will leave me here and I'll ride with the owner to Kermit, who is waiting with the camels and luggage. As I wrote off last letters home for Adrian to take back to the UK, the ger was dismantled beside me. It was like unwrapping a present: the horsehair ropes unwound, the felt walls pulled away, to reveal all the family furniture within the skeleton of support poles. The door was taken away, the chimney pulled down, and soot banged out. Piece by piece it was all loaded onto eight camels, which already looked sick of the job.

Travelling is my profession, it's what I have learnt to do well. But it's impossible not to feel in awe of a family which can pack up their entire lives in one-and-a-half hours. They do it three or four times a year, to keep their animals in good health – knowing which vale offers shelter from Spring winds, which pastures are richest in Summer, or receive good sun in Autumn. If no snow falls in Winter, then into the ecological equation must be placed the need of access to a river – which will be cracked open, and the entire herd led over the ice perhaps thrice weekly to drink.

Next the sheep were gathered and pointed in the direction of the river. The entire herd plunged down the banks for a pre-migration drink. Finally the camels stood up, knowing it was time, once again, to trudge round the hills to the next grazing. The family saddled up their horses and led off, tailed by the camels and then the flocks.

Left: *With Kermit, who is riding the chestnut, crossing the Mörön river. The valley had been stripped by goats which are valued for their cashmere wool. Free enterprise has exploded in Mongolia and with it a steep increase in the number of herds.*

THE THREE GERS

Ermek and I were left in their dust cloud, leaning on the jeep bonnet, doing final admin. work: wages to be paid, food supplies to be brought through to Ölgii, the Kazakh provincial town in the north-west, up in the Altai mountains, where we hope to arrive in about a month. In addition, Ermek must now secure the secret co-ordinates of the military wells across the Gobi. I won't feel happy until I have them in my hand.

Ermek wished me luck. He looked at the three horses, which without exception had their heads down, and were rootling like pigs for something to eat. 'I hope you all get through,' he said.

It seems very early for anyone to have doubts.

I stood for a moment with the horses, watching the jeep disappear, then the ger owner led me to the steppe through the last of the rolling hills. Larks twisted in the sky, marmots stood watching us eager-eyed beside their burrows. A dog came across the grasses and for a while padded alongside us. We lay down by a stream, and while the horses chopped at the thick meadow grasses, drifted to sleep. In the mid-afternoon we mounted up again and my guide began singing a ballad, an unabashed, rich melody such as – elsewhere in the world – comrades in arms might sing, gathering strength to achieve heroism in battle. But this was a song of heroism in the hills. The man sat in his saddle with a stiffened back, arm out, singing as if to the grasses, marmots, falcons and larks. The ballad had a resonance, I felt, with the hills. It seemed as if this was a romantic cadence shaped not only by the human spirit but the natural laws of geography, the sweeping steppe of Mongolia.

We have arrived at Kermit's camp, though he is not here and nor are the camels – nor is there sign of the Mongol dog he's meant to be acquiring. It is 10 p.m. and there is still light, though it is grainy and pale. I look with pity at three camels which are over by the stream. They are skinny creatures, hairless and meek, and seem on their last legs.

What has happened to Kermit? He will come back here to sleep, I'm sure. He's left a Russian army sleeping bag and various photos of girls are wrapped up inside it.

LATER: For want of anything else to do, I went over to the three weakling camels. The nearest had no humps at all, just flaps of skin hanging down the ribs. The second camel had one-and-a-half humps but had a glassy-eyed, vacant face. I turned to look at the third camel. Much bigger and pacing restlessly, it was tied to a huge boulder which it was contemplating how to shift. I chuckled – memories of T.C., my top camel.

Then I stopped, looking at the big camel again. I walked forward, still looking. It couldn't be true, but it was. These were my camels: T.C., No. 2 and Freddie. I went up to reassure the youngest, little Freddie, and stroked him for a while. Suddenly I realised he wasn't Freddie, he was No. 2, the medium-sized camel. He had shrunk.

The throaty cough of a motorbike and Kermit came up. He had a variety of grasses stacked up behind him on the seat. *'Temeenii Khool!'* he said, cheerfully. Camel food. I guessed he'd borrowed the motorbike, somehow, to bring different grasses for them to try. Kermit left the bike and began distributing the grasses. The camels looked at their portions and then back to us. They weren't interested.

'Yasan be?' I asked Kermit. What's up?

Kermit paused, putting it into simple Mongolian for me. 'The camels are crying,' he said.

We went back to the tent, and lay down on the grass with my torch and the dictionary. Around midnight, I at last had the whole story. The camels had been off their food, ever since their arrival, a month ago. I remembered something from before that I wrote in this notebook about camels: 'they will get homesick away from the Gobi'. They were the words of Mr Avirmed, head of the Gobi National Park – not someone, one would have thought, prone to flights of fancy.

Tonight, I won't sleep. I'm so angry – angry with Kermit's uncle, who was meant to be looking after the camels, and left them to pine away and angry with myself, for bringing them up here. I'm also left with a sense of guilt. This evening I didn't even recognise my own camels, these animals that are depending on me.

Kermit is oblivious to all this. He's tucking into a can of meat, something Ermek put into my hand as a treat, as we parted. 'I have found a Mongol dog,' he said excitedly, between mouthfuls. 'We can meet him in Sharag *sum*, 10 kilometres away. You will see that he's a very pretty boy.'

We will leave tomorrow, when the horses have had a full day's grazing.

I asked Kermit to help me treat some potential saddle sores on the chestnut. He held the horse while I unscrewed a tube of cortisone. Kermit inspected the tube and smelt it, then watched me apply the green liquid, entranced as he is with every piece of Western paraphernalia. But he is also mystified at the effort I'm taking – last week giving the horses anti-worm treatment, today checking for the sores. It's the job of the winter to eliminate the weak.

Kermit anyway is never one to dwell on things. He matily slapped my shoulder, and said, '*Khool id*!' 'Come and eat! as I put the cap back on the tube and gave the chestnut a reassuring pat. 'Later we sell the horse,' he shouted cheerily into my face. 'Good meal for someone!'

I happened to catch sight of the writing on the bottom of the tube: 'Not to be used on horses intended for consumption'.

Too late, I thought.

While Kermit went off to look for pack saddles for the camels, I stayed at the camp, sorting stores which must last us until Ölgii. No. 2 is the weakest camel by far, and the success of the journey rests with an unlikely combination: Big T.C. and little Freddie. T.C. is the only fit camel – but surely can't carry luggage just yet … He still has anger in his eyes; he circles like a hungry carnivore around the boulder which anchors him here, stopping him from escaping to the Gobi. I half wish he would break free in the night, and make a run for it. I took the camels to drink, and they seemed to me to be crying, just as the Mongolians believe – that silent, most painful sobbing, when you have run out of tears.

The horses are not in a good state either. They are strong enough for the moment, but that has more to do with the Mongol temperament than their physique. Bones project, like those of concentration camp inmates. To cap it all, my best knife has remains of sheep gut on it; someone has borrowed it to do a bit of butchering.

Right above: An average ger weighs approximately 250 kilos and is constructed from lattice wood walls, with poles added like the spokes of a wheel into a hub at the apex, and bands of felt and canvas bound round.

17th June

We should have been off by eight or nine this morning, but things did not go well from the start. First, we brought forward Freddie. Like many a novice camel he wasn't interested in carrying luggage and kept springing up during the loading, hoping we'd finished. I'd never loaded a Mongol pack saddle before and had to be nannied along by Kermit, and all in infernal Mongolian with Kermit trying to augment it with sign language, while holding ropes with his teeth. The saddle padding was placed either side of the humps and bound tightly on, followed by the black luggage bags and tent poles: it was like building a bird's nest.

And then T.C. He was roaring even before we got him to sit down. A pair of shepherds, who'd long since been watching us from a peak, rode up and waded in to help, securing him with hobbles. I stepped back and watched them. But T.C. would not be beaten. He bellowed, he swiped at the men with his enormous jaw, and finally stood up and walked away, hardly noticing as he snapped his hobbles and miscellaneous obstructive ropes.

We would have to use No. 2.

Right below: In little more than an hour, the ger and every household possession, are placed on camels – these freshly shorn – and are on the move.

'He's too thin,' I said to Kermit, though there wasn't much choice.

Kermit said No. 2 was all right. He was a Mongol camel, tougher than the 'foreign ones' that I knew.

We loaded him up while T.C. stood around like a thug, menacing us with glances.

So we are ready to leave, the camels look forlornly about, hoping we are going back to the Gobi now. Actually, we are, though it'll be a three-month route via the Altai mountains in the west. We do not have much luggage – maybe 150 kilos between Freddie and No. 2, which is half what I would consider a decent load – but the sooner we get T.C. on our side, the safer the expedition will be.

LATER: I volunteered to ride T.C. We know from the Gobi that he will tolerate carrying a passenger at least and he must get used to us as quickly as possible. I climbed on, without incident, and led the way with No. 2 and Freddie while Kermit, riding The Beast, brought along the other horses.

Passing Sharag *sum*, Kermit disappeared to go and get the Mongol dog. I rode on, controlling all three horses and all three camels. T.C., sensing I had my hands full, also sensed an opportunity: he became frisky, testing me. But before he could rid himself of me, Kermit reappeared with a Mongol dog, only a year old and running on the end of a long piece of plastic string. Kermit was jubilant about this little character, Bankhar, enjoying its antics: the way he rolled over as he took fright at the horses, pounced floppily on crickets, yelped in terror as the horse hooves clipped him, swallowed the little lark chick that I was filming. Then, let loose, he went marmot hunting. The marmots watched him come, plopping down their holes at the last minute, the wisest ones taking their time.

I found that T.C. walked with a slow, easy manner, a result of his almighty strength. It was reassuring having such a huge creature along with us, but he is no more use at the moment than a lucky mascot – and he is not particularly lucky. In the mid-afternoon, out in the plains, he tossed me to drop 3 metres down to the ground, seizing the chance when No. 2 sat down in protest at all this work. Kermit is blaming the heat for No. 2's poor performance, but I heard him say to a horseman we met on the road, that the middle camel was 'bad'.

We came to a lake in a bowl of rich grasses, and decided to sleep there, where the horses could drink. At twilight Bankhar was still running from marmot home to marmot home, on and on, until he flopped down beside Kermit, hoping for his mutton. Already, his instinct – to set out and destroy, then return to master – is strong.

A feeling of release, now that we are off, sleeping under the open sky. A cool but not cold evening and we are too tired to pitch the seven-pole tent. Kermit is battling with my stove – but just to play, not to cook. He enjoys nurturing the flame, teasing it by withdrawing its petrol supply. In my little red notebook, I have fifty verbs written down for him to point to, but he rarely uses them, and I rarely have to guess what he is saying. He communicates with me using the same instinctive nods and whispers with which he masters the camels and horses.

We slept in full clothes, cold air creeping up the hill from the lake. T.C. was more-or-less free all night. He broke another set of hobbles and there was nothing we could do to contain him. Only his loyalty to the other camels, I think, kept him here. My hope is that gradually T.C. will take us home to the Gobi with him.

18th June

Kermit came over to watch me treating the chestnut with cortisone, holding the tube while I applied the cotton wool. 'You would like to learn the Mongol way?'

'Yes, I would,' I said. And I meant it, though I knew he was trying to stop himself laughing.

He pretended to wipe a wodge of faeces off his bum to slap like butter on the wound. '*Baas*!' he said, releasing an explosion of giggles: 'Shit!'

On through dull yellow hills. Riding Ulaan, the white horse, now. I wonder if we should let go of No. 2 camel. We passed a herd of male camels that regarded him fondly. Yet our three camels have already established their own loyalty to each other and are determined not to be separated. Other camels we meet block their way, behaving like little boys recruiting members for their gangs, but the three camels resent this, and barge their way through. I also feel my own loyalty to No. 2 – I don't want to lose him. My hope is that my camels, brought up in the Gobi, are far tougher than I can possibly imagine. Minus 40, their typical winter, is no laughing matter.

Sometimes, we call in at gers for a cup of tea and cheese or *bordzig* deep fried flour biscuits, and stock up on dried curds, *aaruul*, or *aarts*, fermented cheese. By now I am aware how many of our movements are prescribed by custom, even the tea pot: it is placed with the handle to the door, towards those entering. Some beliefs are said to be echoes of more treacherous days – vodka is offered in a silver bowl, which might help show up any unwelcome impurities, like arsenic, and

Overleaf: *The departing family home and goods. The Bactrian camel is related to the endangered wild camel of the Gobi but has been bred for its strength and fur. Mongols say their camels can carry 300–400 kilograms and travel 30 miles in a day. However, in practice they never travel loaded for more than a few days and the wild camel – small-humped and with comparatively little hair – though less powerful can survive in even harsher conditions.*

Kermit takes a cigarette himself, before passing the packet to strangers. The most famous case of poisoning is still that of Yesugei, the father of Genghis Khan – who else? A leader of one of the numerous proto-Mongol clans, he encountered members of another confederation on his way home from concluding a marriage agreement for his oldest boy, Temujin. Offering hospitality in the steppe tradition, the men also recognised him as an old enemy, and mixed poison in with the food. With the death of this powerful man, Yesugei's widow and children were in danger from rival factions and the family fled, eking out an existence hunting small mammals on the banks of the Onon River. Gradually, Temujin, though still a teenager, gathered support and began eliminating rivals, showing an early facility for this by shooting his half brother Bekhter – who'd stolen his fishes – as if for target practice. As other factions were wiped out or won over, the miscellaneous Turkic-Mongol peoples were unified into 'Mongolia'. Temujin was created Genghis Khan, 'Universal King', in 1206 and now found he had an army on his hands. As if looking for a job for it, he set about eliminating troublesome neighbouring powers – which meant, for all practical purposes, an invasion of the rest of the world.

Shepherds leave their flocks and ride up to look us over. We are still in Khövsgöl *aimag*, and Kermit is still a local, and rejoices in swanking with his mates. He is now sporting Ermek's sleeveless jacket; it has innumerable pockets in which he keeps losing things. Sometimes young horsemen stop us to say that our baggage is badly tied down, which it isn't. It's all bravado and makes me very irritated. But Kermit is immensely gracious, letting them 'show' us how to load camels, before they gallop off flamboyantly, leaving us with the ropes in a far worse state. Until another man rides up, looks at our baggage, ticks us off for poor workmanship and insists on re-doing it.

And so it goes on, everyone having to show his participation in the mutual effort of getting by, out in these arid lands. As for the women, when we call in at gers they bury themselves in household tasks. A stranger comes, a foreign one at that, but they spend their time rolling pastry for noodles, cutting meat from the bone. The point is to show your willingness to offer shelter, even if it means offering the same old food as everyone else – boiled, vegetable-less sheep. My theory: meat is the staple food, so it must be made bland, like other staples – rice, potatoes, sweet potato, corn or maize. And bland they most certainly have made it.

A wind blew up, and soon was blowing so strongly into our eyes we could not see for our tears. We decided we ought to stop at the next ger.

At long last, it came in sight. But there wasn't one, there were three. THREE! Tsend's warning about a cluster of three gers – completely forgotten until now – came back with surprising clarity, shimmering across the plains. Should I bother about it? I'd wanted to respect her religion, but quite honestly, it was a bit of a nuisance right now. Besides, no-one would know…

Kermit sped up. I suddenly realised that he hadn't been around when Ermek and I heard about the Curse of the Three Gers, and we hadn't told him. There'd been so many things of obvious importance to be done: kilos of sugar to count, doses of animal antibiotic to sort. In the end it hadn't seemed important. The gers were right ahead, and the sky worse: yellow in shafts, smoky blue in angry clouds. Should I stop Kermit? It did prick my conscience: I need to respect these people if I am to succeed in seeing their world.

Then children and adults came out to welcome us, holding our horses and inviting us in. It was already becoming too late. A storm was threatening, the horses getting skittish at the onset of horizontal rain. Kermit dismounted and the camels quickly sat down before we could change our minds. I looked at the gers again and convinced myself that really, if you counted a storage tent at the back, there were three and a half.

We unloaded the camels, as the rain flew with the dust. The women milking yaks had already covered their faces completely in scarves. As we made our way up to the gers, I noticed Bankhar for the first time defending me against oncoming snapping, snarling dogs. He was too small to offer much of a deterrent but he curled his lip in his apprentice-killer way.

Indoors, all was calm. We were not only given tea, but also a huge bowl of boiled sheep innards. '*Gedes*' the host announced excitedly, digging his knife through a stomach wall. The best bits were cut off for me: entrails stuffed with blood, intestines, heart. I took some liver, muttering appreciative words in the hope that this would stop my hosts insisting I had a second helping. However, they simply warmed to me more and proffered overly generous dollops of fat. I ate, knowing there was no escape. Those innards which I discretely left aside now, will be saved up for me for breakfast – warmed up in tea.

There was a break in the rain. A girl child was helped up onto the ger roofs to tie them down with horse hair rope. I went to check on my animals. A horse herd, stirred by the moving air, marched by. The camels munched at the grass, unmoved by the storm. It's what I've been waiting for: they are eating again – not pining, but living in hope of seeing their desert. Maybe it's all going to be fine.

Vodka was produced last night and we woke late – to find T.C. gone. He'd done it! I felt a perverse joy. He must have left with the early dawn, marching to the horizon before any of us was awake. Freddie was upset, he looked abandoned. A young camel should look like that if his master leaves him, but his loyalties are still to T.C. – he is Top Camel and I haven't earned that place.

Above: *Children are sent away to board at school, but lend essential support in the summer when livestock must be fattened in the pastures and goats, sheep and horses milked.*

Three horsemen rode off to look for him, but I knew the direction T.C. would be heading in – that desert – and caught up with him in the tall marsh grasses. I felt so sorry for him. He knows where the Gobi lies and yet has to go the long way round, with us. Never mind, T.C., one day perhaps you'll succeed.

We left soon after, but in the mid-afternoon, on a gentle up-slope, No. 2 sat down. This time, he would not go further. Kermit tugged at his nose line; he simply groaned, not caring what we might do to him. Kermit and I sat down with him and Kermit waited for me to pronounce. There was really no choice. No. 2 would not reach the Gobi, let alone walk with me through it.

Kermit said, 'He is crying.' Sometimes I wonder if the Mongols are too fanciful. They seem incurable romantics. Their ballads, their names: Baatar, which means 'Hero', Bold which means 'Steel'. In the Gobi the herdsmen play music on the *morin khuur*, a two stringed fiddle of horse hair, to mother camels when they refuse to give milk to their young. Finally, their hearts soften, it's said, the mothers cry with sadness, repent and give of themselves freely. Now, No. 2 was crying, or perhaps there was a little piece of grit in his eye. I do not know.

We walked sadly into the nearest permanent settlement, Tsetserleg *sum* – more houses than gers – the horses' hooves clattering on the dust and pebble streets. We drew up at the house of one of Kermit's lady friends. She is an unpromising, plump, serious lady, who turns out (shockingly) to be only four years older than me. She let us tie up our team to her fence and chuck our baggage into her yard. She served up

a mediocre lunch in a kitchen, which had been slowly smoked, like kippers, but for several years. As we ate our mutton, I wondered which room I'd start with if I were redecorating. She had no such plans.

She is a widow – there is a blue scarf around the portrait of her military husband. He looked a decent, authoritative type; he had died of liver failure, like many a vodka-prone man before him.

The vet came to assess the skeletal camels – I'd already dispatched Kermit to buy two more. The vet was short, stout, incompetent and drunk, but did not charge me a penny; seeing the camels he felt sorry for me.

No. 2 got the thumbs down straight away. He was in a bit of a daze – not unlike the vet – and the skin was stretched tight over his bones and now tender, where the luggage had rubbed. Then Freddie's assessment. I dreaded the thumbs down for him, but the vet passed him by. He'd be all right for a while at least, if he carried no luggage.

'The camels have been on a long journey,' the vet said in conclusion, steadying himself on the wooden fence. 'They need a long rest.' But the camels have been walking for two days! They've been resting five weeks! But such is the feeling, it seems, of the Mongol creature for his fatherland. Let's hope Kermit, creature of the mountains, doesn't fade, as Mr Avirmed prophesied, in the same way …

20th June

Kermit came this evening, reeking of vodka, but less than the vet, who has been on another spree. He has bought two camels to replace No. 2. They look ghostly in the fading evening light, peering around, sizing up T.C. and Freddie.

21st June

This morning, I had a good look at the new camels: one has a wart on his nose, the other is smaller, the same height as Freddie, but has two perky humps. Kermit's friends, the camel owners, were also here – on motorbikes, wearing fake leathers. They looked like the local bike gang.

Time to say goodbye to No. 2. He looked pathetic by himself in the yard, facing the wall. I felt terrible. I'd promised myself I'd get him to the Gobi and had failed within days.

I then noticed that Kermit and the bikers were staring, hardly able to believe that I was lingering sadly with the decrepit beast. Kermit cut me short, trying to restore some dignity to the expedition by ushering me away. 'Bye bye!' he called happily to the camel on my behalf, copying the English word I'd used parting with Ermek. The bikers were still staring.

Kermit wanted to pop into the doctor's to see about his ribs – an injury sustained mysteriously with a motorbike last night. So one of his biker friends escorted me out of town with the animals. Kermit caught us up at dusk. He was being carried on the back of a motorbike and the driver was very drunk. Kermit was apologetic: '*Uuchlaarai* Benni! *Uuchlaarai* Benni!' and at his most charming. The bike looked more battered than before. He'd had another accident.

'Bankhar *bairhgui*!' 'Bankhar isn't here.'

'Lost?' I asked, slightly losing my patience.

Kermit leant his head to the side and closed his eyes, miming sleeping. I strutted backwards and forwards. 'Where is he? You'll have to get him back again.'

'Bankhar berhqui,' Kermit said, this time without humour, and he didn't mime the sleeping dog. He sat down in a sorrowful heap.

The story began to come out. The motorbike had somersaulted, throwing them all off, and had landed on Bankhar. Later, as we pegged out the horses for their night's grazing, Kermit wanted to tell me more about Bankhar's last minutes. I looked up and saw, even in the dark, that Kermit's eyes were glistening with tears. He said he had taken Bankhar in his arms and laid him down, and he'd stopped breathing. He had found a place for him on a hillside and covered him in rocks so that he would not be disturbed by the carrion birds. Then he'd sat down and cried.

I can hardly believe what has happened. Another expedition member lost. Tsend, where are you? It's becoming a tadge more than a run of bad luck. Am I failing in my ability to give leadership on my expedition – as Mongolia is failing to find another Genghis? I chose Kermit because I felt he'd be up to the job, but this isn't the Mongolian way. Western systems place their leaders by election or appointment. Mongolian culture lets them emerge naturally: you end up being governed by a strong, good herder, that is, someone skilled in the art of managing resources.

I want the horses and camels to have a good graze this morning, so I'm sitting outside the ger with my notebook. The sky is so rich in tone that I feel awash with it, as if the indigo dye is coming away and staining me. A view across the steppe for 30 kilometres. A long, low hill rises from the flatness, like a ripple coming this way across a pond. The only voices out there are those of sheep and goats being marched off by horsemen to graze. Spiralling in an uplift, a dozen crows. They look idle and free, drifting over the land, harnessed only to the breeze. Of course when I see them I think of Tsend, and wish that these, her friends, would give me the support through the steppe that she has in the spirit world.

Overleaf:
June, and summer growth at last coming through. Except in the empty, southern Gobi, Mongolia is spread with a thin population scattered remarkably evenly across the country, lessening the burden on a land of temperature extremes and aridity.

22 June

But I do, of course, have support – from the local herders. I keep a little red notebook in my pocket, and whenever I stop at a ger I write down the names of our hosts. Now I have a list of names that reaches right the way back to the edge of Siberia: 'Gana', it begins. Then 'Sainbayar of Ulaan Nuur … Baatar of The Hills South of Ulaan Nuur … Damdinbaatar of Bilutin Davanee-am … Chalongbaatar of Bayanzul … Batbayar of Emtimbargat ….' Each person knows the previous name on the list. It is a chain, a safety line which is gradually being extended for me, further and further into Mongolia. One day, the list will continue right through to the Gobi. Then it will stop. There will be no more people. But for now I have my safety line.

23rd June

The elements are working to undo us all the time. If I lick my lips, they will crack – the air is so dry, the wind so constant. The Mongolian treatment is to rub urine on your mouth. Sensible, I'm sure, but, like Kermit as regards my muesli, I'm not that desperate enough to want to try it yet.

The two new camels are being obedient, carrying the load dutifully; but they seem in T.C.'s shadow already. This is worrying. We still have two leaders: T.C. and me. Unless I can take T.C.'s place as Top Camel, we'll have a mutiny before long. But I see no way of surpassing T.C., even I am under his sway, willing the giant and beautiful creature to escape.

Horsemen ride alongside, at times. Without exception, they ask to buy Freddie, who plods along at the back. He may be thin, but he has a pedigree which places him above all local camels: he is a creature of the Gobi, tempered by its sands and winds. But I cannot leave Freddie behind. When T.C. lifts his head from the grass, Freddie also lifts his head. He stalks him everywhere. I've never seen such a relationship. To leave him behind would be to devastate him.

We erected our tent this evening and an old man rode up, plied us with half-fermented mare's milk, lit his pipe. He laughed away with a malicious bass voice, trying to coax me into parting with Freddie. He mimed lameness, slumping tired or dead. 'He will not get as far as Ölgii.'

But I shall not dump Freddie yet.

The mare's milk, bubbling, explosive, soon gave us both diarrhoea.

The old man got back on his horse, still roaring with laughter, and left Kermit and me planning where we'd have to crawl from our sleeping bags to squat after dark.

The light is very yellow, spreading a buttery glow over the green plain. Gers in clusters emerge like toadstools from the levels.

The old man came at dawn and harried me again. Riding alongside, telling me to swap his horse for Freddie. I said Freddie was a friend.

'My horse can be your friend.'

'But I am happy with this friend.'

'What a friend to have!' he said, wheeling his horse around, to ride back home. 'He's weak and useless!'

Today, Freddie actually sat down and refused to budge for a while. It was quite a scare. After a while, I encouraged him back onto his feet, and coaxed him onward. Kermit as usual blamed the heat, but he is just being kind to me. Like the old man, he thinks Freddie should be left behind. But if, as the Mongols believe, every animal has its home, it seems important to get him back to the Gobi. It's bad enough that I've lost a dog and a camel. I feel weakened, that part of my family has died.

On, beside a large salt lake – whooper swans, teals, and a couple of pelicans. And Freddie faltered again. Was the old man right? Would he even get to where Dundoi lives, in Bayan-Ölgii?

Over a hill, on the crest of which was an *ovoo*, one of the shrines which, throughout Mongolia, reach to connect us with the spiritual dimension. The communists tried to rid the countryside of them, but the stubborn Mongol could not be prevented from communicating with the land and sky which supported him. Sometimes he has a precise prayer – the lame, who placed a crutch on the *ovoo*. Sometimes his mind is empty – the drunk, who chucked on bottles, not knowing why anymore, but was reaching out to the supernatural forces anyway. And now Kermit, not a believer in anything much but drawn to do this gesture, stopped as Mongolians who've felt drawn to do this gesture have stopped for decades, and circled three times clockwise around the *ovoo*, tossing on stones. A steppe eagle prescribed an arc a thousand feet above us.

I'm lying in my sleeping bag in the tent. Kermit lying beside me. I told Kermit that we had to get T.C. trained to carry luggage. We must prepare him now, before we are forced to by circumstances. We have no spare camel.

Over a brook. On the banks, fescues and sedges and reeds heavy with moisture. Between here and the scattering of sharp-edged hills are pastures that seem as green and level as a billiard table. Freddie is still eating well, and I still have hopes of getting him home.

It's a hot morning; we have stopped for tea. Kermit is a little way off, urinating against the leg of The Beast. The Beast is uninterested. He's seen it all before. It seems that urine is a standard treatment for infections. I am in favour of using such practical treatments, though I haven't tried the faeces procedure yet and can't see how a substance with so much bacteria in it can be helpful. Perhaps it merely soothes and protects from the ravages of the dry Mongolian air. Even so, this Mongolian tendency to make-do-and-mend – the consequence of having a countryside patterned by welcoming gers – I have to watch.

Right: *Two conflicting worlds. Settled peoples like us have progressively taken over the land of nomads the world over. In Mongolia, although the Russians encouraged the population into such sums (administrative settlements), ironically the Iron Curtain fended off consumerism and the authorities introduced health-care and social support, such measures helping to maintain the age-old rural existence.*

But when I tell Kermit that our animals must last, we are not rounding up a herd, the concept passes him by. He just does his best to cheer me up, perhaps pointing out a Tolai hare which is crouched ahead hoping we won't spot it.

LATER: I was riding along on Ulaan when he suddenly sat down. I found myself just standing on the ground, my feet still in the stirrups, the horse flat out between my legs. I carried on by foot to give Ulaan a rest, and later he was helped by a change in weather. The sun was all of a sudden

swallowed up. Grey-black clouds menaced the hills, then us. We veered towards Songon *sum*, and beyond the outlying gers we came to a barbed wire fence of what must be a military outpost. Ahead, gyrating above a vehicle which had lost its wheels, an antenna. It looked frail, like a large wire coat hanger.

We were stopped by a small, unshaven, greasy-shirted man in an old uniform, who led us to his commanding officer's ger. The officer, a lieutenant, had watery, cruel eyes. On a stack of suitcases sat his hat, with its red, communist star shining outdated on it. Kermit explained who we were; we showed our papers and were led into the barracks and told we could stay as his guests. He got out a bottle of vodka and sat us down.

Outside, the corporals began unloading the camels. With only half an hour to go before parade they set them to graze freely within the compound – rather rash, I thought.

A little bit intoxicated from the vodka, Kermit and I went over to a neighbouring ger for some mutton, and from there watched the evening parade – the camels and their pursuers criss-crossing through the assembled ranks. In the ger we ate with Chinbaatar, a small sixteen-year-old shepherd who showed me sketches of tender foals and hunched wolves that he draws when he is out in the steppe, sitting with his flocks. It's a talent that will stay with him here, never to emerge into the world beyond. Kermit is more interested in Chinbaatar's sister, Erdentsetseg, whom he spotted on parade. She spends HOURS rearranging our wardrobe, which is very limited. First she changes out of her military uniform, then into an array of fluorescent athletic outfits, changing them every hour. Kermit watches her fashion parades, but he doesn't actually address her. Maybe because he's playing hard-to-get, maybe because she smells of cabbage water.

Kermit kindly walked me back to the army dormitory to sleep, then disappeared. I'm now looking out of the window at the camels tidying up the parade ground weeds – I don't think I'm revealing any state secrets if I write that, though Mongolia is emerging into the world, this time it is not ready to take it by force.

26th June

Morning parade. Men in uniforms left over from Russian days, all unshaven; Kermit's girl, Erdentsetseg in the ranks, decked in multiple layers of powder and lipstick. The flag was jerked up the pole; it looked like a red duster – I'm afraid it'd been chewed by T.C. overnight.

At Chinbaatar's ger we had a farewell cup of tea and Kermit was just securing his photo of Erdentsetseg when the dogs tried to get T.C.

But T.C. was unimpressed and it was Wart, the larger of the two new camels, who lost his nerve. He bolted, scattering my belongings to the horizon. After a moment of indecision, Jigjik, the other new camel, followed. T.C. and Freddie monitored their progress, saw they'd made it to the horizon, and ran off themselves. The Mongolian cavalry, more or less asleep since the last of the Khans, once again launched into action. This time they were on motorbikes as well as horses, but they were an impressive sight. It no longer mattered that they were unshaven: once these people were out in the steppe, combing the grasses, they knew what they were doing. You wouldn't want to be their enemy.

Spoons, cameras, knives, ropes came back in dribs and drabs, borne by men on two wheels, men on four hooves. The soldiers sped to me, dropped all they had foraged, then headed back out into the dust for more. Finally, the camels were back – all of them jubilant, unrepentant. Wart was unmanageable, having worked himself into a state of euphoria. We are forced to use T.C., just as I feared.

LATER: Kermit brought T.C. forward to load him. The crowd gathered round to see what would happen. Before we'd got anywhere, there were lots of kickings and scufflings. Kermit walked him round in circles, trying to contain that energy. Then I noticed that T.C.'s eyes were actually calm – the look of someone with nothing to prove – an aristocrat, a world champion. Kermit worked patiently, giving the camel lots of time to show his dignity. Finally, he agreed to sit, and then, after one or two minor incidents, he was successfully loaded up. But we journeyed only 5 kilometres before Wart bolted once more, this time spotting a far camel herd to join, and T.C., sensing an all too obvious weakness in us, embarked on his own plans. We were forced to retreat. I watched Kermit battle with him by twilight, steam rising from them both, as the light changed from warm yellows to metallic blue.

'THE FLIES, THE FLIES'

Genghis shared the nomad attitude towards

the way of life of civilized nations, finding their

activities strange and threatening.

Paul Ratchnevsky, GENGHIS KHAN: HIS LIFE AND LEGACY, *1991*

This time Chinbaatar will come with us until T.C. settles down – if he settles down. We first loaded Jigjik. Though small, he's a polite, reliable camel. Then T.C. We loaded him quietly, trussing him like a chicken to keep him down.

Onward, through plains bordered by grey, worn hills. T.C. resents carrying the load because it hampers his attempts to snatch grasses as he walks. But we are making progress and decide not to stop for breaks but to keep going while the going's good. Chinbaatar snoozes along the way; he is so small he can curl in his saddle, like a cat.

Torrential rain – sky slate grey, jagged clouds on one side, friendly, open and light on the other. Rainbows looping in the plains. We put up the tent in the wind, and stayed awake all night, holding down the poles.

At dawn Chinbaatar helped us load up. A brief goodbye – casual almost. He handed me his entire collection of sketches. At first I refused – so much talent given away – but he thought I didn't value them, so I took them and he galloped off without another word. People come, people go – nomads. Possessions just don't have the same value. They are a hindrance to the nomadic way. So nomadism encourages sharing of what little there is and discourages envy. The Mongolians don't say, 'The grass is greener on the other side of the fence.' There are no fences.

The grazing fell away and we found ourselves in a patch of desert country, geckos and other lizards, slender and chunky and cross-banded and all the colours of the stones. This is *terra incognita* for Kermit; we are

Left: *Like these herdsman, we always approached gers mounted, to protect ourselves against the mongol dog, an ancient and formidable breed.*

now a long way from his mountain realm. Though this means little to me – all the land is alien – he is noticeably quieter.

With the onset of desert, Kermit wants to buy another horse to support the others. Especially because The Beast – of all horses – has a sore on his spine. Kermit had tied my tripod too loosely to the back of his saddle. He confessed it mournfully, '*Uuchlaarai! Uuchlaarai!*', Sorry, sorry. Then brightened up again and whistled that one dire tune he knows. Suddenly, The Beast is a burden, as well as a menace. I hadn't appreciated how important it is to have this powerful animal on our side.

We saw a ger 15 kilometres away through the empty desert air and homed in on it. After three hours we were drawing close. Kermit spruced himself up, buffing his James Dean sunglasses and we went in for a cup of tea. The head of the household sucked on his pipe, produced a bottle of vodka and ordered his sons to round up some horses for us to choose from. They'd already had a job on their hands outside, starting to break in a foal: every time they placed a child's saddle on him, he keeled over in a dead faint. There was nothing anyone could do but wait a year, until he had grown up to recognise the duties of his kind. Our horse was lassoed in. He was a beautiful piebald, and I had an uneasy feeling that Kermit had fallen for him because of his decorative colouring.

With our matching set of horses, through an empty, barren plain until dusk. A cold night in the tent, and I am lying awake thinking of The Beast, worrying about him and wishing that, like Kermit, I didn't. I am beginning to appreciate that the Mongolians simply cannot afford to get too attached even to their beloved horses. In the future, I must not give them names. I must somehow learn to see them as implements only. There are maggots in The Beast's wound, which writhe when we disturb them. I've never been keen to use imported medicines, so we'll do it the Mongol way and let the maggots stay; they'll feed on dead tissue and will clean up the infection.

29th June

Level steppe around us, and all the larks give a feeling of peace. But far off the hills around descend to meet the grasslands steeply, like crashing breakers.

At dawn a herdsman rode up, got off his horse and sat in the grass, waiting for Kermit to wake up. With him was a spare horse. It looked rather like Kermit had been doing one of his business deals.

'One of your friends?' I said to Kermit, shaking him awake. 'Looks like he's been riding for days!'

'One-and-a-half days,' Kermit said, unzipping his Russian military sleeping bag and straightening his hair. Kermit walked blearily over to our pile of horse tackle and gave him one of my own precious bridles to examine. They were made of cheap silver, but they were silver nonetheless, and ornately moulded.

'That's one of my precious silver bridles,' I thought. 'Kermit's going to sell one of my bridles.'

The shepherd grinned, seeing the bridle. Exactly what he'd come for. He waved gratefully to me, jumped on his horse, and cantered off into the ether leaving his spare horse behind. The horse looked over his shoulder to his vanishing master. Then he turned to look at us.

'The boy thought the bridle was silver!' Kermit said, cheerfully giving the horse a slap.

'He was right,' I said.

The horse, which hasn't even come with a bridle of his own, is a 'grey' – identical to Ulaan, but with less of a beard. He is slow and stupid, and has hooves that point in. Even if the boy had ridden a whole week to catch us up and dump this specimen on us, he'd have had a bargain.

'I'm going to make myself a stiff cup of tea,' I thought. The British and Mongolians share one custom at least: they both stop for a cuppa when the world has got too much. Sometimes Kermit, now investigating the properties of the tea bags, sucking on them, makes me want to scream. 'Make haste slowly ...' I keep having to remind myself.

EVENING: Through the gravels. No water. A vulture chopped at the stomach of a dead antelope. We let the horses drink from puddles, though Kermit said it is bad Mongol practice. We are looking for the lake that we spotted on the horizon in the mid-afternoon. Was it a mirage?

The clarity of the light, the absence of even a dent in the gravels, made the walk slow. The lake could have been 30 kilometres away when we first saw it. By the time we arrived, there was no light to pitch the tent properly. We merely rammed the poles into the lakeside mud, and threw the canvas over them. Then wind blew in from across the lake, sucking at the water, tugging it our way. Later still, rain spiralled with the wind and we spent much of the night hanging onto the poles, or darting out to tie down luggage, horses and camels. However, Kermit has taken to my pasta, which I mix with dried soup as our staple food. He has a collection of dried sheep meat, and cuts it up almost lovingly before dropping each chunk into the pot to boil up with the rest. To me the meat is rancid and its fat is exactly what my stomach and I have been trying to get away from. Had I had a lovely juicy carrot out here to put in, Kermit would say the same: a great shame that I'd spoilt an otherwise decent meal.

We woke late, feeling like half-drowned rats. We spent half an hour treating The Beast's sore. Kermit has given up on the maggots, which are meant to be cleaning it, and is now trying our 'Chinggis Khan' vodka. He bathed the wound, while I held The Beast. Maggot after maggot came out, each one either drowned or drunk.

On along the lakeside, and we have now stopped at a ger. Another stranger, a woman, has just come in with a small boy with a threadbare del with large, obvious needlework and patches. Both have gone down on their knees, in quiet supplication, waiting for the owner to address them. They have a modest bundle of furs to sell and must have got here on the back of the lorry we saw. But the owner simply lets them wait. For reasons I can't understand he is utterly dismissive of them. He shuns them: they are an embarrassment in front of his important guests – Kermit, me and the nine motley beasts.

Perhaps it's because the treatment is counter to everything I've seen from Mongolian behaviour that I find it so worrying. Is this woman known – a persistent nuisance? To me, she looks desperate. Perhaps her sheep herd is already below that fearful minimum, a hundred. She knows that now she can only slide downhill.

I want Kermit to greet her at least but he is too busy trying out the owner's pipe, teasing tobacco from the embroidered silk pouch into the traditional tiny pipe bowl – room there for a thimbleful, enough only for a moment's sweet repose. He concentrates on getting a good draw on the tobacco, with half an eye on the inevitable vodka, now appearing from the cupboard. Sometimes, Kermit seems only to be able to discern what is delicious in the world around him. God knows what'll happen when we reach Ölgii, our first proper town.

LATER: After waiting a full hour for an audience, the woman and her thin child got up and left. I wonder if soon she will abandon her child to live under the manhole covers of Ulaanbaatar, where others have ended up.

As we continued swifts swirled, running down mosquitoes. Our little camel, Jigjik, carries the luggage with T.C. Neither shows any tiredness, but I keep catching Kermit examining Wart, the camel that ran amok beside the army barracks. We'll never be able to trust him again and Kermit is waiting for him to get back into prime condition to sell him – no doubt one of his special deals.

3rd July

We seem to have lost two days somewhere. Of course, one expects Mongolia to be timeless – if Genghis Khan turned up again, only the scars of the meandering jeeps would draw his immediate attention – but in every ger is a moon calendar, guiding the Mongolian through a barrage of inauspicious dates. Everyone knows when Tuesday, that dreaded day, is coming around, and under the Russian education system 98 per cent of the population was literate – even though this figure has dropped now, it's certainly higher than the US. They've even had a cosmonaut in space.

We proceeded today along the north side of the lake, the land still waterless, the water itself sulphurous. I found T.C. walking alongside me. We are colleagues, almost friends. Slowly, he is giving up his crown, handing over his trust, his team. Sometimes I miss seeing him angry, indomitable, determined to break free. Now it's up to me, and I'd rather not have the responsibility of getting him to the Gobi.

Swifts, black headed terns, a pair of cranes escorting a grey offspring with no flight feathers – sticking with it despite us, five horses and four camels. The new grey horse, the one with wonky feet, not only walks at half a pace slower than everyone else, but has also taken a dislike to the camels. He is obsessed; he keeps his head down, watching them with the corner of his eye, waiting for an attack, but then makes a pre-emptive strike himself, biting at the camels. The camels don't mind: they just turn to look at him slowly and disdainfully.

Along the cobalt lakeside, negotiating old lava, burnt brown biscuit escarpments.

4th July

Ahead are hills and plains of stones, the beginnings of the giant Altai Range. We must get the horses shoed and so are heading towards Naranbulag *sum*.

LATER: There wasn't much of it. Telegraph lines were leaning, their lines whistling, broken in the wind. Some were a hazard to our animals, capriciously flaying in the air.

We rode into town in the heat of midday. Every house seemed empty, their occupants out in summer pastures. But we found the blacksmith and he came with his kit. This consisted of some 10-centimetre nails, which would be banged into more suitable dimensions, a hammer and a motorcycle tyre. Motorcycle tyre? Yes, for the man was more a cobbler than a blacksmith, and shoed horses with rubber rather than iron.

With the help of his assistant, a gentle man who wore what seemed to be a lady's velvet del and clutched the hooves delicately, worrying about spoiling his ruby nail varnish, he cut out tyre blocks, whacked on the nails, by now flattened and halved, and trimmed the tyre to each horse. We will leave tomorrow, bouncing along on our rubber tyres, each with plenty of tread.

6th July

Suddenly, the horses are able to walk on stones. But we stopped at a ger in the afternoon because T.C. is very slightly footsore, favouring his front right pad – we have no shoes for the camels.

We are staying with a huge bellied man who should be – and perhaps is – a wrestling champion. He marches around in big Mongol boots, and tonight I saw him strolling along the skyline with a goat on either shoulder.

7th July

As if T.C.'s sore foot wasn't worrying enough, when I rounded up the horses this morning I found both the chestnut and the piebald were lame as well. The Wrestler was handy in these matters and said they just needed to be re-shod – Mongolians are generalists, kings in the art of making do. He flicked a rope under the first horse, and pushed it over as easily as if it was a puppy.

Meanwhile, T.C. lead the camels in another dash to the Gobi. Freddie got the furthest, but then, turning round to see that Kermit had headed off the others, he gave up, walking straight towards me to be captured, like a prisoner of war with his hands up, defeat in his eyes.

I, like T.C., long for the desert. For my part, I'm driven by curiosity. What's more, I'm bad at sitting still, and seem to need a challenge. Put these ingredients together and you get someone who immerses himself in a far-off place, and comes back feeling invigorated. This anyway to me is exploration: leaving what you know behind, interacting with a far removed world and then reporting back. So, T.C. longs for the desert because it's home, security; I long for it because it isn't.

LATER: We have ridden on for a half day, through brown, scraggy hills and I've asked Kermit for us to stop, so we can brew up some tea. Even having been re-shod, the piebald is limping badly. And I'm fed up because I came riding through Mongolia ready to 'gather skills' – that was my guiding principle – and again and again I find people who are apparently unskilled even in the tying of knots: they simply make do. I remember a friend in Ulaanbaatar telling me how she visited the country in the winter, and heard a puppy start screeching. It had licked a metal pipe, and its tongue had stuck fast. The locals came running up with a knife! She managed to stop them cutting off the dog's tongue and released the dog by pouring on warm water.

Their gers operate like a super social security system, a safety net, and they don't maintain their cars, their camels, even their most cherished horses.

But I mustn't be so hard on these people. Possessions do not rule the nomad as they do us. What's more, Mongols work by consensus, achieving it by lengthy talking, everyone pitching in with their own (often contradictory) opinion. And if achieved by consensus, as the Japanese also find, ideas are in the end far easier to sustain in a community. Besides, the same ger social security system also gives me support. The Mongolians extend the same hospitality to me. And it's this that is enabling me to do the journey: the open door and open heart of the everyday Mongolian.

EVENING: On, into steeper hills which rise to a snow-capped ridge. An electric storm danced about us, sparking against the slate-blue sky. A large, handsome chestnut rodent, one of the normally nocturnal jerboas, looked up at me. It was a friendly face, and scarcely afraid. He just sat there in his bush – his large feet, large ears, long tail with a flag on the end. Maybe he knows that dogless horsemen are not herders but travellers, and will not loiter to harm him. We tacked through slopes of high shrubbery – easy for the camels to snack on, impossible for the horses – and descended into a plain cupped by red, copper and ochre ridges.

Progress has been a little slow. T.C. was slightly lame again, so we used Wart, even though we had decided we'd never use him again. He is naturally a complainer, making it difficult to judge when he's in real need. Jigjik never complains, making it difficult to judge him as well.

We are now resting in a ger, the old granites of the hills bright in the last light, and I have a horrible feeling that T.C.'s foot is getting worse. That I therefore didn't deserve his trust. The animals need a rest, and my plan is to leave them for ten days – two weeks if necessary – to fatten up in the foothills. We are approaching Bayan-Ölgii *aimag*, Kazakh country, and I'll go off with Kermit and try to track down my friend out here, Dundoi.

Yesterday, we came over a pass, and down into a depression dominated by a large, still lake reflecting the blues and greens of the sky and valley bowl.

Each morning, as I round up the horses and camels with Kermit, I fear that one will be totally lame. This morning the piebald was. There was no point in postponing the inevitable, and Kermit and I didn't even need to discuss it. It was clearly kinder to leave the horse – either the blacksmith or the Russian motorcycle tyre was inadequate. Kermit asked if we could exchange our piebald for a fine cowhide lasso, which he has had his eye on.

As we rode away, Kermit's saddle adorned with the lasso, I noticed that the piebald was being tied up by his new owners, not let out to graze.

'What are they up to, Kermit?'

'*Khool*,' he said. Food.

'What! They're going to eat my piebald?'

'He'll be supper,' Kermit said. 'Or lunch, if they hurry up.'

I looked ahead, hoping we'd be round the corner before I could hear the horse's protests. Kermit stopped his horse. 'Benee, I am very hungry.' He put on his puppy-like face, the one the women can't resist. 'Can we go back to eat him too?'

Dusk, and we've come to a wide river – the Khovd, which flows right through Ölgii. I'd like to follow the river for the grazing, but there are biting flies down there, and they bother the animals even up here in these bare hills. All day today the horses have tossed their heads; the camels, given the chance, closed their eyes and sat down. I don't think they have eaten a blade of grass between them. One day without food and they are noticeably weaker.

Onward early, to get out of the fly zone of the valley floor, the camels and horses tiring as we worked along the hills. The Beast and Chestnut were exhausted and when we rested they would stand around in a stupor, troubled by the flies, not eating. After another five hours we were away from the flies, and took the caravan downslope towards Lake Achit, where they might rest. But the chestnut and The Beast were so slow by this time that Kermit had to stay behind to steer them along at their own pace.

Now we've all made it through to the lakeside. Reeds and irises along the bank. Wheatears and tawny (I think) pipits. Terns bombing the water, great white egrets, spoonbills and what looks like the relict gull.

We'll rest the animals right here. We are on the road to Ölgii, and should be able to get someone to come and look after the animals for a couple of weeks.

LATER: A Kazakh coal lorry came by in the late afternoon and stopped to investigate. We sat in a circle, talking over what we should do next, only interrupted when the sun went down and they placed their hands in their laps and muttered prayers. Soon after, we struck an agreement by which the oldest man and his son would tend the camels and horses. We would leave them all our food and saddles.

Kermit took the men's Polaroid photos for identification, rather theatrically, and we loaded ourselves onto the bed of coal. We stopped five times in the night to repair punctures and arrived to see Ölgii at dawn.

The town is in a mountain bowl; there are mud-encased houses, the Soviet style apartments and chimney-stacks; around the edge, a halo of Kazakh gers. The town trees lean permanently from the wind. All was quiet, just sheepskins being loaded in the street, flung expertly up onto the lorries like pancakes.

The coal lorry dropped us at the hotel, where there were chandeliers of plastic and posters of puppies. We slept most of the day, waking in the evening to find that the restaurant wasn't offering food. The hotel staff

Below: *The medieval Mongol cavalry rode with five horses to a man, changing mounts each day to rest them. We had no such provision and, reaching the Khovd river, near Ölgii, the animals – T.C. seated to the rear, Freddie standing – were tired from the march and weakened by the drought.*

had eaten it. There isn't water either, or electricity. Wallpaper curls from top and bottom. This is the opposite of a ger. No welcome, and the hoteliers spend their time cooking for themselves – they are already obese from their pickings, a life of putting their feet up, watching Kazakh telly. Here, socialism has achieved the impossible – reduced the Mongolians, the most hospitable people I've ever known, into people who hardly care.

Yet these people have already had their day. They, like the hotel, like the Communist party building next door, its clock set at ten past ten, are from the 1950s and 1960s – outmoded, outdated. The town market is meanwhile humming with old ladies selling Chinese jeans, Kazakh rugs, Russian toothpaste. Mongolia is moving forward without them.

10th July

We have found food! It's available in the little hut that's like a train carriage opposite the hotel. Inside, a weighty coat stand, as thick as a railway track, and posters of Schwarzenegger.

We had our *khuushuur*, mutton fried in batter, and went outside. A man with a long face and excellent moustache drove up, and got chatting with Kermit. He seemed a little bit drunk and his hand was bandaged as if from a punch-up, but he had quite a bit of local news and he began talking about some horses outside the valley: they were being eaten to death by flies and he was almost sure the owners didn't even know about it yet.

'Terrible,' I thought. 'It could so easily have been us.'

Then I saw Kermit's face. 'The black horse as well?' he asked the driver, miserably.

It was us.

With the help of the driver we found the house of Murat, a distant relative of Kermit's, commandeered a jeep, and sped up the road for a look. Before long we came across a lone figure walking up the hill with Freddie and Jigjik. It was the older of the two men. But where was his son? Where were all the other animals? We pulled over and got the story from him. 'The flies, the flies,' he said, like a Conrad character racked by something beyond all comprehension 'They must have been blown from Khovd river.' The old man said they couldn't think what to do, so they'd decided to get the animals out as soon as possible, risking taking them to me the quickest way, along the Khovd. The boy was further down the road, coming along with the others.

The others? Did that mean the animals were all right? I thought of Ulaan, my little grey horse, the chestnut, who I'd never quite got to

'THE FLIES, THE FLIES'

know, The Beast, which I knew all too well. None of them deserved this. My one comfort was the thought of T.C. A giant like him would certainly be all right.

We drove on. We saw the boy ahead, limping. He had a grey horse – so Ulaan had made it. But closer I saw it wasn't Ulaan, it was the horse with the wonky feet. The boy also had with him T.C. and Wart. Even from a distance, through the cracked windscreen, Wart looked terrible. But T.C. looked worse: his humps had gone, somehow deflated in two days. As we drew up and the boy stopped, both camels sat down, letting out a sigh. The herdsboy himself was in a bad way. His eyes were sticking out, the eyelids swollen. His ears were thick, and purple, as if they'd been thumped. He said he'd at first ridden from the lake but the flies had been able to settle on him as he sat in the saddle. He'd had to walk to keep his legs moving.

I got out to have a closer look at the camels. T.C.'s head was still in a cloud of little blown flies. We were well out of their habitat, but he was still carrying a million with him, quenching their desire for blood. The herdsboy started walking again. He just wanted to get back to town.

But where were the three other horses? He just pointed back down the valley. He walked off with T.C. and Wart, the brown storm of flies tailing them. We drove to where the valley steepened and the Khovd wound, through stark rock, billowing trees and rich, lush meadow grasses – all left ungrazed.

There my three horses were, standing on the rock slopes, as far as they could get from the flies of the river. They just stood there, as silent and motionless as the stones. It was a horrible sight, worse than if they'd been lying down. 'Like ghouls,' I thought. 'The living dead.'

It was immediately clear that Ulaan was in the worst shape of all. When I led him forward he kept tripping on the boulders and sometimes he seemed to trip on nothing, unable even to negotiate thin air.

Kermit shook his head. '*Muu*,' he said. 'Bad.' He tutted and looked me in the eyes. He signalled cutting his throat. I shook my head. Such an act of disloyalty. I just couldn't – at least not without thinking this through. Ulaan had been so patient with me, just getting on with the job. Kermit shrugged at the driver, the driver shrugged back. To them my behaviour to animals that I hadn't even been through a winter with was beyond all comprehension. To them the animals were, in the end, tools. The two men lit up cigarettes and shared a joke.

But Kermit did care about me looking so miserable and he went off to forage for water to give to the horse. He came back from the river

Above: *Khovd river, a valley near the Altai Range preserved from grazers due to its biting flies. Unknown to me, as I took this photo, a wind was blowing the flies out of the valley and to the resting camels and horses.*

and splashed it over Ulaan's face. Ulaan gulped at it. But his eyes were sunken, sleepy, lids swollen. As I stroked him, my hands were covered in flecks. I looked closer: these were the flies – hundreds of them. And many thousand more were scrambling over him, concentrating on his eyes, lips and genitals. As I comforted Ulaan, he dropped his head into my hands. He was so heavy, a dead weight.

We retreated back to the town to get a truck, passing the herdsboy limping along with T.C. and Wart. Back in Ölgii, Murat put the matter of the truck aside for a while – he wanted to throw a big lunch for Kermit, his long-lost relative. He invited his three brothers round and the vodka flowed. There was an atmosphere of jollity which was difficult for me to cope with and was compounded by the menu, which was potato and horse.

Then back again to the horses, armed with a truck. It was a picnic atmosphere, everyone laughing, joking. We came to the steep valley, the brothers shoved on the horses and drove back, still singing, to the very edge of town, where there was water, moderate grazing – and no flies. For the men this was just another day. They were desperately keen to help, but their compassion was for me, not the animals.

By way of thanks, Kermit arranged a meal for the men, back at Murat's house. They toasted me, and I toasted them, 'Kazakh *Khun sain*!' Kazakh men are fine. I did mean it. I could have left the horses out there on the hillside to die, instead saving my cash to share among these men. But I'd indulged myself, and rescued horses that might die anyway, and they'd been good enough not to be sour about it.

I'm meant to be joining in the festivities. For today is Naadam, the big annual holiday, a chance to celebrate the three Manly Sports – horse riding, archery and wrestling – and also the time of plenty. Everyone will sing, everyone will drink – for although the Russians introduced their industrial vodka, alcohol from mare's milk has always been an important ingredient of the Mongolian summer. The horses have had their foals and are producing milk that can now be fermented and distilled for everyday consumption. However, my mind is still on the animals, which I'm determined to save.

The man with the long face and moustache came back again, finding me at the reception as I haggled for tap water. Kermit hadn't come back last night and was still nowhere to be found, so the man sat me down and made me understand that T.C. had not managed the walk to town. That he was still out there on the hill.

We drove off to look and, somewhat miraculously, happened to pass Kermit in a back street. He climbed in, smelling of an unhappy blend of vodka and lady's perfume. With Murat's jeep, and some of his family for the ride, we went up the dust road to the hill top. We found T.C. slumped on the ground. When Kermit made him stand up and walk forward, his feet were chaotic. He staggered drunkenly, then fell. I went over. Such splendour reduced to a lump of hair, the blood sucked out of him.

'*Yasan be?*' said Kermit. What do we do? '*Muu baina,*' he said sympathetically, and shook his head with a tragic air. But he seemed fairly sure himself because he gave the cutting-throat sign to the driver.

'Tomorrow he'll be better,' I said. He needed a long, long, rest.

'Not here,' Kermit said.

'We get a lorry.'

'He's too heavy to lift in.'

'Then we get a crane.'

'That's 170,000 tögrögs!'

'Then I pay 170,000 tögrögs,' I said defiantly. US$ 200.

On the way home, Kermit explained to Murat and the others that I wanted to rescue T.C. with a crane. 'That's 170,000 tögrögs!' they shouted, in disbelief. 'I know,' Kermit said sadly. 'That's twenty-five bottles of vodka and change left for a pair of Chinese Levi jeans.'

Back in Ölgii I paid a shepherd to go on his motorcycle and wipe oil on the undersides of T.C. That would stop the flies. It was impossible though to get a crane – the holiday.

'What about a vet, at least.'

'Drunk,' five people answered in chorus.

In the end, as there was nothing I could do today, I agreed to go along to the festival and try to forget the dying friends on the hills. Freddie, Jigjik, and maybe one or two of the horses had made it through. I could be thankful for that.

Everyone was out in their finery, Kazakh womenfolk in scarves and bright dresses, the men with their Russian leather flat caps. Once Kermit was back from checking the horses – it sounded like the chestnut at least was better – we went to watch the wrestling.

A man tapped me on the shoulder and I recognised him as the shepherd I'd dispatched to coat T.C. with oil, to keep off the flies. '*Tom temee muu*,' he said. The big camel is bad. We set out once again, this time in the jeep of a man who spat louder and slower than I've ever heard before. Then T.C. was ahead of us, on the right. Even before we got out of the jeep, I knew he was dead.

It was so difficult to fathom. This creature, which had been so indomitable until he had decided not to escape but to accept my leadership and which I had bought because I thought he would get me back to the Gobi, above all animals, was now lying in the dust, his tongue a plank for ants. Kermit took a tuft of hair, and tied it in a neat knot to keep. This is the Mongol way, a tribute to a parting animal, a gesture to show that, although its life might have been hard, it had been valued. Kermit will now take the hair and place it on an *ovoo*, and his spirit will be with the spirits of innumerable camels and horses which have gone before.

I undid his blue silk sash. This was meant to have gone to the Gobi, where it was given him.

Kermit, trying to take an interest for my sake, attempted to close T.C.'s eye. He couldn't. Then he tried to put on a pebble, but it rolled off. Finally, getting impatient, he placed an extremely large chip of shale over his face. This was something he thought I'd like done, nothing running deep within himself. But I still appreciated the thought. He is not heartless: had this been his camel of some years' faithful service, his eyes too would be watering.

The driver began honking the horn. He wanted to get back to the festival. Kermit kindly put in a word for me, suggesting that while we were out here we might as well look at the horses as well. 'Benee will feel better.'

'I don't think Benee will,' the driver said, loudly delivering one of his loads of spit out of the window.

And as we drove down the hill towards where we'd brought all the horses on the town edge, I saw he was right. I didn't feel better. No sign for the moment of the remaining camels or of the chestnut and wonky-footed horse, but there were Ulaan and The Beast on the roadside. They lay side by side, back to back, their mouths open – as if still gasping. They had been dead since this morning, and no one, not even Kermit, had thought to tell me.

Ulaan looked in peace, The Beast anguished. What more can I say about the subject? It was as if my organs were being yanked from me, one by one. The dog, No. 2, T.C., Ulaan, The Beast. My expedition was all I had in Mongolia; it was my existence out here. I asked Kermit, who was himself looking sorrowfully on at The Beast, for a couple of minutes quiet, so I could gather myself – just as I had up the hill for T.C. 'And tell that driver to stop spitting, or I'll scream.'

Ulaan, the horse with skinny legs who never complained, the treads of his rubber shoes hardly worn. The Beast – what a waste. And his saddle sore healing nicely.

I glanced at the other animals. Wart looked mauled, but all right. Freddie was not eating: he was spending all his time looking around for T.C. The chestnut was standing there staring, the flesh around his eyes so swollen it was forcing his eyeballs forward. His genitals bulging, a football bladder. He was weak legged, but recognised me, and his ears flicked forward for a second. I think he'll be all right.

The only animal of my entire team that certainly is all right is the wonky-footed grey horse. It's a good reminder. He may have looked like a cripple, but like all the others he survived the winter: there's no such thing as a delicate horse in Mongolia.

Now I am too tired to write anymore. All I can think about is that I must get Freddie to the Gobi.

RUNNING REPAIRS

When the Mongols decide to have a party,

the rest of Asia locks its doors.

Chinese proverb

Yesterday I felt I was, like my expedition, falling apart, but there is much to look forward to: today is the day of the four horse races, each of different horse classes, each a charge through the plains by child jockeys. That thought, of the children willing on their mounts, without stirrups, without saddles, is enough to quicken anyone's heart. Today is a day that four children, pelting over the grasses, will achieve glory.

However, it's now 9.30 a.m. and Kermit has yet to return to our room from his night's activities. I can look forward to his appearance any moment, staggering in apologetically – and no doubt wearing my Marks and Sparks boxer shorts, which I notice have gone.

10.30 A.M.: Kermit has now appeared and, because there's no water in the taps, he can't wipe off his lady's perfume. He's going to be smelling like this all day.

LATER: A misty, drizzly, cold day after a sunset of extraordinary beauty last night – smoky puffs of yellow and crimson right across the sky. We set out for the races in a jeep full of Kermit's distant relatives, equipped with a picnic they'd kindly put together. As we rocked over the plains, I could hear the ominous clinking of vodka bottles.

Out into the grazing lands – draped in low, rolling grey cloud. The grasses seemed to swell, drawing on the moisture, fattening and rising before our eyes. The children were already sitting on their mounts, patiently waiting for their fathers and uncles to stop muttering last-

12th July

Left: *A Kazakh woman at dusk milking time. Still only July in the Altai and snow is already dusting the slopes behind. In Mongolia even lowland pasture only grows between May and September when day temperatures average above zero.*

minute instructions. Some jockeys had thin cushions tied between their legs, to buffer them against the horse's spine, but all were bareback, their feet dangling to the side, often only in socks.

The other spectators were almost all on horseback, the women together in their best dells and glittering scarves, looking like radiant flowers, even in the drizzle, as they promenaded on horseback. Kermit walked off to intercept groups, my cameras swinging from his neck. Women gathered in twos, threes, tens, trotting up on their mounts, slipping into poses, trying to tempt him to snap them.

I walked about, soaking up the excitement. The women out in their finery, the men sitting in circles, swapping snuff, their horses' manes draped over them. Spectators were still arriving, reaching from their saddles to buy soft drinks from ladies issuing them from babies' prams. Here, there was not yet Pepsi, not yet Coca-Cola, the flotsam of the American incoming tide. There were few motorbikes, and fewer jeeps. This was a horse day. The Mongolians can still claim to be the best in the world at something. They were proud, and I felt able to claim a little part of that pride, and at last felt I would be able to continue my journey – because my journey was being achieved with the help of these people.

We were mainly interested in the Big Race, run over 35 kilometres and with 70 horses in the field: Jockey No. 66, 'Shamarowal', was the driver's brother's cousin's nephew. He had a very bright red face, black, vivid eyes, and was fifteen, which made him something of a veteran – the youngest jockey was said to be five.

Those jockeys not yet mounted, hopped up on their horses and walked away from the crowds and out between the hills to the starting-point. Occasionally, one or two boys sang. The girls were quieter. We drove off to a vantage point, and settled down for a picnic, Kermit generously offering to drink all my share of the vodka so that I could film. Sitting there in the rain, it was all very like an English point-to-point meeting, except we didn't have green wellies and Barbours and we were eating horses as well as watching them.

By the time the horses got underway, stirring dust into the heavens, Kermit was, like the driver, the worst for wear. We bundled them in the jeep, then set off in pursuit, calling encouragement to No. 66. The sight of so much horse power, with frail jockeys on top, was immensely moving. They seemed to fly, the children unattached, above their horses. There was screaming, there was yelling, there was crying. The hooves thudding on the moistened soil, the women screeching at their younger brothers and sisters to get a move on. Owl feathers, secured in the horse manes for Kazakh good fortune, fluttered from the horses' heads like small birds. Down the children's faces, mud ran with the sweat and some with tears of disappointment – already, before the finishing line. But it was very beautiful.

Where was No. 66 now? He was slipping back. One by one, other horses overtook. Call and scream as we might, it was no good. The horse was ailing. Then a police car, no doubt following our erratic progress over the plain for some time, came from nowhere and the police driver, as if a herdsman heading off a steer, blocked our path. He asked to look at our driver's documents. While the driver fumbled around for them, the winner sped past the flag. It was quite a long while after, that No. 66 went by. Everyone sat still in their seats, rather quiet. 'Thirtieth' Kermit ventured, gingerly. He tried to think of a positive thing to say: 'Such a fine style of riding …' No one else spoke and only the policeman slowly shuffling through the driver's documents could be heard.

I got out of the jeep. I still wanted to congratulate Shamarowal: with the other jockeys he'd cast a spell over me, told me I could carry on. I looked and looked and I came across his mother scurrying about, also looking for him among the jockeys. But Shamarowal had slipped discreetly away.

The crowds closed in, fathers gathering around their children, who were radiant but quiet, perhaps disappointed but being brave about it. The winner of the race was brought forward, still on horseback, and a cape of blue silk tied over him. He was a nonchalant ten-year-old, the runner-up jockey, even younger. His mum came and wiped his nose.

An old man, propped up by two walking sticks, sang an oration. He had a dry, tickly throat that rather ruined his performance, but the message was clear enough. The horse was being given the ultimate accolade, that thing denied all everyday animals, a name.

On the way home, Kermit sang songs to cheer everyone up, especially the driver, who had a police fine. I was thinking that I'd now be able to put my troubles behind me and gather my expedition together, but no sooner was I back in Ölgii than the shepherd who's been looking after my animals came to me and said the last of the original horses, the chestnut, was weakening.

He put me on the back of his motorbike and we sped through the puddles until we came to an obstruction in the road. The obstruction was my chestnut horse. People were walking by, as if he was just a roadworks. Children didn't give him a glance, just skipped on with their day. This death was everyday life in Mongolia.

Overleaf: *Kazakh gers are larger than those of the Mongols and more lavishly decorated inside. However, they share all the same features of a perfect mobile home, being light, easily collapsible, white (to reflect the heat) and having felt layers for insulation against cold.*

Only when I squatted down beside him, did the crowds gather. This show of interest was unusual, worth hanging around to watch. The chestnut was still breathing, but his eyes were glazed, as if all the light had been snuffed from them. His breathing was hard. It wouldn't be long now. The Kazakhs crowded round to stare at me, everyone laughing and joking. I had to work hard to be tolerant of their curiosity of me, their indifferent attitude to the horse. How would Ermek have put it in English? 'This is something extraordinary for them. For Mongols and Kazakhs, when a horse is dead, it is dead. That is it, finished.'

As before, though, when the Kazakhs saw I was upset they did have a heart for me, and a man took a knife from his boot and began doing an emergency operation, opening up the horse's nostrils to ease the breathing. The horse appeared not to care. I stayed some time with the chestnut, and everyone got bored and tried to engage me in conversation in broken English across the horse's body. 'Hello, good morning teacher, thank you, how are you?' I got up and walked away, angry at yet again being denied a few quiet moments with a dying companion, and angry at not being able just to accept this loss by being, for a minute, a Mongolian.

13th July

I wish I could retreat all the way back to Tsend and gain some sort of strength from her, the guidance she has from her crows. But I am forgetting Dundoi, the Kazakh herdsman up in the mountains. I remember that great bulk of a man, the ice flying over his head as he chopped at a river for ice, the eagle resting on his arm as he rode. He will give me a breather; he will launch me out, as she once did. Shortly Ermek is coming from Ulaanbaatar with supplies. Then I'll need to reassemble a team, learn the animals' faults and gain their trust, all over again.

14th July

Kermit was nowhere to be found after I wrote the above and I went back to the chestnut to have the body removed before the dogs moved in. Two men tied a rope around his neck, fixed it to their jeep, and dragged him off, his head clonking through the dirt, swishing through the puddles. 'Like the others, died of a blockage of the flies' maggots in his urinary tract', I said, trying to be all objective as he disppeared forever. Then I went to check on the other animals. The grey horse with the wonky feet is fine, as are Jigjik and Wart. Freddie is the only camel who is conceivably fit enough to go on towards the

Gobi, but they can all rest for another week while I stay with Dundoi, and then we'll see.

The driver – the one with the loud spitting habit – found Kermit in an outer ger, where he lay on his back with his new sunglasses still on. I left a message for Ermek to meet me at Dundoi's and the jeep took us twisting into the hills, Kermit in the back sleeping off the drink. Sometimes we stopped at gers along the way to ask directions. These were the high gers of the Kazakhs, furs of foxes around the walls and dyed sheep wool plaited on camel string in bands striating the ceilings and perimeter walls. Outside, the eagles, now out in the fresh air, placed on river islands to discourage thieves. On the skyline, heaps of stones like scarecrows, but these are to scare off wolves.

After seven hours, near Dayan Uul, right beside the Chinese border, we turned into a side valley and found ourselves swept into Dundoi's ger by his son. Dundoi himself strode in, wearing a dark trilby, and gave me a lavish handshake before sitting me down to to share in the obligatory tea.

I have been here for a day now, resting up. Dundoi and I can communicate very little. His accent is heavy, and mine even heavier. We just look at each other warmly, and Kermit tells the story of the journey and how pleased we are to be able to rest. Some things I understand: he wants to know if all Africans are rich because the one he saw in the Soviet Union was covered in gold jewellery. But mainly he talks of his animals: of winter when you lose 10 per cent of your flock, worse if you are a bad shepherd; of nights awake, nursing baby goats and sheep; and of the summer coming at last, of long easy days riding under the warm sun. Othertimes he talks of his family, who he just wants to be happy in their lives – and not marry Mongols. His daughter Serikgul is getting married, as it happens. She is the first-born, but it would have been nicer if his son – 'now a very skilled lorry driver' – had been married first. Lena is also coming along well; she likes towns and will probably insist on being a teacher.

Around us, all the family heirlooms I once saw in his winter quarters, the log cabin – the photo of Dundoi decked with medals, the photo of his mother – black-and-white prints tinted in yellow, removed, placed on camels, and walked 150 kilometres around the mountainside.

A lone kid-goat sneezes in the corner of the ger, the yaks grunt outside. Upland buzzards sweep the ground, and goats and sheep move over the hills, flowing like amoebas the size of football pitches, down for evening shelter near the ger.

With Kermit flat on his back asleep all the time, Dundoi isn't quite sure what to do with me, but I am content. Yesterday was the day of the milking of the first horses up here in the mountains. Everyone dressed up – the old women in head-dresses like nuns' habits, but embroidered down the front – and walked out onto the hillslope for a picnic. There were lavish toasts, then everyone waded into the giant platters of horse meat and dairy products. This is the season of 'White Food', the time of milk, cheeses and curds, the time of life itself. Foals and mares stood tethered, reaching for the alpine flora. Two tame wolf pups stole a child's red gumboots to add to the treasures they'd secured underground.

This morning, I rode with Dundoi up towards the snowline, through rich sedge swards, mountain saxifrage clusters, where the lichens are brick red, emerald, dusty black, and voles pop up between the boulders, eating the bilberries. Further off, escaping into the ground birch, an Altai snowcock; and above us, up on the cliff, the golden eagle eyries, dark ledges abandoned only two weeks ago, when the young flew.

It wasn't long after our return that Dundoi's children reported a stranger's jeep approaching up the valley. It had to be Ermek.

'What has happened to your animals?' Ermek said, getting stiffly out of the jeep.

'You've heard already?'

Ermek said 'It is a massacre!'

Ermek was then swept away by Dundoi's family, as I had been, and over tea I updated him, and he updated Dundoi. With Ermek here to attract attention, for the first time in two months I was unnoticed, and could walk outside onto the hills to be alone.

Here I am, writing by myself on the hillside, trying to make sense of what's happened. The circumstances which brought my animals to their end was unlucky – a drought, a plague of biting flies, the vet being drunk because of Naadam – but I still need reassurance. And I am getting it from the eternal-seeming, firm hand of Dundoi, who has this partnership with the brutal mountain. I have a moment to reflect on what I have learnt so far from the Mongolians. Perhaps it is to observe better the condition and character of animals you depend on, perhaps it is how to scan this apparently empty landscape – to discern a ger from the shimmering horizon or that distant horseman who may be of no consequence now, but tomorrow may save you by getting your bolting horse back. In the end, no-one can cope alone. In Mongolia, it's a group effort. You rely on each other. As long as everyone plays their part and offers hospitality, you are never at a loss, except in the Gobi – but that's a little way off yet.

Right: In contrast to Westerners, Kazakhs, like the Mongols, breed goats – and sheep in particular – not for leanness, but for their highly prized fat. Little is wasted and the tail of a sheep – a breed known as 'fat tail' – is given pride of place at the onset of a feast. A Kazakh guest, if given the honour of being asked to carve, would, quite properly, show his appreciation by presenting the hosts with the fatty ears.

Today there was again something of a party – it was the drinking of the first mare's milk, which had been carefully sloshed about in leather bags for three days, fermenting into *airag*. A lute was played, children did their party acts, standing before us like the Trapp Family Singers, and a teenage girl was asked not to sing her special sad song about her parents dying and her brother losing an arm when he fell off a horse, but she did anyway. 'Strong on spirit, weak on voice,' Ermek concluded, as she warbled away and everyone watched stoney faced. Finally it was over. Tears were dribbling down her cheeks and a man was ushered forward to strum an up-beat tune to get the party swinging again.

After shooting off Polaroid photos in various combinations, we left. Though it was getting late by the time we arrived in Ölgii, I insisted we drove straight to the camels. There they were, Jigjik, Wart and Freddie. Their winter coats, I noticed, were coming through.

Freddie was still looking around for T.C., waiting for him to catch up. He may yet be all right to leave with me in a few days' time, but I doubt it. I spent a moment scratching the back of his head, something he adores. He nuzzled my hand for more and more, the poor lonely camel. The wonky-footed horse isn't all that fit either; he was sleepy eyed, and stood by himself, up in the cliffs, the furthest he could go from the river, though there were no flies in this section. He seemed to want to be alone, cut off from the world. Loathsome to ride, he is a peaceful, kind horse and I so want him or Freddie to make it to the next stage. I want some continuity, some link: but nothing. Only Kermit – who at the Gobi will also leave – and also my little red notebook, with the names of Mongolians stretching from here back to Siberia.

Late tonight, a discussion with Ermek in the hotel. For the first time, Ermek revealed to Kermit that Tsend had issued a warning about visiting those three gers.

Kermit said: 'I am an atheist fortunately, so these things do not affect me.'

'It seems,' Ermek said, 'they have affected you already.'

Kermit, rather enjoying the opportunities this expedition is bringing his way, asked if he could continue with me into the Gobi. 'We started the journey together,' he told Ermek, 'and we should finish it together.' He added that I shouldn't worry about his life as he is old enough to be responsible for it himself. 'You are tough, but sometimes you have asked to stop riding for a tea break before I have.'

I was flattered hearing this – respect from a Mongolian for my stamina. But I am determined. I am trying to harness something of Mongolia's strength to pull this off alone, and that's what I'll do – unless my animals keep on dying.

Freddie was brighter eyed than yesterday, but a shepherd reported him up on a hill, having got as far as he could with his hobbles. 'He was trying to find his master,' he said. 'That's you or your Kazakh friend, I suppose?'

'T.C.,' I thought.

Ermek said, 'Freddie Camel will fade away, sadly.'

'No-one thought he'd even get this far,' I said. 'But he has.' However, I have to face it: he's not up to coming.

'It is as Mr Avirmed said,' Ermek commented as we drove away. 'A camel needs his motherland and fatherland – the open sandiness. If Freddie Camel sees that, instead of these big black mountains, he will want to live.' This was Ermek speaking – the rationalist, the man of computers and calculators.

I'll come and say goodbye to Freddie, I thought, but as we drove I was already having to begin to think forward to the new team I must build. Autumn is just over the horizon – around the peaks this morning, there were snow clouds. Time is running out and I must buy horses to get us quickly through the mountains; we'll dispense with baggage – camels can rejoin us nearer the Gobi. We'll be two weeks late by the time we're away; another mishap, and winter will catch me before I'm safely out of the desert.

I daren't think too far into the future, of the Gobi waiting for me. For now I must think only of getting there in time to get out again. Ermek has gone and I'm now back in the hotel, building a strategy. Hotel staff sit having natters, eating hotel food – mindless of the distressed guests, wandering dark corridors in search of water.

Kermit is pining for some money for a haircut and a wash in the communal baths, to have one last night out on the town. I think it would be stingy to prevent him – it seems we haven't washed since we left Ulaanbaatar, two months ago.

Farewell to Freddie. 'So, Freddie, go over that hill, take a right, keep going for two weeks, and you're almost there at the Gobi.' Saying this aloud makes me feel better. I can pretend he understands and shift the responsibility from me to him, but I think he will get there. It's a question of whether he can forget T.C.

Right: *Kazakh grandmothers during a feast to celebrate the height of summer, when mares' milk is fermented in leather vats and stirred by passing members of the family to become the refreshing alcoholic beverage* airag.

Will I ever find a camel to replace him? I need that loyalty – but no longer friendship. I want the Mongolian way – to see them as a tool, however cherished. In Mongolia, there is no other way; death is too common, and I don't want to go through that agony again. I handed the three camels over to Kermit's *akh*, his uncle. He is a burly, loud man and unfortunately looks just like my butcher in at home in Shepherd's Bush.

Then, goodbye to the horse with wonky feet. Murat says he will 'look after' him. Later, he was brought down to Murat's house to wait outside the kitchen. I found myself having to say goodbye again. He made one escape, but was caught. It's as if he knows he's waiting for his execution, which he is. I went back to the hotel, leaving Kermit to have a final good night out with his relatives, eating him.

23rd July

Far right: *Dusk, and time to milk the goats. For nomads, the pattern of each day and month is dictated by the needs and life-rhythms of their animals.*

We drove out of Ölgii and drifted through the hills, looking for horses. Boulders high and rounded, a metre out of the grass. From time to time we enquired about horses or stopped for make-shift repairs. Finally, below Mount Tsast, we found ourselves with an old man with horses to sell. He ordered his sons to go and round them up and by the time they returned there was already something of a horse fair: cousins from every valley had brought along their lame, mad and oddball horses, trying to pass them off on us. While the old man sat down with another moustached gent and played chess, the visiting horse-sellers partied in the ger, talking, drinking and picking their teeth with knives, and Kermit whittled the horses down to just four.

We will use two horses as pack animals, and continue with only curds for food, leaving behind nearly everything else, including the seven mighty poles necessary for erecting the tent. Risky to be without good shelter up in the mountains, but Kermit is confident that we will get by.

Later: Our jeep has left. It is good just to be on our own again. All journeys need a momentum to help them over obstacles and I must quickly get us up to speed. A tremble in my stomach.

The horses were shoed, this time with iron rather than rubber. The nails were fashioned inside the ger by a man who had no legs, only one and a half arms, and three fingers. How can he get by, out here? He cannot ride a horse to herd, nor milk the goats and sheep. Instead he makes himself indispensable as an odd-job man, working all hours as only the women do.

Everyone helped saddle and load the horses – the usual committee decisions, young men chipping in with totally contradictory ideas. The animals were unloaded five times before agreement was reached. Even then, there were dissenters, including Kermit, and I was left none the wiser about loading a Mongolian packhorse.

We rode round the mountain, taking it slowly because of our heavy loads. I'd promised myself that I wouldn't name any more of my animals, but my horse is burnt umber by colour and the Mongolians themselves know their animals by description, so Burnt Umber he is. Though he'd be a pony to Western eyes, he is something of a giant by Mongolian standards, and Kermit is sceptical of him – he's 'foreign', probably something left by the Russians. In the same way that I can never be a true horseman because I'm an outsider, he will never be accepted as a true horse. Perhaps that's why we get on. Kermit has a pretty, small red horse – he fell for the delicate white star on his nose – and there're the two slightly dim animals, the packhorses.

Through a squall, then snow, then heat, hale and rainbow mists. We settled into the ride, both of us thankful to be moving forward. For Kermit, it's the chance of a new encounter, a new adventure. For me it's a chance to shrug off the ghouls – after all that's happened, it's hard not to feel haunted. As the light faded, and no ger came into sight, I began to want to strangle Kermit, who was supposed to have asked the whereabouts of all habitation before we left. We both had to dismount to walk, to keep warm in the dusk. 'What if we don't find a ger?' he asked.

'We freeze,' I said. 'And it'll be your fault.'

'I think so too,' he said, mournfully.

However, somewhat miraculously we did come to a ger, arriving just as a jeep with an Ulaanbaatar numberplate drew up. As we came near we saw that this was a family reunion, but our predicament was obvious and once we got talking the family was good enough to let us stay.

The ger was home to only one man, an old Kazakh who had lost his wife and did the sewing himself by machine, tobacco tucked into his lower lip. He must have been looking forward to his son coming for months, but by nightfall he was lying on his bed, wearing his Kazakh cap, staring in astonishment at his grandchildren gyrating to the Mongolian Spice Girls, a cassette they had brought all the way from the capital. This was meant to be a family get-together, but it was a collision of two worlds: these townspeople chose not to sleep in the ger, but instead erected an orange nylon tent of their own. And in the morning, while he was dismembering a sheep, his son was dismembering his jeep. Meanwhile, the children were charging around with spare energy, teasing a pet falcon. Their behaviour was a shock even to me, after two months of living in the countryside. They walked over the laid-out food (almost unforgivable) and barged into their grandfather (definitely unforgivable). Finally, it all became too much, and the grandad put the children to use gathering cow dung and fetching pails of water. I took a Polaroid photo for them: at least they'll have that – so much more of their world will die with the old man.

I cannot be disappointed in the loss of the old world, if that is what the Mongolians choose. But do they choose? Mongolia has something special: a proven way of working a harsh land. Uniquely, out in the steppe most of the population are still doing it. But now the West, having grown rich by polluting the planet and having made a mess of many of the world's developing economies, has come along here with its latest economic model and an offer no small poor nation can refuse.

We rode up and up to the final pass, hardly a blade of grass, just rock slopes and a rubble floor around us. Rising to the high pass, both of us walked alongside the horses, so as to keep warm. Mice ran over the boulders, gathering food while they could. The summer is proceeding apace. Finally, we started descending into a wide, high gorge. It is the beginning of the long descent to the plains and has a scattering of Mongol as well as Kazakh gers; we are edging back into the Mongolian steppe that leads to the Gobi. This is not a place for strangers and certainly not ones without a proper tent. We received a good welcome and some of the very best portions of sheep: cuts of kidney and fat.

Umber is still strong and increasingly gaining Kermit's respect. Perhaps he'll be awarded honorary Mongolhood. However, the horses do need a rest, down here in the lowland grazing, so I went off marmot hunting for the day.

27th July

In a way, I didn't want a hand in the death of these creatures. I've enjoyed the way they pop in and out of their burrows. But I've come here to get to know the ways of the Mongolians and so off I went, following a hunter on foot up a near-vertical slope. The man didn't duck down as normal hunters do. He danced a jig, waving a yak's tail above his head. For it appears the marmot has a fatal weakness: his insatiable curiosity.

Hares sprinted away, billions of small grasshoppers were underfoot and a small party of gazelle nearby, but the hunter ignored the lot, jigging his way up the hill, waving, ducking, jiving – and finally firing.

The poor marmot. He doesn't understand. One moment he is standing on his rear legs, trying to fathom this strangeness. Then, 'bang!' he is no more.

I kept my own head down, trying not to ruin things. Worth recalling, I thought as I lay behind a tuffet, that G.K. had a formidable war machine for three reasons. The first was himself, a leader, who with generals such as Subedei forged an army with precise disciplinary structures, 'making bands of thousands and appointing captains of the thousands'. Each soldier had a clear set of responsibilities, was schooled in specific manoeuvres and advanced through merit, not through feudal or family status. Nor was this army too proud to pick up skills, such as the use of catapults and explosives, from those they fought. Secondly, that flexible and resilient tool, the Mongol horseman – was at his disposal. By not adopting the European armour, shield and broadsword, which could amount to 50 kilos, he kept this advantage, and the horse's manoeuvrability and speed, to a maximum. But the third reason was

Below: Kermit, helped by a committee of Kazakhs, strapping my solar panels onto Packhorse X. These were used to recharge camera batteries.

Left: *Drinking Mongol tea, laced with both butter and salt, kept me hydrated day after day on the ride. Being summer, the season of dairy products, I was continuously supplied with snacks of cheese, curds and bordzig – pastries made from dough deep-fried in mutton fat.*

that the Mongols were not just herders but hunters also. Armed with the state-of-the-art composite bow (from bamboo and cattle horns) and a new, sturdier stirrup to steady the archer, Mongol armies used one hunting tactic, time and again: they simply retreated. The sight of the legendary Mongol army in full flight was a very great temptation indeed. It was in 1241 in Western Poland, that the elite of Europe – Knights Templars, Teutonic Knights, the Hospitallers – each man dressed in chainmail useless against the Mongol arrows and spears, went to their doom. They gave chase and rode straight into an ambush. When the light cavalry had weakened the hapless chivalrous knights, stumbling in a smoke screen released by their Mongol hunters, it was time for the heavy cavalry to move in. Afterwards, nine sacks of ears were sent to their Mongol prince Batu, so he had a true tally of the dead. The next day it was the turn of the Hungarian army. The road to Pest was soon littered with an estimated 60,000 bodies, slaughtered by the arrows of the Mongol light cavalry, and they lay 'like stones in a quarry'. It was the same tactic here. The marmot was a victim not of his enemy's superior force but of himself. He was conquered by his own vanity, his sheltered outlook of the world.

We walked back down the hill, the marmot victim swinging from the hunter's belt. Other marmots popped up their heads behind us, still curious, wanting us to wave that yak tail again. We took up our horses and rode back, snow all of a sudden driving down on us. Around the peaks above, there was already a blizzard. A baby hare, confused by the dazzling snow curtain, sat in the path.

I ate the marmot that night. It wasn't my sort of meat and I kept thinking of the fact that marmots' fleas, and marmots themselves, carry bubonic plague, and that Govi-Altai *aimag*, which we are approaching, was quarantined off last August. Mongolia has an estimated 2.5 million marmots and it was the Mongol armies which probably carried the Black Death to Europe in the Middle Ages wiping out one in three of us. It wasn't just us British, French and so on who suffered. It began perhaps in 1345 when Janibeg Khan, one of the Khans of the Golden Horde, flung diseased bodies by catapult over the battlements of Kaffa, on the Black Sea, to end a siege by chemical warfare.

This morning, as Kermit gathered the horses in the far distance, I could see that one of them was lame. I looked, selfishly, to make sure it wasn't Burnt Umber. I've come to adore him – purely, I think, because of his sheer size. Whether he's actually stronger or not than the standard Mongol horse, he represents a strength that I need. As it happens, the injured horse, though, was Kermit's mount, the red one. Kermit said the animal fell off the river bank, in the night. He has badly torn a ligament.

I couldn't help but despair; I thought we'd left the ghosts behind. What am I doing wrong? I'm not someone prone to religious sentiment, but it's very hard not to feel the victim of fate, of the supernatural.

The hitherto friendly ger occupants laughed when we offered the horse for 60,000 tögrögs – half price. There was nowhere else to sell him. We couldn't very well offer him to the Kazakhs next door. We'd already blown it by telling them we had no Polaroids, which they knew very well wasn't strictly true. In the end we sold him for 15,000 tögrögs – 'chewing gum money' Kermit said disgustedly. I tried to get reassurances from his new owners that he wouldn't end up as supper. 'They say they will give the horse a whole year to get well,' Kermit reported back.

'In other words, they'll wait until I've gone, then eat him.'

'Exactly,' Kermit said. Later, he asked if he could, as has become customary, stay behind to join the feast

Hills around us steep, painted with lichens, and at the bases of slopes are square red blocks the size of bungalows, which have been released from above. We have achieved only 10 kilometres, having to stop at the next ger. Not far beyond here is a mosquito zone. It lasts to Khovd,

114 kilometres away. The first gers are 100 kilometres on, but the mosquitoes will still be bad: we'd be wise not to stop there. It means we'll have to race this distance in a day – the sort of challenge I nowadays feel tempted to shy away from. Are we somehow bewitched? It cannot be. Yet it's even difficult keeping a running total of casualties, there've been so many.

I must have faith in the horses. They are tough. They can do this journey. I'm reminded of what Marco Polo said – I've got it here in my notes: the Mongols were the best army to have for 'overthrowing kingdoms', partly because their men were the best able to endure exertion and hardship and the least costly to maintain, and partly because their horses 'support themselves by grazing', so there is no need to carry hay.' Indeed, soldiers even drank their horses' blood from lanced veins.

Nonetheless, we have gone through the luggage once again to lighten the load, chucking away yet more items of clothing and shelter.

chapter nine

KERMIT FADING

In this country, though the sky waits over you,

the land ushers you on.

Early thoughts on Mongolia from my diaries, NOTEBOOK 1, *14th December 1996*

Both of us were ill in the night, Kermit being sick in a complete circle all around the outside of the ger. It's partly the change from the Kazakh diet of horse to that of the Mongols: despite Kermit's hopes, last night we were back to greasy sheep suppers again. Not a good start, when you have to ride 114 kilometres with baggage in one day. I woke poor Kermit at 5 a.m., then off, the moon a high circle. First light was a startlingly clean yellow that electrified the crag slopes. Down and down the valley into the plains. We waited for the first flies to hit us. We passed the last gers. Finally, not even livestock. We were still waiting for those flies.

I realised how accustomed I had become in lowland country to the distant bleating of sheep. All we could hear now was the iron of horse shoes, the running water, the wagtails and larks. Waiting for the flies, waiting ... Ten kilometres done, 100 or so to go ...

We trotted, slowed, trotted, slowed. So far the horses were doing fine. Kermit is now riding one of the former packhorses, a shaggy mount with an 'H' branded onto his bum. His mane has not been cut, this often meaning he was a prize animal of the herd. There's absolutely no sign of why he should be prized by anyone.

The valley opened out: old granites, crumbling pale red, huge boulders, rearing jagged hills. The mosquitoes hit us quite suddenly, as we passed through river-bank trees which had been combed by flood water. The air was droning with them; they bothered Kermit, who'd never met such swarms in Khövsgöl, and lay heavy on the horse flanks.

Left: *Descending the Altai, and at last into the Gobi.*

They made the horses nervous, and when I tried to film from Umber I was thrown off, down onto the pebble terrace.

We made it to the first gers only at nightfall, but the men we saw steering their flocks were waving yak tails in their faces – mosquitoes, albeit fewer. Another 14 kilometres to go. We kept on through the dark, reliant on the horses' eyes. Far ahead, the barking of dogs, which sensed something alien out there. Kermit headed towards them. Where there are protective dogs, there must be people.

This was an otherworldly sensation, riding in the dark – one of floating, as my horse carried me over the streams and pastures. This was like the world that Tsend journeyed through in trance, guided by the faculties of her spiritual ally, the crow. I listened ahead through the dark to Kermit's horse crossing pebbles, sand, water. Four or five seconds later I would cross the same – the pebbles, the sand, the water. Only this way did I know how near I was to Kermit, whether I was falling behind.

At last we arrived at a ger, though we were accepted in only after Kermit had talked coherently for a while, so the man inside knew he wasn't a drunk.

30th July

Rose late this morning. Old ladies are sorting wool in the morning light, children are walking out with the sheep and goat herds. Other ladies collect scissors for shearing. Past the gers is the lacy river system that we came through last night and behind, steeply rising, pale rust boulder hills. A line of telegraph poles lead to Khovd.

There are mosquitoes here too – Burnt Umber is covered in dust. He's been rolling, trying to scratch his insect bites. The other horses seem resigned, and stand about being sucked by mosquito proboscises. The news from the gers is not good. Though the mosquitoes are tolerable here, they get worse again beyond Khovd, and continue for 200 kilometres. The horses have to withstand yet another dash, this one almost twice as far as the last.

2nd August

The horses are rested. Time to continue. We must manage the 200 kilometres as quick as we dare – say three days. Again, I will ride Umber and Kermit will take Hairy H, leading Packhorse X. We have very little luggage – no tent, food or thick clothing – and are extremely vulnerable to the cold, and of course mosquitoes. Only when we get some camels, on the other side of the range, will we be fully operational again. But the prospect on that front isn't good either. From all we gather, there are simply no camels to be found. In the summer the females are needed for their milk and the males are spread over the hills, enjoying a bachelor life of freedom – or as much as a castrated bachelor ever can.

LATER: Up over a rise, down into a plain, the lakeside rolling hills sinking away, the red escarpments merging into crinkly green hills. As we rode, Kermit would fall asleep, then whack Hairy H, pretending it was his fault that he was going round in circles.

We rode and rode some more. Umber was undaunted, but Hairy H tired and was constantly goaded by Kermit – when awake. After 50 kilometres Kermit sighted what we thought might be a ger, but how could it be? No-one could be subjecting their herds to these quantities of mosquitoes. Sure enough as we came nearer I saw no sign of grazing, but nearer still, we saw it was definitely a ger. Then we saw that a vehicle track led right alongside it, and guessed what it was: a *guanz*, roadside café. It provided passers-by with fast food.

We tied up the horses, and immediately decided it would be wisest to shelter here for the night – this ger seems almost armour plated. There is netting over the roof apex, and a glass window either side of the door. The woman here runs an efficient operation, and even has potatoes to add to the mutton. From time to time, motorbikes and lorries call in, often to do that very traditional Mongolian thing, the running repair. Here there's a broken lorry cab that acts as a toilet facility for travellers, and an *ovoo* which is part shrine, part roundabout. Passing drunks pay their respect by chucking their bottles on.

Kermit watered the horses in the swamp, then stayed out in the mosquitoes to chuck all the vodka bottles off the *ovoo*. Like all the Mongolians I have met – a dozen drivers, a hundred townsmen, three hundred horsemen – he chucks his litter carelessly to the wind. Yet to Kermit, an 'atheist', the contribution of vodka bottles to the *ovoo* is not on. Perhaps he sees it as an empty gesture, therefore a defilement of what it means to be Mongolian. Whatever the true reason, he lobs the bottles out across the plain to shatter there and he does it with the sincerity of a religious ritual.

We plunged into the mosquitoes again, heading south. What are these insects living on? Where is the water they emerge from? Out here, it is just dry, dry, stony barrenness. This is a huge, ancient river bed, the whole wide valley floor. Everything is rounded by forces long gone. Mudstones, old granites. We passed a dead horse. He hadn't been very unfit – he'd been in no worse shape than ours – but we knew he was dead, not sleeping, because the surfaces of his metal shoes were rusting.

Again after only 50 kilometres, we have come to another roadside takeaway ger, sealed from mosquitoes, like the last, and will rest here.

With the slow but steady progress of the horses, I feel I'm at last leaving the ghosts behind. It's a good feeling, the approach of the Gobi: I can almost smell it. I am strong and feeling stronger, but the horses are weakening and so is Kermit. He sleeps as we ride and asks to stop to adjust his girth straps – an excuse to get out of the saddle and rest. It really is as the Mongolians say: every creature has his home: the camels their scrub, the horses their pastures, the Mongolian his mountain, steppe or desert. So Kermit, man of the cold north, like the horses is fading.

But at least the horses are still going. They haven't been eating – the mosquitoes – but they won't give in yet. I want to salute them somehow.

4th August

The hardest day yet for the horses, as we crossed the final range. Umber, Hairy H and X ploughed on up the slope in automatic drive, head down, just getting on with it. Hairy H's left eye is closed, swollen over from mosquito bites, but he continues regardless, carrying Kermit slumped asleep.

We wound through the hills, coming across gers in pockets – we'd made it through the mosquito zone. Sometimes, skinny camel mothers looked up, their shaggy infants gazed. However, as we'd been warned, the big males that we need were not to be found.

There was a heavy downpour, releasing soft, musky smells which reminded me of the fern-clad shales of the Scottish Highlands. The horses chugged on and on, up and up, Umber undoubtedly the strongest. We dismounted to help the horses. Then, cold, damp and wet, we crossed the pass, bare hills spread around our feet, and walked down to the nearest valley gers.

As we approached we mounted our horses to get protection from the dogs. I saw there'd been flooding here; but for the ger, a piece of technology that can cope with all that the elements offer, it was simply a matter of undoing the perimeter skirting strip to let the water flow right through unobstructed.

We were made welcome as ever, given tea, then the mutton. That's two months of boiled mutton, so far, excluding my time eating horses with the Kazakhs – oh for a decent horse to eat now. Presently I am relaxing, flat on my back, made to feel at home. I have a growing

KERMIT FADING

158

optimism. Whatever fate has left to throw at us, it can't be enough to stop the horses – not all of them – because we are over the final pass and into good pasture for a day or two. All we need is camels.

Through a wide green valley in the district of Möst *sum*, the wind growing, the hills around a patchwork from the light glancing and fading from the clouds. The thought of being near a sum has filled me with dismay: visions of Kermit led astray, despite his best intentions.

In the pure yellow light of early dusk a herd of thirty or so camels was coming our way, steered by two horsemen. I dared not hope too much, but it looked as if there were three males among the thick copse of camels.

Below: *Purchase of Bastion, Jigjik and Bert. A moment captured by aspiring photographer Kermit.*

The camels thundered up, and came to a chaotic halt, standing about, staring indignantly at us. We got off the horses and introduced ourselves to the owners, the traditional pleasantries going something like this:

Kermit: 'I hope your sheep and goats are fat.'

'Yes, they are well indeed.'

'And your cattle are fat?'

'Yes, my cattle are fat, indeed.' In Mongolia as in Europe, it doesn't do to unburden all your own woes: 'Well, as you ask, it hasn't been an easy year, no not with the snows carrying away the last five sheep. And then Batbaatar taken bad with the plague … Remember that dog we had? Rabies. And sweet little Tsetseg? Pregnant again.'

Still holding the horse reins we sat ourselves down, crossing our legs and hunching ourselves against the wind, while the horses stood over us. We accepted their snuff and there were more niceties while Kermit explained who I was. Sometimes I stole glances at the male camels. As we'd thought, there were three. Perhaps it was a trick of the light but it looked as if the nearest was one-eyed.

We established that the two men, a father and son, were willing to sell them. An enormous piece of good fortune. And so I handed Umber's reins over to Kermit and went over to put the camels through their paces. The first was the youngest by far. I made him sit, stand, walk. He was clever, perhaps a little too clever? Otherwise, I couldn't see anything wrong with him. The second, the largest, was much older, maybe twenty years old – teeth worn to nothing very much. Once upon a time he would have been very strong. Now, to be blunt, he was past it. The third camel was even older: he seemed to be hardly a camel at all. One of his humps was bent right over and, as I'd feared, he was missing an eye.

What a sorry pair. Camels live to thirty years – thirty-five in the olden days, when they were vital for moving the ger and looked after with greater care. That didn't leave much mileage.

I trotted the one-eyed camel back and forth, seeing if he would trip up. He seemed to cope with his handicap well. The two owners huddled with Kermit, smoking, bent forward to block out the wind but watching fascinated as I examined the misshapen creature. Here was a prospect of dumping the ancient thing on a foreigner. But I was looking for more than just physical fitness. I wanted placid camels, gentle camels, camels that would stick by me. In the Gobi, there would be few if any gers: I couldn't afford to be abandoned.

I made my decision. Two of these camels might be old, one of them might be half blind, but yes I could see myself working with this eccentric collection. I went over to the men and said I was interested in all of them. I wasn't sure, but as we got on our horses and went together to a ger to get out of the wind it looked as if both men were smirking.

Once we had had a warming cup of tea, we went outside again and sat down to negotiate out of earshot. Because of the cold, I tried to make it quick for everyone. Kermit had already whispered a starting price and he helped me along through the negotiations, joyfully bashing out numbers on my calculator so there would be no misunderstanding between the men and me. At last we agreed a price that was fair, Kermit thought, and the money was counted out. Notes scattered in the wind as we did the counting.

'Agreed?'

We shook hands – not something such rural Mongolians do that much, being a custom only introduced by the Russians. But Russians were foreigners and I was a foreigner, so they understood this was what was expected.

Then, when all was done, the older man suddenly handed back two fat bundles – some 40,000 tögrögs in each – one for me, one for Kermit. I was confused. Had we miscounted? *'Beleg,'* the old man said. A gift. He let out a sudden gust of laughter, then clapped me on the back. 'You should have haggled more!'

6th August

Today is a rest day: we have camels to carry baggage and can be more self-sufficient again. Now I am checking equipment and gathering poles so that we can use the tent. Kermit is counting out his newly acquired tögrögs. Just as I feared, he wants to make the most of them, right away. You can almost see the bright lights, vodka bottles and women reflected in his eyes.

'I'm planning a trip to Möst *sum,*' he said. 'Please …' I began, but it seemed he'd already arranged a lift on the motorbike of one of the camel owner's because he then put on his sunglasses, jumped onto the bike and the rest of my sentence was lost in the explosive din of a broken Russian exhaust pipe.

So off he goes to seek his fortune – or rather spend it. Meanwhile, the horses have their heads down, grazing for all they're worth. The camels are tied beside the ger, not allowed to eat at all. The old Mongol rule is that a camel must not eat or drink the day before they set out on a journey. The most common explanation is that it toughens their metabolism for the journey. Others say that if there's too much water

Overleaf:
In summer, male camels, such as these in the Desert Steppe, are left to graze free, while mothers are kept nearby with their young for milking.

in their system, the camels' feet get soft. In fact, no-one seems to be sure of the reason. The Mongolians just pronounce that it is the Right Way, it must be done, and though it makes no sense to me I'm here to learn, so I obey, and turn away sadly from the tied-up camels.

The trouble is, I am losing a sense of right and wrong. I can't be right because I know little of horses – and, I suppose, Mongolian camels. The Mongolians can't be right because they don't do such long treks. Furthermore, we come from opposite viewpoints. As a child I was taught that a good cowboy always looks after his horses before himself. Not Kermit, not the Mongolians. Sometimes, the Mongols don't seem to have earned their reputation as horsemen at all. But then I come across a teenager sitting quietly alone at a brook, letting an old, beautiful horse have its fill, and I see respect akin to worship. I have judged too harshly again. Meanwhile I end up secretly hoping that when the horses are next 'neglected', tied up after a day's ride so that the next *airag* session can begin, that they'll sit down – as the most cunning horses do, yanking their lead reins down the pole to the ground – and grasp an illegal blade or two.

LATER: Kermit is back. He arrived on the motorbike with a box balanced on his knees. He wasn't drunk, but the box was full of Chinese beer. 'Oh no,' I thought.

Kermit pulled out everything else he'd bought. Apart from some new sunglasses and the beer, there was only flour and sugar. 'No eggs,' Kermit said, handing them to the lady of the ger, 'and you can use your own butter.'

Flour, sugar, butter, eggs? They sounded like ingredients for a cake. Then I remembered. 'Oh my God!' I thought. 'They ARE ingredients for a cake.' How could I forget? It was Kermit's birthday.

'Party?' Kermit asked, hopefully.

The drinking and singing began and I slipped out for a quiet word with the camels. They must get used to my voice. Up ahead is the desert, and out there they won't need me as the horses do. They can simply walk away, if they want, snacking as they go. All I can offer them is security, the leadership that every camel craves.

Thankfully, the party is ending – only two hours. Kermit has restrained himself, even escorting the drunks into the night. I'm so grateful, I feel like kissing him. I do know he tried his best for me and I also know that his way of living, for the day, for the month, for the next swig of *airag*, is as full as mine. The Mongolians are tougher than the Anglo-Saxons and

Celts, but their energies are invested only in the moment. Notions of extended expeditions, of progress, don't belong; they invalid their contract with the timeless land, which does, after all, provide for them.

Kermit was slow to wake, as usual, but finally responded to my shakes at 9.30 a.m. As we departed – now with the three camels as backup – I noticed that Umber's front right foot, the pastern, was swollen. It is an injury caused by a loose nail in his shoe – slipshod workmanship – but fortunately it is minor. I can breathe again; Umber still stands by me.

As for treatment, it's the usual procedure: I must urinate on the injury. It does seem to be most effective.

We were away, with our new team. Once more, the sound of padding flat feet. Their strength on my side. Now I can start spreading responsibility onto them and away from the horses. I must do it quickly. The horses will not be with us for much longer, just to where they can no longer tolerate the Gobi. Having learned the hard way, I'm meant to be maintaining some detachment from my beasts of burden, but the camels have already somehow developed names: Bastion, the biggest, then Jigjik 2, the clever one, then Bert, with bent humps and one eye, lumbering along at the back.

We are being led by an infuriating shepherd boy called Amgalan, through the last hills and down to the Gobi edge, which we'll reach in a few days. He has been leading us up and down hills, taking bad lines across the land. My camels' feet have been getting damaged on the rocks as they scuffled uphill and then skidded downhill. Finally, unable to stand it any more, I insisted we stopped early and we put up our tent. The light is in split tangerine sunset bands, grey rain smearing it. On the slope below a young man, dressed up like a sheep, two little horns on his cloth cap is stalking marmots.

Not long now before the Gobi Desert. 'It would take a year to go from end to end,' Marco Polo wrote. Whatever route he was talking about, it can hardly be much longer than mine. I have 1000 miles ahead of me, and I'm now almost three weeks behind schedule and the summer is drawing to a close. I'd say I have five weeks, until mid-October, to cross – later than that and there's no telling what degrees of cold we'll have to face. I'd feel better if I'd already received the co-ordinates of the military wells from Ermek, who is presently meant to be tracking me down. 'Twenty-eight watering places in all,' noted Marco Polo in his *Travels*. 'Beasts and birds there are none, because they find nothing to eat.'

Meanwhile, Hairy H's left eye has been cured. 'Mongolian urine,' said Kermit with satisfaction. The Mongolians take pride, even in their urine.

Granites of red, skies of blue. Hills and ranges, and empty stone cottages – winter quarters. A possible sighting of Ermek: a shepherd rode up and said he'd seen a jeep with three men aboard, one of them had 'little hair and big blue spectacles'.

Crags like chipped-edged knives. And always above us one summit covered in snow, and as rounded as a knee cap. The camels have yet to complain. Yet damage IS being done. Amgalan takes stupid short cuts through sharp rocks, despite my pleas, and thrashes the animals, despite my demands. What can I do? I feel like nudging him over the cliff.

Finally, on an upslope, only twenty paces from the summit, Bert sat down. 'Lazy,' Amgalan explained and began beating him. Kermit, seeing my eyes go red with anger, told him I didn't like it and after a rest we continued on our way. The irony is, one man who would understand about maintaining animals on the march, is the man I've been trying so hard to get away from: old G.K. And his general Subedei, who took an army 10,000 km, a circuitous route from the Eastern steppe to the Danube. Not for him a day or week trip with the flocks.

Where is Ermek? I picture him in his jeep, enquiring at gers which weren't even there when we passed through.

The animals need rest and grazing, so I said we'd start late today. I lay writing my diary stretched out across the ger floor, thinking of the camels and horses out there gratefully munching. But when I shoved on my boots and went outside I found that last night Kermit had tied the camels together on a gravel patch. So, no food.

We all make mistakes, I tell myself, but, once again, like the Mongolians, I find myself seeking to rally behind Genghis Khan. It's something I must fight, as they perhaps must. There IS strength for me in the here and now, as there is for Mongolians, if they choose to look here rather than Japan and the United States. For me there's Tsend, Dundoi and Mr Avirmed, the Head of the Gobi National Park, who's letting me walk through the Gobi because, he says, I'm like a camel.

LATER: The walk started badly, Jigjik 2 refusing three times to set out at all. I cannot blame him, after no food this morning. He seemed to be making a point. He is so intelligent I fear he'll outwit me one day, when

Right: *With Umber. Generally, manes are cropped by Mongolians on all but prized horses and the hair is used as rope to bind around the outside of gers, for example.*

I'm alone … He agreed to come in the end, and we descended steadily into the Gobi. It must lie ahead down there, at least the beginnings of it. 'Not far now,' I said to Umber, meaning Bayantooroi oasis, where the horses and Kermit will leave me at the desert proper. At home, you'd say 'not far' meaning your destination was five minutes away. Here, I mean a fortnight.

We made our camp in a narrow gully of grey and red granites, sides of grey grass tufts and red lichened boulders. Here, the sound of running water – the stream weeds weaving in the flow, the fish darting. In an arid land, this seems almost magical. Indeed, Genghis fixed a death penalty for anyone who disturbed the spirits by bathing in fresh water.

10th August

Packed the tent, and as we were about to leave, a green jeep trundled slowly over the boulders of the rock road. Ermek with Adrian [the photographer], both looking pale – three days in the jeep looking for me. After a few preliminaries, I wanted to hear the news. 'The big question is, have you got the military well co-ordinates?'

'Yes, they were most helpful, really. They said "No one has done this before, and he'll die if we don't give him a hand." But first they did another check on you with the KGB.'

'And what did they tell them?'

'They said, "Oh yes, we know all about that Englishman. It's funny: he is walking right across the Gobi! Yet he is quite, quite harmless."'

Ermek and I walked over to look at an ibex skull – both of us, it turned out, looking for a chance to confide about Kermit. There were a billion wild chives in flower, beds of them in a purple haze, stretching into the plain, the dustlands which are my first sight of the Gobi in khaki summer starkness.

'You are not thinking of taking him into the Gobi are you?' Ermek said as I lifted up the great goat skull from the giant red lichened boulders. I could see that he was worried I'd succumbed to Kermit's legendary charm. 'He is too young,' he said, though Kermit is, like him, in his mid-twenties.

We settled by the riverside, a paradise protected by mosquitoes which had been blown away. There were reeds, deep grasses, swaying willows, and around us crumbling dry, red hills.

I read my mail from the UK in the night. Home seems unimaginably far away. 'Dad as chirpy as ever,' Katie [my sister] wrote, and, with terrible brevity: 'PS Bramble has been put down. Ran out in front of one too many cars.'

Urgent packing of final supplies. Kermit seemed excited at the prospect of entering desert and got the driver to draw him a map of his very own. It was a simple endeavour, drawn on the back of an envelope and like a map of the London Underground, but instead of the tube stops there were silhouettes of peaks. They ended with that of the giant Eej Uul, Mother Mountain, near Bayantooroi.

'Good luck, Benee,' Ermek said. 'See you when I collect Kermit in Bayantooroi.' He slammed the jeep door, and a net of dust descended slowly over us. 'Oh, and the driver wants me to warn you about the Almas.'

'The what?'

'The Abominable Snowman. From the Himalayas. We get him out in the Gobi too.'

'But there's no snow.'

'He doesn't seem to mind.'

Then the jeep was gone. The silence, and the realisation that I was at the Gobi edge. I'd reached the third and final zone of Mongolia. The desert, where an awareness of the fragile nature of all our lives is thrown at you.

Today is a rest day. Yellow stringy 'dandelions', and the stemless thistle. The camels stuff themselves, mowing the river banks, standing mid-river and working their way down.

chapter ten

SPIRITS *of the* LIMITLESS FIELDS

They are, of all men ... the best able to endure exertion and hardship and the least costly to maintain, and therefore best adapted for conquering territory and overthrowing kingdoms.

Marco Polo, THE TRAVELS *(A constant reminder as I tried to learn skills from the Mongols.)*

The tracks of a wolf around our camp – but very cautious. Swifts swooping through the mosquito clouds, which are gathering now that the wind is dying. It's dawn: I can hear the butting of ibex, their heads meeting with a loud clack, the sound echoing among the crags. There's a herd of thirty, a mother and kid perched on summit rocks to view our camp.

12th August

LATER: We rode off through the last thick grasses, within a few paces finding ourselves among shingle and the spread dust of the Gobi flatlands. Kermit ahead, frowning at his map as he's seen me do with mine over the months. The horses were lively from yesterday's excess food, and were reluctant to come along with us at all. Only the camels were happy to keep walking ahead, into the limitless field of hazy light.

THE GOBI: Grass tussocks which have been tortured by the winds and wheeled in the ground as if in agony, leaving scars in a circle around them; bright sun and a bitterly cold wind as sands, gravels and rocks grow in place of grass species. To some humans this place is just a wasteland, I thought. A good place to dump your nuclear rubbish. To me it's special: the life and death drama played out here is so very tangible. I especially prize the Gobi Desert because I've fought so hard to get here. Underfoot, grasses snapped; to my left, north, the brown escarpments of the Altai Range, slipping away.

After 30 kilometres we came to a few gers, as promised on Kermit's envelope. I have a resurgence of respect for Kermit – not for his navigation

Left: *Mongol saddle with its characteristic ornate metal studs and high wood seat. Almost unbearable for anyone not used to life on a horse, Mongolians take as much pride in their saddles – which provide them with a firm platform for capturing livestock with the uurga pole-laso – as they do in their equestrian skills.*

SPIRITS OF THE LIMITLESS FIELDS

171

skills because he leads me like a mole, meandering short-sightedly this way and that, but for his ability to see distant objects. Like all Mongolians his eyes seem at times telescopic, focusing on images which are only black slithers, lifted from the horizon by a shimmering haze.

The gers crouch behind livestock enclosures made of scrap metal: car door panels, bonnets. All to keep off the Gobi summer and winter. These things are worth noting. I am still over two weeks behind schedule. We cannot afford even a day's rest. There was a severe frost last night and this is mid-August! Have I cut it too fine?

A view from the ger of a line of magnificent camels, walking as if on patrol along the base of the rich brown hills. They began calling to our camels, luring them away. Kermit was at his best, flying up onto a horse, riding out and separating them off. How I will miss him – not just for the ease with which he deals with animals, but the very thing that has exasperated me most, the way he deals with the days, whistling through them with the one tune he knows.

13th August

Covered 35 – 40 kilometres today. Progress of Bert disappointing. He slumbered along in second place, pulling back the lead camel, Jigjik 2. Finally, Bert just sat down, head resting on the sandy ground. He must be strong with all that muscle, but he is slightly misshapen – not just his lopsided humps, but his hunched shoulders. He got himself going again, but in forthcoming days I will have to lean more on Bastion, who is today having his day off.

Knobbly hills, pitted and denuded, red rocks protruding like knuckles. The sky velvety blue, the same lustre in it as the scarves of Mongolian shrines. Out in the plains, an immense herd of wild asses. They swirled away from us in a mist of dust. A second later, the rumbling sound of the thumping hooves as they travelled as one body, all those legs moving in the harmony of the wings of a flight of birds.

We came, thanks to Kermit's eyes, and no thanks to his use of the Underground map, to a very minor settlement, Takhiin Tal, whose only claim to significance is the presence there of *takhi* or the Przewalski horse. They are named after Nikolai Przewalski, a Polish explorer who helped push forward the Russian empire as part of the Great Game against British expansionist aims. When he came across a skin of one in 1879 he immediately recognised its importance. This was, he saw, one of the few wild strains of horse to have survived the Ice Age – another had emerged as the domesticated horse in northern Africa or the Middle East, some 5000 years ago. By Przewalski's time there were no other such wild strains and steadily this horse too was to be driven to extinction by Kazakh hunters and the growing military presence. The last of *Equus przewalskii* was seen in April 1969. Now its fortunes have been revived through the importation of new stocks from the zoos of Europe and the United States, where some 1500 horses flourish; they have been resurrected from the abyss of extinction through the genes of a mere thirteen individuals.

I trotted over on Umber to the paddocks where they are nurtured. Beyond the barbed wire were small, light-weight and very skittish horses. They came over to examine Umber, their short ears pointed, very alert. These horses were strange, yet familiar. They were wild in looks and manner, but had the stocky body and large head of a Mongol horse, their descendant. They had a fawn underside and dun top half. Their tails and manes were short, as if both thinned and savagely cropped by a hairdresser. They had beady eyes, like those of a rodent, the erect mane of a donkey, and thinly striped legs. But to me, having just crossed Mongolia, more impressive than anything else was the fullness of their stomachs. What a cosseted life they lead.

A steely frost down by the stream. The leaves crisp and silver, and made solid, like cutlery. I take this as another warning: it must have been minus 5 at night.

The day itself warmed quickly. We headed to the full moon, as it descended into treacly orange hills. Umber was fitted with a new shoe – the original iron shoes are now as thin as potato crisps. The horses are bearing up, but Kermit is continually tired and by the time he gets out of his sleeping bag I have gathered all the horses and camels, bringing them from the hills and marshes where they've ambled in the night.

Off again, over pea gravel studied with small yellow-tipped flowers which rock in the breeze, wrenched by winds, their roots exposed – another sign of the violence that can be inflicted out here. The camels also give an indication: their coats are a thick felt and growing visibly by the day in readiness for extreme cold.

On through a rocky gully, then below a range created from layers of sediment. At dusk we stumbled across a ger tucked up in a grey hill nook.

The horses are becoming a burden. We are now nurturing them along, no longer risking a trot because we never know where the next water is. Yet the horses are at least constant, loyal; the camels are still untried: they cannot yet be relied on. Jigjik 2, the clever one, continues to assess the situation, looking at the landscape, turning his head to juicy shrubs, wondering why he is being denied them. The other two, Bert and Bastion, plod on, though it is unclear what goes on, if anything, in their heads. Kermit and the horses must last ten more days, my estimated distance to Bayantooroi. I believe they can do it, but will the camels carry on alone with me?

16th August

Below: My tent's Mongol motifs were a source of pride to both Kermit and passing herdsmen.

In the night, the camels made their first serious bid to escape. Kermit found them by moonlight. Even with hobbles, they'd achieved 8 kilometres. It is almost admirable, and it means that they still have lots of energy. The man we are staying with asked where the camels are from and when I said Khovd *aimag* he said, 'then they will fail in the Gobi, and they know it. That's why they want to go back home now.' It is the old Mongolian lore: Every person and creature has his rightful home.

Left: *Inspecting wear and tear on Jigjik. Spending time with each camel, at least in theory, helped to build up their trust in me as we approached the desert.*

Difficult country, up through scree slopes, and around hills. Soon it became clear that Kermit was leading me in a semi-circle. It got worse. We headed out into rocklands, damaging the camels' feet all the way, due south, not east. It became all the more startlingly obvious as the sun sank in the west. 'Everything all right, Kermit?'

'Everything,' he said, lying superbly. So we continued on our course into a rockland oblivion, Kermit slipping glances to his side for other possibilities. Sometimes he looked down hopefully at the scrap of envelope, but it offered no solutions. As we had no water for the horses I had to find a way of getting back on course without hurting Kermit's pride. So I waited a little longer for him to stop and pretend this route was all part of a plan to get a good view from the hill ahead. He purveyed the landscape, singing a song which celebrated – as far as I could tell – the life of a horse which had carried him through the wind, one night. I envied him, wishing I could forget about the journey, this Western idea of progressing onward, and that I had his freedom of mind to simply sing a ballad instead of drumming my fingers impatiently. His peace is achieved by acceptance, mine is achieved only by striving – finding more to wonder at: the crow overhead, for example. It had tattered wings, which clacked as it flapped on by. Black-tailed gazelle were visible as delicate pale lines, their fawn colours lost in the dirt. Falcons scanned the ground. Rodents ducked down.

Finally we were heading eastward, back on course. As the sun dropped from sight, we came across some gers and pasture. By then, the horses were almost audibly sighing with relief.

This is a delightful spot, harboured by the dark brown hills. A few streamside willows – a rarity in this dust land. The four gers were packed with people – some sort of party. They stripped off our camel luggage in seconds, telling us they'd assembled for a wedding, which is all set for the day after tomorrow. Some people are already in their brightest, newest dels; there is a continual hum of light-hearted chatter. It is tempting to stay and savour this last company. From here on, humans will be few and far between.

18th August

More and more people are arriving, drawing up on horses, tying them to the gers while they cool, sitting themselves down for tea, then taking the horses out to graze, before returning to drink *airag*. Girls and women scoop up toddlers and kiss them on the cheek. It would be too sad to miss the wedding – like a slap in the face of humanity. So we are staying. Our wedding gift is two Polaroid films.

19th August

Everyone checked their watches. The bride was late. In the Gobi Desert, as everywhere else in the world, the bride doesn't want to appear TOO keen to get herself married off. The men sat on the sheep enclosure walls, smoking pipes, looking out into the plain for the approaching dust cloud. The women set up stove operations out of doors, boiling water for the expected rush. Then the cry went up that she was coming. I looked and I saw only an immobile speck, one more rock on the flickering horizon. Only a full 15 minutes later did the speck turn into a lorry. Ten minutes on, we could hear its cargo of singing relatives. The vehicle ground through the dust towards us, eventually swinging alongside the ger. The passengers tumbled out, along with bits of furniture for the newly-weds, and piled into the main ger.

Indoors, there was soon a fug around the bride and groom, both of whom stood modestly accepting greetings. For a while the crowd was intertwined, a criss-crossing of arms as the men exchanged snuff bottles, younger men placing their arms to gently support those of their elders – this the *zolgokh*, the traditional greeting.

By noon everyone had settled in, the men on the left, women on the right, mopping their brows with neat hankies. Tea was served, children eyed the pile of Chinese sweets with cigarette packets on top invitingly opened for guests. Then the bride and groom shuffled forward and the bride broke a ritual brick of tea, crumbling it into the hot water, and she moved through the crowd serving guests dutifully, as she will from now on until she dies.

The couple were steered towards the next stage in the proceedings, a high chant by two men, one with huge velvet blue cuffs and a fine voice, the other a dopey and altogether forgettable man who wore a Chinese plastic Panama. Together they sang away, heroically trying for the high notes, all the time bearing a silver and wooden bowl of *airag*, presented on a blue silk sash. The *airag* was offered to the groom and bride. Then there was present giving. Every visitor unwrapped a bundle, often of material, and gravely presented their gifts laid on silk sashes, with kisses on the couple's cheeks, and whispered words of congratulation – and maybe advice.

Afterwards, proceedings were informal, men and women joining in all the old favourite songs as the *airag* was passed around. The tunes were strange to the Western ear, a warbling and a wailing that was an otherworldly sound, right for this otherworldly place of the spirit-filled skies that oversee the life of the Mongolian. Time went by, and while the women remained alert, the men's eyes were glazing, their minds and spirits overcome by the *airag*. Their hats tilted at more and more rakish angles – until mid-afternoon, when they were sliding off altogether.

I was sure that at any moment now Kermit, who'd been on his best behaviour so far, would succumb to temptation. But by mid-afternoon the party was breaking up, drunks riding off slumped upon their horses, or being dunked like tea bags in the stream. I decided to leave and avoid any invitations to late-night drinking. I had already seen the very best of Mongolia: stout heartedness, civility and unquestioning hospitality. Alone in the desert, I'd be able to remember the Mongolians like this.

We were away in the mid-afternoon, Kermit's waterbottle mysteriously having got itself filled with *airag*. Kermit got out his envelope map, and took us straight into a minor hill range, startling gazelles which had every good reason not to expect travellers to take this route.

LATER: We camped by a minor stream fenced by reeds. I didn't see the need to erect our tent and curled up to sleep. I woke in the night to find Kermit patrolling the sand for snakes. I realised I'd been selfish: this was our first night in the desert without a tent and Kermit was uneasy. A Khövsgöl man, he feels further from home out here than I do. He turned on my stove, as one might light a fire to keep away wolves, and huddled by it.

20th August

Above: The Mongol system for loading baggage requires two people. Mongols almost never travel long distances without a companion and as my time alone in the Gobi drew close, Kermit and I still had not developed a new method.

A laborious day across a plain towards a lone black peak. The envelope map didn't distinguish it from any of a number of the same. It was up to me to sort out our route and, because the military allowed me only a map of 1:1,000,000, I was pushing my skills beyond their limit. I became less and less confident, and the peak seemed to remain unchanging ahead of us, never getting nearer, dancing away from us in the quivering horizon. We sat behind a shrub and had a break, coffee and noodles. Then, suddenly we heard someone let out a yell: 'Yeaaaaah!' We both looked up from our noodles, startled. Not a fox, nor a wolf, more like a human cry. But humans do not come out into the desert, least not here – we were on the way to nowhere.

'What is it?' I asked Kermit.

'It's a spirit perhaps,' he said, slowly. I'd never seen Kermit looking so humourless. He took off his sunglasses.

Marco Polo talked of spirits leading you from your path. 'Sometimes, indeed, they even hail him by name … Yes, and even by daylight men hear these spirit voices, and often you fancy you are listening to the strains of many instruments, especially drums, and the clash of arms.' But the locals had one solution: 'Round the necks of all their beasts they fasten little bells, so that by listening to the sound they may prevent them from straying off the path.' These stories still abound in the Gobi. I said to Kermit, 'I thought you were an atheist.'

'I am, in Khövsgöl,' he replied. He cast his eye gloomily around these alien miles of uniform pebbles, each one, it seemed, painstakingly measured by God to exactly 1 centimetre in diameter.

'Not to worry,' I said. 'If it is a spirit, all we have to do is ignore it.'

'Perhaps it's only a small one …' Kermit murmured, lightening up a bit.

We rode on. And I still haven't an explanation for the sound we heard. A trick of the wind? Or maybe simply a lost Abominable Snowman, calling for its mate.

We slipped around the southern edge of the black peak, and entered a ravine of gully-eroded ochre rock, disturbing Mongolian Desert finches from the saxaul scrub. This brought us to a hidden-away oasis. The grasses were so thick that, after the dust of the plain, even I felt like eating them. Held between a hill of naked sand and a mountain of brittle rock, a grove of stout poplars. Up in the branches of one tree, a lammergeyer. In others, scores and scores of crows. But no water for the horses.

Below: Into true desert. Now the horses (Ulaan left, Hairy H, right) became fractious and insecure - and also increasingly loathed the desert-adapted camels (Jigjik left, Bert centre, Bastion right).

This morning, Kermit let me load the camels alone – practice for the days ahead. I found it next to impossible. He tried to work out a way himself, using sticks to prop one side of the saddle against the camel while he secured the other side, but even he struggled. All we've done is show how dependent the Mongolians are on each other. They just do not operate singly.

Neither of us sure how I'm going to manage, we headed off through the grove, listening to the wind in the leaves. A red fox trotted away; the crows lifted and circled. The poplar leaves flickered in our faces. For the first time in three months of travelling through mountains, hills and steppe, other lifeforms were pressing in on us, sharing our air, and it was as unsettling as it was beautiful.

Soon after, in the lee of the peak, there were small dunes which seemed all the more dead for the life we had just experienced. But the sands soon dissipated, spreading to a pebbled, wide plain.

On and on, no sign of water. A horse can be ridden for two days without water in these temperatures, then fades fast. We've already had those two days. Now they have stopped eating – they cannot digest the food. Kermit is dozy and no longer helps scan the horizon. If the horses are going to make it, it's up to me.

LATE AFTERNOON: I spotted what I thought was a well, positioned against stabilised dunes at the base of the northern range. I left the caravan with Kermit and rode off with Umber for a closer look. It took me half an hour before I was even sure it was, indeed, a well, and a whole hour to get there and see if there was water. As we approached, Umber pricked his ears and quickened his pace. I knew we were all right. He could smell water. I waved Kermit to come over with the rest of the caravan. Suddenly, no more crisis. The horses could drink and eat and we will set out tomorrow with our containers full.

Night-time: Wolves call to each other, back and forward. To me, not an aggressive sound, but friendly. However, Kermit looks about warily – the reputation of the wolf goes before it. To the Mongolian, they are the embodiment of intelligence and strength, all that the head of a nomadic family should be. They were the only animal that once threatened their mastery of the grazing lands. Not surprising then that the wolf has been accorded supernatural powers. 'If you get a cold,' Sergelen, Wilfred McKie's secretary had said, 'you must take a tongue of a wolf and put it around your throat. We believe this.' And in the past, when the Mongols raided their Chinese neighbours, it was as wolves, descending from the plateau down onto their opulent neighbours in the south, like wolf packs to a sheep herd, picking out the weakest. The truth is though, now – late summer – there is food and the wolves are content. It's only in winter that you'd perhaps have to watch out. Pity the poor old Abominable Snowman.

One mountain continues to dominate the horizon, ahead. I suspect it is Eej Uul, Mother Mountain, near Bayantooroi.

22nd August

The horses are getting scared. Day after day they walk further away from their grazing, towards what is, for horses and humans, a land of death. We don't bother keeping Packhorse X on the lead rein now. He trots along behind, neighing. He doesn't want to be left behind. Only the camels are happy. They seem to spend time thinking of the next escape plan, then testing the ropes, leaning on them and finally, having found their weaknesses, breaking them. They are not interested in escaping the desert – only us. We are a hindrance. They want to be free out here to potter about, eating bushes on their way home. Only if things get very much worse will they actually stop, turn round, and march back to Khovd.

We are at the base of Eej Uul, Mother Mountain, a massif bursting out of the Gobi dust. Closer, the Mother seems worn down; her wind-rubbed granites, smoothed and scooped. She is ancient and crooked, her skin disfigured by warts of protruding rock, but she is magnificent and though of course just an extrusion of magma – a lobe of granite that forced itself from the earth – it would be a sorry person who could not sense the wisdom of old age here. This is something from the living core of the earth itself, like the sap which has squeezed itself out from the heart of a tree.

24th August

According to Tom McCarthy, who is studying snow leopard activity nearby, the snow leopard has crossed through the barren sandy plains to be up in this peak. It is the only time this secretive animal has been recorded in a desert and at first it's hard to imagine a leopard, creature of ice and scree, sleekly making its way over pebbles, through scrub. Yet it's entirely to be expected that the snow leopard accomplishes strange feats. One expects magic of this elusive animal, acts of the abnormal, the incomprehensible. It is also to be expected that, while the snow leopard was tracked through the desert, no one actually saw it there.

Skirting marshes, through brush and salt encrustations which have hardened into plates, we saw, in the late dusk, the tell-tale Russian chimney-stack. We'll be at Bayantooroi in the morning.

We arrived before the settlement was awake, riding in along the poplar groves, and tying our caravan to a telegraph pole. The horses' duty is done, and they look as fit, or fitter, than when we bought them. 'You've come through,' I thought. All the way from the mountains of Khovd. I was so proud of them – Umber, Hairy H and Packhorse X – I'd have given each a carrot, or any other vegetable, if only there was one anywhere.

Ermek has arrived, after a day or two's search with two jeeps. The lead driver is in a bit of a state. His vehicle got ruined, while Ermek tried to look for wells for me nearby. And his wife gave him a hard time for equipping Kermit with the envelope map: 'You might have sent

Right: *Bride and groom (left), receiving gifts from wedding guests – in this case dress material all the way from Ulaanbaatar, with the traditional blue silk scarf of blessing.*

Left: *Waiting for the bride. Her home-to-be, bought by her husband, also awaits, stacked with a welcoming array of new furniture and old relatives.*

those two young men to their deaths!' It's true, if we'd been depending on the Underground map, we'd still be out there, perhaps adding on to it our last will and testament.

We've taken over one of the offices of the Park Headquarters, to plan my launch out. Mr Avirmed is being very good about it – his office now a camp-site, his neat poplars outside being devastated by the three camels. It was he who gave special permission for me to cross through the park, and even hearing of the losses of miscellaneous horses and camels, he has faith in me.

Ermek has obtained all the remaining military well co-ordinates and a new military permit. There's still a lot of arranging to do. While I check my food provisions and equipment, Choinjin, one of the Park's trackers, an old-timer, will make up new ropes and repair saddle packs and try to think of a system whereby I can load the camels alone. The tent stays behind – I'll take an emergency bivvy bag, my sleeping bag and mat. I shall carry 40 litres of water, enough for five days certainly, and spread the containers on the two camels. Most items have a backup – for example, if the stove breaks and I can't boil water to drink it, I have a simple water purification system.

The feeling is, it will take me fourteen days to get to the next habitation, Ekhiingol, where Ermek will meet me in case there's trouble there from local military. Up until then, I may bump into a herder, but it's unlikely. If I'm in trouble, I must try to make it all the way back here, or head on.

I needed to gather myself, and decided to go over to Eej Uul. Kermit decided to come for the ride and in the end I had to take refuge at the back of the mountain. A hermit had once done the same, secreting himself away in the 1930s. His modest home was perched on a ledge, completely invisible to the passer-by – had there been any. It was a cave sealed off with a neat, mud-brick wall. Inside, a smoke blackened ceiling – the smoke designed to leave by a separate exit, so as not to betray the hovel. The hermit was a lama and was supported by locals, who brought him provisions. He had a stone block for a seat, dust for his bed. His hand prints were in the clay he'd moulded for windows. I sat alone, looking down on a wild rose bush, comforted to think this was once a view from a home.

I thought to myself: what skills have I learnt from the Mongolians? How to observe the land more keenly; perhaps an ability to make do. But there's something more important. And, sitting here on a rock, as the hermit once sat, I find enormous encouragement in the Mongolians.

I feel like I've been in the presence of a special people, one a cut above the rest of us. Because day after day the Mongolians have sheltered me, building me up to be ready to complete this journey. Not just Tsend, or Dundoi, but every Mongolian: together, they have something greater than the individual. The Mongolians exist out here through co-operation, through consensus, using the ger as their common unit of currency. The ger is open to all. It is perfect democracy: whether president or pauper you get the same treatment – a face to face meeting over tea. Europeans feared the Mongols as barbarians, yet in some ways they were more democratic. The Europeans didn't have one man, one vote, not for another seven centuries. They already had *liberté, égalité, fraternité*. This is why Mongolia doesn't need to look back to Genghis Khan, or forward to the United States and Japan. It is a great country without them.

chapter eleven

MUTINY

The Mongolians don't say the grass is greener on the

other side of the fence. There are no fences.

From my diaries, NOTEBOOK 4, *28th June 1997*

Choinjin has re-worked all the camel equipment and everything lies ready. He's given me my lesson on loading a camel by myself, propping up the other side of the saddle with poles, and Kermit's tested me on my slip knots. Finally, Choinjin put halters on all three camels. It is an extra precaution to help me grab them should they try to run amok.

I am ready. Choinjin pointed out a hill range, Edrengiyn Nuruu that I should aim for. We looked together through the dust, tracing a line of mountains like a black gecko's spine. 'There is so little water to find,' he said quietly, taking off his bleached, cloth cap. 'I do not know why someone as clever as Mr Avirmed is allowing you to go without the help of me.'

Nor do I, really. Of course, before our meeting in Ulaanbaatar Ermek and I had had to convince Mr Avirmed that I had a track record in deserts and ever since, we've been trying to remember if we overstated my skills. Actually, I'd been disappointed at the time that the route he indicated didn't take me further south still, through even drier, emptier realms, but they were devoid of even military wells. And am I actually up to this route? Choinjin wished me luck anyway. He said I should be wary of snakes, though they will not bite unless I tread on them. I took the opportunity to ask about Almas, the Abominable Snowman. Choinjin has knocked about the desert for years, poaching wildlife and now safeguarding it. 'You've seen him?' I ask.

'I haven't seen him, no. But there are many who have.'

It's what people always say.

28th August

Left: *With Jigjik. Camels always keep survival in the forefront of their minds and, for example, 'memorize' the route they have taken. When Jigjik decided he wasn't able to trust me with his life, he walked 700 kilometres home.*

MUTINY

187

Changed into my desert clothes, put on my little emergency waist bag. It'll have my current map, a compass, a spare compass, a pencil, a Mars bar, a penknife (with pliers for taking stones out of camels' feet) and a torch (for looking for escaped camels at night, etc.). I have a GPS [global positioning system] navigation device, but I resent its intrusion and will keep it tucked away for emergencies, relying instead on the map, compass and all I've learnt here in Mongolia.

Kermit brought the camels into the yard, and Ermek, Choinjin and Kermit helped me load them up. I was nervous. What had I forgotten? 'THINK!' I kept saying to myself. 'You'll be alone out there.' I have grown lazy – like Mongolians I'm used to the safety net of the gers. I kept reminding myself that in an hour I'd be out there without a radio transmitter or friend. I asked Kermit for any final thoughts.

'My thoughts?' His mind didn't seem to be on the job. He was polishing his sunglasses – now striated by grit scratches, but still apparently able to reflect his face as an adequate mirror. 'I am thinking of the Top Ten,' he said.

'The what?'

'That new bar in U.B.,' Ermek explained, snatching away Kermit's sunglasses. 'Stupid kid. He's already thinking of the Top Ten Club.'

'Oh well, Kermit is Kermit.' But I couldn't help but feel a little hurt. It's not every day you walk off to spend six weeks wandering alone in the wilderness.

Ermek reminded Kermit that I was filming and he must do his bit for Mongolia. So he gathered himself and reminded me that the true personality of the camels wouldn't show until they were tired and out there alone with me.

'And which camel is the best?'

He pointed at Bastion. Then Bert, the one eyed-camel. What does that say about Jigjik 2? That he's worse than a mono-focal, misshapen camel? But I too am worried by Jigjik 2 – difficult to put your finger on it, but I suspect his 'intelligence' is actually low cunning.

A few more words, and then Kermit dived excitedly into the jeep. All he could think of were the flashing lights of Ulaanbaatar.

Ermek: 'He doesn't mean to be unfriendly. It's a big thing for him – the city.'

I said that of course I understood that. I would have been the same in his shoes.

'He has asked me for advice about how to behave in public. He wants to improve himself. I can teach him about it all on the plane, he said.' Ermek climbed into the jeep. 'So, Benee, let's hope it's a long long flight!' He laughed, and the jeep was gone.

Mr Avirmed stayed out in the sun to see me and my camels off. A brief wave, and he turned, idling back home with his son. A sinking feeling: that he has a shelter to turn to and I have none.

I turned to the camels and said aloud, 'Well, time to get on with our job.' A relief to be moving again. And I walked out alone into the desert out across a scrubby pan, with Bastion my lead camel, Jigjik 2 behind and Bert, having a rest day with no luggage, at the back. Watching the oasis sink behind, I caught a view through the trees of the three horses, now given a home by Mr Avirmed. Hairy H was eating and Packhorse X also had his head deep in the grass. Umber, though, was watching me steadily and continued watching until I had gone into the desert.

I cut across another grove of mature poplars, hugging the shade, then out into the wind, earth and sun, slowly up into the hill range. Before long, Bastion caught sight of the unpromising looking hills and simply sat down. I had to act quickly – a rebellion, and so soon. They were testing me. I took a pole from Bastion's baggage and gave him a whack. No choice but to stop this nonsense NOW. They've been watching me over the last weeks and think I am a soft touch: if I am, they are right not to follow me.

I entered a gully, and have now stopped for the night by a huge grass clump, a dried-up spring. The camels are scything through the grasses. I have them securely hobbled, and lie beside them, keeping a watchful eye – I shall take no chances and tonight I'll tie all three camels together. The only sounds are the camel burps and sneezes, a few crickets and the clitter-clatter of mouse feet on the bare rocks. I'm not lonely – there again I am, as yet, within reach of help.

I woke at 7 a.m., first light, and released the camels. While I packed camp, they ate and ate. Then I turned to Bastion and hoicked him out of the vegetation. He had to carry luggage again today; after yesterday's unhappy performance, I had to prove my dominance over him.

But before we set foot anywhere, I had to load the camels by myself for the first time, using poles on the other side of the camel to prop up the saddle in lieu of humans. After an hour, it was done, and we plodded on through the gully, the padding sound of the camel feet echoing off the rock sides. Flocks of Pallas' sandgrouse scrambled up the cliffs. A bald, crimson caterpillar loped heavily over the shales. A white and dun-brown striped snake, a slender racer, sunning itself, stretched like

30th August

disused hosepipe across the track. It moved off reluctantly and even then the camels didn't notice it.

On through narrow, secret valleys – red succulents spread over the black pebbles. I was clear of the mountains by dusk, and skirted along the southern side. I was looking for a spring, which I have failed to find, and I am now camping in the open.

The day has grown bitterly cold. I have assembled my emergency bivvy bag, but with all the layers of clothes I need, I can't get out easily to check the camels through the night. All is miserable. As I write, it's well below freezing. It doesn't bode well for the future; this is only the beginning of autumn.

31st August

A bright morning, promising warmth. I defrosted my numb hands over the stove, realising I'd better take things slowly – I'm slightly feverish and mustn't make mistakes. I shall put Bert as my lead camel, for the first time since I bought him.

Later: I am increasingly impressed by Bert. As we wound through gullies, circuiting around, getting lost in a maze of them, he showed his intelligence by trying to race ahead, then cut me off so that he could graze. When that didn't work he tried to intimidate me by breathing down my neck. But I trust him as the lead camel – the camel that, being nearest at hand if there's an upset in the caravan, always carries the bulk of the water supply.

A single *khulan*, the wild ass, powdered in red dust after having had a good roll on the ground. A Henderson's groundjay, reluctant to hop off and abandon something it's found. Then three domestic male camels which ambushed us, thundering up like delinquents, hoping to cause my team to panic, throw off their luggage and be free to join them in liberty. No such luck – this time. We made it to a spring which Choinjin told me about, but only after three hours bending down to look at animal tracks, trying to discern a pattern of animal movement while my impatient camels were stamping out the information with their flat feet.

1st September

Gazelle spring across our path and sometimes domestic camels bar our way, trying to recruit my team. When they've failed, they sometimes tag along behind us for a while. Through a rock land, old lava in stacks, a portion of moon that has been reclaimed and dusted off. I stopped for a tea break, and turned to loosen the camels to discover that I had only two. Bert had gone.

I quickly assessed the situation. It was his turn to be at the back, not carrying anything, so I still had all my supplies. But I cannot risk losing a camel – if Jigjik 2 outwits me, then I'll need Bert on my side. I secured Bastion and Jigjik 2 then turned and ran and ran, thinking, 'why Bert?' He is misshapen, partly blind, but he'll stick by me if ever the worst comes to the worst – and I'd like to think it's not simply because he is less physically competent than the others. I found him 2 kilometres back, sitting in the middle of the trail, waiting for me with a look of total innocence on his face. It did rather look like he'd decided on a nice little rest. At least he didn't walk off home. I took him to join the others and then Bastion tugged on his lead rein, probably deliberately, and the nose peg, which is what it is attached to, snapped in two. I had to haul him along by the halter. It was like pulling an oversized dog by the collar.

I found a spring, a little trickle coming from a river bed woven with algae, and decided to stop for the night. Jigjik 2 sat down in the gravel, soaking in the cool water, the others waded through grasses 2 metres tall, stuffing them down. A squad of Pallas' sandgrouse chase crickets. I am nursing my left wrist, which I very severely sprained tugging Bastion along earlier today. I don't know how quite, but it is now

Above:
Self-portrait in my camp on the edge of Death Valley. Jigjik (left) had decided to go home. If Bastion and Bert (far right) now followed his lead rather than mine, I'd be in deep trouble.

completely disabled. I have managed to take the camels' packs off but this is serious. Mongolians do not load their camels even single-handedly; tomorrow I will have to do it with one hand.

My hand is worse, swollen, and thanks to yesterday's cold night I have a slight fever, but I want to load the camels and move off today if I can. Ermek will worry himself sick if I don't make contact at Ekhiingol approximately on schedule, after two weeks. We have no back-up plan, no emergency procedure.

I'll let the camels graze until midday, the time they normally settle down to daydream. It gives me a chance to watch the visitors to the spring; a baby hare, a tortoiseshell butterfly on what looks to me like knapweed, small pigeons chittering, Pallas' sandgrouse on foot, picking their way up the cliff.

Later: At midday, I had to insert a new peg through Bastion's nose and then begin loading the camels. I took it slowly, strapping my wrist to be able to use the hand at least as a blunt instrument, and tried to keep my temper with myself as I fumbled about. After, bit by bit, the luggage was lifted off the desert floor and bound onto the camels. Some ropes I held taut with the help of my left elbow, others with the aid of my feet and teeth. I felt like a frustrated old man, whose vigour has gone and now can hardly tie his shoe laces. Normally, it takes an hour to pack camp and load the camels; today it took two hours before I was on the road and maybe an hour to unload and hobble the camels again. It hardly seems worth moving at all. But again the clear, clean views, the never-ending skies, keep drawing me onward.

I broke out of the hillrange, back again into the northern plain. A hard day, and I fear for the camels' feet on these stones. I need to rest up for my own health but I hope to carry on for two more days to the last spring – then it'll be five days with no water, through to Ekhiingol.

A ruddy-coated fox flitted away. A pair of desert ravens seemed to follow for a while; what are, I think, saiga antelope sprang off to watch from a distance, hares bounded out from bushes at my feet. They vanished in silence, flicks of dust rising from their feet and dissolving into the wind.

We have reached a hillock which will give us shelter if the wind continues from the north. The camels are grazing. Bert sticks with me when his old friend Bastion doesn't draw him away. Jigjik 2 wanders off alone, seeking out the best shrubs. Though the youngest camel, he doesn't follow the lead of the others – nor that of me, for that matter. I try to develop an alliance with him, plucking herbage as I walk and shoving it into his mouth. I don't get the feeling he is grateful and recently he's come to expect it. But my worry is Bastion. On the march, he is becoming a nuisance. He drags me back, knowing that he is wearing me down. I think he is hoping his nose peg will break, so that I will have to spend an hour fixing a new one again. But I suppose I enjoy the tussle I have with the camels. With my duties to these, my fellow team members, I keep alert; they don't allow me to slip into dispondency.

3rd September

Bastion is increasingly difficult – more of a millstone than a bastion. He has to be cajoled, chided. Once, he became detached from the back of the caravan and I had to walk 3 or 4 kilometres back before I found him obscured by a bush, his dark face for a moment like that of a Gobi bear. Is he weakening, or lazy?

I have walked all day, and now should be at a military well. No sign, though the army gave very precise co-ordinates. Anyway, there is said to be a well after another 30 kilometres. Let's hope it's got water in.

I have made camp, which consists of building up the bags into a wind shelter and putting on my layers of night clothes. By the time I had done this it was dark and it was time to make my pasta supper, but the stove was broken tonight, and my fingers too numb from the cold to fix it.

After dark, wolves were calling. I continue to find the sound cheery – fellow mammals surviving out here with me. However, I don't want them coming for a visit and spooking my camels.

I am not lonely, but today I came across desert rhubarb, sitting as if in a neglected vegetable garden. Though this specimen has probably never even been seen by a human, the familiar rhubarb leaves were poignant somehow.

4th September

Walking and walking, half an eye on the ground to look out for snakes. At midday I looked up, sensing something, and found myself facing a wall of horses. It was a terrible shock after the emptiness to find myself being blocked by animals. They snorted, challenging us. Then I took a single pace forward and they broke ranks, scattering. People must be near – they've released these herds for the winter. Now these horses must begin to fend for themselves and forget human company; it looks like they are reverting to the wild in front of my eyes.

As for human company myself, I don't miss it. The help that this nearby family might give me is outweighed by the interruption they'll cause to my system – my slip knots, my daily allowance of petrol for the stove. We are self-sufficient, we have the beginnings of a family here – for all the faults of some of its members.

Now I'm having a tea break. The camels have elected to sit down and rest, rather than graze. Jigjik 2 has positioned himself beside me and I'm using him as a back rest. He has an enormous appetite and is also, as I feared, a scheming, not just intelligent, camel. He keeps turning to me, thinking to steal my Mars bars, though I doubt he'd like them. And he has appalling breath. It is from the wild chives that grow throughout the Gobi. But I am winning him over. He's almost on my side, I think.

Later: I'm tracking better and sometimes almost by instinct, not checking my map but following gazelle, camel and ass tracks to water-holes. However, I wasn't prepared for my next encounter. I came through hillocks and was met by a gathering of camels. There were hundreds of them and they weren't going to bother to get out of the way. We walked steadily on and I saw that they were centred on a water-hole. Three hundred camels, each and every one better value than Bastion. As we drew closer, all 300 stopped their musings and turned to look us over and when we came nearer, trying to barge through to the water, they closed ranks. They wanted a closer look, and my camels became flustered and dragged me away, ignoring the water. It is signs like this that tell me my camels are already a tight little family, distrustful of outsiders.

Then I saw humans – a girl bareback on a camel, rounding up strays, a boy in a Russian flat cap, slaving at a makeshift pump – and a flock of sheep and goats assembled around a well. Some newly arrived camels were striding right through the flock, trying to skip the queue. Neither boy nor girl were surprised to see me. Considering there's no habitation within a week's walk this was rather creepy. Somehow, everyone out here knows of the man walking alone with three camels. The girl came up, weaving through the sheep, controlling her camel with a flick of the lead rein. I asked if my camels could have a drink, but she had difficulty understanding me – I hadn't seen a human for a week and had hardly been in a position to practise my Mongolian grammar.

My camels were given preferential treatment at the well and then I was led to a ger which was positioned nearby, in the lee of a hillock. As we approached it they proudly indicated a metal structure behind the ger. I took a look, and discovered a generator and a shiny silver satellite dish. I'm in one of the remotest inhabited regions on the planet! Yet they can watch Oprah Winfrey. The girl smiled, gratified by my amazement.

From the oldest girl, I gathered that the boy was only a cousin and that this was a family of five daughters and a little boy toddler. Their mother had died in childbirth having him: there was blue silk draped around her portrait.

The father, a man called Mendee, arrived just then, on a motorbike. Strapped to the back was a canister of water – in case he'd broken down in the desert – and a canister of petrol. He greeted me in Russian, but when I couldn't understand he turned to his daughters and said, 'He's Japanese.' These are the foreigners on the telly, people who are always coming over in trade delegations.

'British,' I said.

'Tokyo?' he asked, trying a new angle.

'London,' I said.

'Near Tokyo?'

'Not really...'

'Japanese countryside,' he confirmed to his daughters. 'He is a countryside man and THAT is why he knows about camels.' At last: it all made sense.

The girls made me tea and Mendee sat listening to my broken Mongolian. He was patient and interested, the way the genuinely alert or very stupid people are. I was never sure which he was, though his children had a grasp of the outside world that he lacked almost entirely. When I got out my map, the girls took over, explaining to their dad that close contours meant slopes, and that north was upright. He was from the passing generation, the Mongolia of the closed days, yet these children were Mongolian enough to reserve utmost respect for their father. When he turned on the TV, they tactfully let him fumble with the generator for half an hour before getting on with it speedily themselves.

The family worked in harmony, popping in and out of the ger to fiddle with the satellite dish to get a better reception, with the fluid movement that they'd earlier shown rounding up the sheep herd. When Mendee had a good picture everyone settled down. They shuffled me forward so that I could watch with them. It was Mongolian TV, a story set in the days of the medieval Khans, and Mendee was transfixed. He'd crossed the desert on his motorcycle just to buy petrol to watch the telly, but to me it was an unnecessary trip: it was only a black-and-white version of the life already going on outside the tent. Never mind. Perhaps tomorrow it'll be *Jurassic Park*. [It wasn't, but I was close. It was broadcast to the Gobi Desert a fortnight later.]

Then something extraordinary. Mongolian TV had borrowed a clip from CNN, and on this I saw, quite clearly, a map of central London, then pictures of Hyde Park, Piccadilly – places that I (loosely) call home. I was watching this and outside the tent was an arid wasteland and my camels! But nothing was so remarkable as the caption across the top: 'Princess Diana's funeral procession.'

What? She's dead or something? It took me a moment to realise what I'd seen, and by then Mendee had turned over the channel to some cartoons.

'Turn it back, turn it back!' I couldn't help yelling, probably in English. Ever the perfect hosts, the Mongolians snapped to my aid, but the news item was over by the time we got back the channel. So, Princess Diana is dead. Or is she? And who killed her? Mendee didn't know who Diana is, which is understandable. But if the news is true [it was], then I am living in an age when even the inner Gobi is owned by the outside world.

6th September

Bastion disappeared for the night. The boy rode out and found him some way away shuffling westward, still in his hobbles. If Bastion had broken them again, that would have been that. I'd never have seen him again. I take it that he's saying he would rather not follow me much further into the Gobi. It's as if he knows that it'll get worse, which it will – today onwards. I'll turn back after two days if I haven't made enough ground to Ekhiingol, where the next water is in five days.

Later: I took my camels to the water trough, to top up the camel stomachs and the water containers. Twenty horses were already there, kicking and biting their way through all the sheep and goats.

Mendee helped me load the water onto the camels. I realised, to my sheer amazement, that even with my one hand I was quicker than he was. Camel skills that he must have had are being lost in the Gobi – that motorbike. The teenage girls, however, were very deft indeed, working quickly to strap the solar panels around the camels' humps. Furthermore my camels instinctively liked them. They possessed none of the loudness or bravado of Mongolian youths, though they could, I had no doubt, deliver a decent thwack if any camel misbehaved. Sad to depart – sadder than when I left Ermek and Kermit. Here was a home, and it seemed all the warmer for the hot and cold desolation awaiting around it.

The girls shook hands and Mendee's eyes twinkled as I presented him with spare tea and biscuit rations. They gave me *aaruul*, dried milk curds, to eat for the road, stuffing them in Bert's saddlebags.

I walked off on a south-easterly bearing snatching plants for Jigjik 2. I really seem to have won him over. I think he'll stick with me through thick and thin. I think.

We were breaking through into a black plain, when I had a bad shock. We were being followed – dark quick shapes cautiously stalking us. Wolves! I thought. But then I saw they were in fact Mongol dogs. They must be Mendee's two pets.

I walked on a bit and the dogs kept following. I knew I ought to send them home and reluctantly began lobbing stones their way. Yet I also wanted them to stick by me out here. Dogs are reliable companions at least – man's best friend. 'Oh well,' I thought. 'They'll soon turn back of their own accord.' But now it's night-time and the dogs are still with me. How immensely loyal dogs are compared to camels. Dogs, of course, are dependent on humans out here – the camels are not, and don't they know it.

These Mongol dogs, however, though dependent, are adapted to the rigours of Mongolia. They are sitting beside me as I write and while they look at me hopefully for water, they haven't begged for my pasta. Now they are settling down for the night, simply digging a nest for themselves in the sand to keep off the night frost.

I did 30 kilometres today. Not good enough. Need to do 45 tomorrow if I'm going to make the crossing. Otherwise, I turn back. My nose is bleeding – the dry air cracking blood vessels.

The dogs left this morning, as the heat gathered. This is the hottest part of the Gobi; it's not too bad now that it's September. Bert stumbles sometimes – tripping on stones due to his bad eyesight? Or just tired? The camels look thin for the first time, their ribs out, their stomachs in.

Bastion and Jigjik 2's turn to carry the luggage. Jigjik 2 is my only strong camel and Bastion doesn't like leading him. I suspect Jigjik 2 gets up to something while my back is turned. I now prefer to lead them separately, side by side, to give them more space from each other. Bastion's rein stays in my left hand, Jigjik 2 in my right, stronger one. Jigjik 2 prefers this special treatment; in fact he is beginning to insist on it.

Black stones underfoot, each of them oval, as if off a factory production line. Ibex, startled by us, look up and get a horrible shock, then kick up dust as they scramble up apparently sheer cliffs.

I have done 45 kilometres today, which is good. I have decided to 'commit'. There'll be no turning back. But the difficulty I had achieving this distance puts a slight question mark over the future of the expedition. The days are getting shorter — there is less room for mistakes, less grazing time for the camels — and I fear I'll have to do 50 kilometres a day to get through the Gobi before winter.

A slender moon tonight. I have to lie with my arm across my eyes, it's so bright. But I enjoy the moon, the knowledge that later it will shine equally on Britain, and my dad and sister's home in Gloucestershire.

Right: *Tseshuu, veteran of the desert, with a camel herd as I prepared to launch out with a new team. The old lady would have been milking camels all her life, and even at seventy years of age would think nothing of riding such a powerful beast into the desert to round up some goats.*

I set out across the open plain – firm sand underfoot – and from what I could see there was only one physical barrier between me and Ekhiingol. On the map it was nothing, a few creased contours, but I soon saw it ahead of me, a black chain of hills fencing me off from my objective. I kept walking, hoping it would reveal a way through. Nearer, I did see a possible chink in the black wall. I headed for it,

climbing a gentle rise and then scrambling with the camels up a narrow gully. Halfway up I looked back through the notch, down onto the levels. It was red Marlborough Country: a plain with mini plateaux close at hand. I headed on up and shortly we made the summit, where we had another view. This was rather different – a Death Valley of greys. There were chain upon chain of hills, crinkling back and forth across my line of travel. Jigjik 2 stood beside me, also taking this in. He used his eyes as I did, scanning the horizon, assessing what to do about this unpromising prospect.

Already I knew I'd made a mistake, letting the camels get a good view. Camels have very good eyes and use them to work out the potential of the land. In this case, there was very little potential. In survival terms, a minimum number of edible plants, a maximum number of energy-consuming slopes … I carried on forward, calling to the camels, immediately aware I had to break their despondent mood. On we went a few paces – to find we were standing on a cliff edge. No way down! There were a few possibilities, sand-filled crevices which led down at a gentler decline. But when I gently led Jigjik 2 forward, he took one look and his knees started shaking. I tried coaxing, but it only made it worse. He had a real phobia – camels are top heavy even without loads – and I was asking too much. There were other gullies that led down, but all the slopes were precipitous and the more I tried the less co-operative Jigjik 2 became. It wasn't just the slope, it was the view. Hardly a bush down there. Just ochre and charcoal stones! A home not for camels but lizards. Jigjik 2 became first belligerent, then adamant. I had overplayed my hand – the camels didn't need me, I needed them. Finally, Jigjik 2 decided he didn't want to go anywhere.

I left the camels where they were for a while – with Jigjik 2 in this mood, they weren't going to wander away – and after an hour found a route off the ridge. However, Jigjik 2 still wasn't interested. He'd worked himself up into a state and was standing there roaring, his back legs spread, anchored into the desert. I appealed to him, entreated him. I was now worried. This was not good: Jigjik 2 was my strongest camel. If the others copied, then I'd be stuck. At the risk of making it obvious that I was backing down, I took off Jigjik 2's luggage, painstakingly putting it all on Bert. All the time I was wondering about the loyalties of these other, older camels, Bert and Bastion. To me, or to Jigjik 2? Neither had shown themselves as Top Camels. The question was, whether I'd earned my place as the Top Camel. Regarding Jigjik 2, it seemed not.

But the battle wasn't yet done. My last chance: I turned him around and pretended to offer to lead him back home, away from Death Valley. He thought about it and came. I worked my way back, then after a few hundred metres I gradually altered course, making a large circle, travelling back into Death Valley down a gentle slope. I thought then that everything was going to be all right. I think it would have been if Jigjik 2 hadn't been such an intellectual. He would not be fooled. Now that he knew I was trying to deceive him, there wasn't a hope. He sat down in protest. He would not budge. I knew then that, even if he eventually did decide to come with me, he could never be trusted again.

I remained as calm as I could, simply untying him from the others and pretended to head off with them, ostensibly back the way we'd come. I was hoping he'd get worried at being abandoned by his kinsmen and follow us. He did not, and there he sits now. It is dusk and I've set up camp here. I have tried whacking him, but it's no good. I even decided to leave him and carry on with the others; it's vital that I get my other camels away before the strike spreads. I went as far as to hobble him so that I could find him later by launching a rescue attempt from Ekhiingol. Then I thought it through. If he is restrained by hobbles, there is a risk that wolves will get him. It's a small risk, but it'd be horrible to be gnawed to death.

My only other chance is that he'll change his mind in the morning. So here we are, perched on the hillside. No grazing, no water. Will the other camels strike tomorrow as well? My feeling is that they'll stick by me. Yet they are in poorer condition than Jigjik 2, their ribs like that of a radiator's. Jigjik 2 was always the one who ate at every chance. He seemed to be rather enjoying the walk.

Bad night, worrying about Jigjik 2 – that I'm letting him down. But he's letting ME down! Either way, it may lead to the other camels abandoning me. I keep recalling what Kermit said, about how the true personality of a camel only shows when he is tired and out there alone with you. I feel depressed: these were my companions, my substitute humans. And one is about to walk out on me.

This morning, Jigjik 2 is rowdy. His roars of defiance echo on the cliff walls. Clearly, he has not calmed down overnight.

A little later: I have managed to get Jigjik 2 to stand up – and that's all. Now I must leave, with or without him. I am running out of water and cannot lay my life down for a camel. I owe it to my friends and family back in Britain to get back and so will abandon him if he insists. 'Don't make me do this Jigjik 2!'

LATER: I tugged him to follow. He anchored himself. I walked away with Bert and Bastion, seeing what would happen if I left him. He looked surprised, but not distressed. If I was going, that was fine by him. Final chance: I walked back again. Bert and Bastion waited for me, watching. But Jigjik 2 would not come. So that was that: I had to act immediately, to stop the other camels catching on. I quickly undid his lead rein and walked back to the others. I swept them up, saying soothing words. We walked off down into the blue dust valley, taking a very gentle slope. Sometimes I looked back to see if Jigjik was following, but he just watched, interested, standing stock still. For two hours, my mind focused on the camels that were still with me. It was nerve-racking. Would they also let me down? Bastion did not have a good track record, and Bert also had had his weak moments. Bert in particular became a worry. Twice descending steep slopes he tugged at me, scared to follow, and I quickly changed direction to a less severe angle, doing it nonchalantly, pretending a change of route wasn't a victory for him. Slowly, slowly, we wove through the moonscape and scary views of barrenness. Here there was hardly even a lizard track. Sometime later, we chanced upon two wild asses, which galloped off, kicking yellow dust out from under the metallic black pebble surface. If asses can survive out here on water obtained from vegetation, then so too could Jigjik 2.

Then, thank God, the lunar scape gave way to a flat expanse. There was a clear route through to Ekhiingol, the oasis where Ermek may or may not be waiting. I ushered the camels along with gentle words, conscious of a sideways, crab motion from Bert if I veered towards the unappetising mountains on our right, the south. Neither camel has eaten or drunk for 3 days. I'm not sure how long they will put up with this.

Why isn't Bastion complaining? Maybe he is too weak. Perhaps Jigjik 2 was the only camel fit enough to go on strike.

LATER: Now it's 3 p.m. and we've stopped – a grazing break for the camels. I can afford to think back. It is a terrible sadness, losing Jigjik 2. This was the camel I shared my tea breaks with. He sat and I used to lean against him for shade – putting up with his bad breath. Othertimes, as we walked, I used to slip him choice snacks from my hand, building up a good relationship so I thought. I feel the loss, and I feel anger – I've been stabbed in the back. But I'm also disappointed in myself. In the end, Jigjik 2 hadn't felt able to trust me to take him through the desert.

Such is our pace – I don't dare let the camels slow – we might even reach Ekhiingol tonight. If we don't, I'm not sure at all if I'll be able to get my two camels to carry on with me tomorrow. Today may be my last chance. Several times this morning, abruptly Bastion sat down, but I was stern, and he reluctantly followed orders. He still cares enough, to continue.

LATER: Another stop, just now, when Bert started limping sharply – his front right pad. I sat him down, took my torch and wrestled out his foot from all the new winter fur to examine the pad. I found a rock splinter. I yanked it out with the pliers on my penknife. He stood up immediately and now we can continue. Everything's going my way I can afford to tell myself. I was prepared – I had torch and pliers to hand in my hip bag. My emergency system worked. I'm still in control.

EVENING: Towards dusk, I stopped increasingly to examine my map, I saw an unnatural sheen on the horizon. After another hour, the sunlight dim, I identified it positively as a tin roof. We descended from a sequence of convoluted hills to a wide valley floor carpeted with olive brush and occasional poplars. As the sun died, I walked into the settlement of Ekhiingol, a run-down outpost with a smattering of gers around the edge. One by one, men and children ran from their cement or felt homes to walk alongside. They led the camels for me, chattering. They all knew of me and said that Ermek had safely found his way here, and was waiting nervously. 'He thinks you are dead!' a child said, laughing hysterically.

I was so glad to see Ermek – to reassure him that I was all right but also to ask him to lend a hand. Apart from seeing Mendee's family, I have been alone for twelve days. He can shield me from these people, give me time to get used to beings which are not flat-footed, humped and hairy.

A restless night, wondering what Jigjik 2 is up to. He must be still out there somewhere. Also, I felt stifled by the still air of indoors. I couldn't leave the windows open – Ermek would have frozen. I now have thickened skin – I mean it. There are copious extra epidermal layers on my hands, as if I'm always wearing leather gloves.

I got out of bed at dawn as usual, and waited for two hours for Ermek to wake and put on his blue glasses. Together we then checked on Bastion and Bert. They had been installed in the communal vegetable patch and were laying waste to the greenery. The settlement had been developed by the Russians for the production of vegetables. Now it is run by the families here, who produce watermelons, honey

10th September

melons, tomatoes, carrots, pumpkins – and the camels were threatening their livelihood.

Next I wanted to find out what happened to the traitor Jigjik 2. Ermek and I walked over to Tseshuu, a retired park warden, now living in a ger with a pension of 8000 tögrögs, or $8, a month. He has wispy facial hair, and his skin is mottled brown. He was wearing an old military cloth hat, sunbleached except for where there was once the red star of communism – it'd been removed rather ineptly, as if in great haste. His wife brought camel milk in a wooden bucket, carved from the trunk of a poplar, and we had tea while we explained about Jigjik.

Tseshuu is extraordinary. He is seventy-two, the same age as my father, and though he is gentle – and organised breakfast with great aplomb, placing fruit before us, 'Za!' – I think he could knock me out with a swing of one of his heavy hands. He is large and a little slow, and big hearted. He'd help of course, he said. He asked me about the nature of my camel, and where I'd left him, listening carefully, occasionally emitting a cackle of laughter at my predicament out there with the treacherous Jigjik 2. From time to time he emitted a decisive 'Za!' to show he was following the story so far.

The procedure for finding Jigjik 2 wasn't what I was expecting. As we got the jeep ready, Tseshuu sat himself slowly down beside his ger and plucked up lots of gravel stones. Then he counted them in his lap, making sure he had exactly forty-one. Next, he sorted them and resorted them, and then shuffled them some more.

'It's a technique used by country people for finding their lost sheep,' Ermek explained. 'A sort of numerology or something.'

Tseshuu stared at the forty-one stones, trying to discern a pattern. 'Good,' he said, stiffly getting to his feet. 'The camel that you call Jigjik will still be out there, waiting for you.'

'Waiting for me?' This didn't sound like Jigjik 2 at all. Perhaps he had the wrong camel.

I asked Tseshuu if the ancient technique usually works.

'Usually works?' Tseshuu repeated. He thought about it, pulling his hat down and climbing into the jeep. 'With me it almost never works!'

Off we went in Ermek's jeep, guided by Tseshuu towards the ridge where I'd left Jigjik 2, 50 or so kilometres away. Immediately we were in trouble – Tseshuu took us on a shortcut right across a steep sided valley. He was rather too used to travelling by camel. We had to retreat and start all over again, this time taking the vehicle down the centre of the valley. But it didn't diminish the admiration I have for the old man.

He has careful, observant eyes, which are almost covered over by the slipping, loose skin of his eyebrows.

'Let us eat a melon!' he said, unexpectedly as we drove. We got out of the jeep, rummaged for the melon. 'Za!' he said, giving Ermek the knife to cut it up with. And then he pottered to the lee side of the jeep and did what he really wanted to do, have a pee.

Some time later, we arrived in Death Valley, skirting the worst of it, then driving through the lunar dust up to the slope where I'd left Jigjik 2. No sign of him. Ermek and I backed off, while Tseshuu scoured the ground, reading his tracks. The old man picked up the trail and we walked along, following each other in line – Tseshuu walking stiffly in Jigjik 2's footsteps, me in Tseshuu's footsteps and Ermek in mine.

Ermek translated Tseshuu's observations, a stream of consciousness, as we went along: 'Very healthy camel … Long stride … Feet strong, pads undamaged by rocks … The weight placed on the feet evenly. Body weight heavy – either muscle, fat or water reserves. Nibbled a dry plant here – good teeth and still lots of water in his belly to digest it with.'

Tseshuu stopped. 'He has stood here a while, waiting for you for an hour or two. You must have headed down the valley, heading out of sight exactly over there.'

He was right. Looking down the slope, I remembered how I'd nursed Bastion and Bert through the grey dust. 'Where was Jigjik 2 heading?'

'Home,' Tseshuu said.

'But home is Khovd. That's about 700 kilometres away!'

Tseshuu bent down to the ground. 'You see this? The camel stopped here. He was wondering about going back to follow you. He must have quite liked you!'

Not enough, I thought. In the end he decided he preferred a 700 kilometre walk.

Tseshuu pointed to the far horizon, beyond the red-hot valley with mini plateau, the Marlborough Country, to where the two Mongol dogs had decided it was not a good idea to follow me. 'He'll be there, by now.'

'Already?'

'Only if he's stopping to chew bushes on the way. Otherwise he'll be even further.'

I remembered writing about Freddie, how the Mongolians were proud that their camels memorised as they plodded along.

'He says a Mongol camel remembers every juicy twig, every inviting dust bath,' Ermek said. 'If he wants to go back, he replays his journey in his head, like a tape recorder in reverse.'

Overleaf:
There are few dunes in the Gobi. However, the area – long ago part of an inland sea basin – has an extreme climate. Rain may fall only every few years, temperatures rise to 40 degrees Celsius in summer and drop to minus forty in winter, while in spring and autumn, dust storms can reach 130 or even 140 kilometres an hour.

Ever an optimist, Tseshuu sat down again to try another method of divination, this one using old coins. 'Yes,' Tseshuu concluded, tucking away the coins into a neat cloth bag. 'The camel's gone home.'

'Is this any better than the Method Of Forty-One Stones?' I asked.

'Oh no,' Tseshuu said. 'It's a sad shepherd who relies on this.'

We piled back into the jeep and returned to Ekhiingol. Somehow, this suspect Mongol method of devining the truth did make me feel better about the whereabouts of Jigjik 2. And maybe that's its true value to the shepherd – a shifting of responsibility back to the mysterious forces which run the desert, mountain and steppe.

Back in Ekhiingol, Tseshuu gave Bert and Bastion a medical examination. Strangely, we found that they had already earned a reputation among the locals for violence. They had kicked a total of four passers-by – Bastion one, Bert three. When both camels stood up as we came near, Tseshuu stepped back warily.

'That camel with one eye,' Tseshuu said.

'Bert?'

'He's a menace.'

I was slightly disappointed with Tseshuu. I admired the old buffer, but he was accusing my most loyal camel of being a 'menace'.

'These are difficult camels', he went on. 'You are very brave to have tackled them.' He looked Bert in his eye. Bert looked back. 'Especially this one.'

Just then, a lady, passing by with her vegetable produce, received a glancing blow from Bastion's back leg.

'Sorry,' I said on Bastion's behalf. I told Tseshuu that they'd never kicked me. He said in that case it must be devotion.

I made Bastion and Bert sit down, suddenly very proud of our special relationship, that I was the only person who could get near without a flesh wound. I looked at them differently now: they had been such friends to me and I'd hardly even realised.

'Let's take a closer look,' Tseshuu said, edging up behind me. I opened Bert's mouth for Tseshuu, and he burst into laughter. 'He's got the same amount of teeth as I have!' He indicated his lonely incisor. 'He's like me, virtually in his grave!'

'He's fit, for his age,' I said.

'It's a miracle,' was all Tseshuu said, walking away puzzled but smiling, as if he'd witnessed a strange phenomenon. 'All the way from Khovd,' he said. 'He must have loved you very much.'

I could take comfort from this thought, but nothing else, because, all in all, the camels failed their medical exam with flying colours. It is time, yet again, to say goodbye to team mates. Bert and Bastion will stay here in the vegetable patch – it's like a very expensive camel retirement home.

11th September

There's nothing to do but find a new team, but the nearest camels are with the nearest people, and that's 140 kilometres away – meaning I have a 100-mile walk just to see them. But they are said to be good camels, owned by a friend of Tseshuu. He indicates their exact condition in the traditional way, with two curled-over fingers, each representing a camel hump. These humps were erect and fat. Tseshuu has kindly agreed to escort me there and it's not too far off my route east. But what with the demise of Jigjik 2 – enemy of the people – and collecting a new team, I can expect to be another week behind in my schedule, that's three weeks in total. This is not funny. Ermek and I have studied the maps together, and IF I can keep up 40 kilometres a day without resting, I should get through the Gobi to the Trans-Siberian Railway, my end-point, in about a month – that is, before the winter comes and camels go on strike. The actual distance I'll cover on the ground – dodging rock fields and minor hills, and looking for wells – I estimate at 50 kilometres a day for a month. For some reason it sounds worse in miles – '30 miles a day'. I'd feel better if I wasn't setting out with untested, unknown camels. It breaks all the rules in the book.

'Is this what he eats?' Tseshuu said, picking up a bag of muesli from my supplies. 'Or is this for his camels?'

'It's for him,' Ermek replied.

'Za!' Tseshuu said, nodding politely. 'Fair enough,' he turned his head slowly, to look at the packet's contents again. 'If this is what got him here on foot in eleven days I must buy some for my best camel.'

My luggage will be carried on this three-day walk by two young camels which Tseshuu is training; a third youngster will carry Tseshuu himself. He has been looking up his moon calendar and says the most auspicious time to leave is 7 a.m. or 10 a.m. I need to double check all my equipment again tomorrow and so have elected for 10 a.m.

14th September

A smattering of rain in the night. It dribbled down the window panes, channelling through the coat of thick dust. Then it was gone. The rain had only the chance of dampening the Gobi ground before being blown away.

The outpost looked ugly, as I did my equipment checking. The damp, poor light was greying the remaining plaster, darkening the exposed lattice. Chunks fell away in the breeze. The Russian empire, still crumbling.

We were ready at 11 a.m., a full hour past the auspicious time. I feared that Tseshuu would say we'd now have to leave tomorrow, but I should have known better. 'It's a sorry man,' he said, 'whose life is dictated by a little book.' He mounted his camel – 'Za!' – and I led off the two young pack camels by foot.

Without much of a goodbye to Ermek I'm afraid, off Tseshuu and I went, the three young camels energetic, wondering, curious.

After a while we bumped into Ermek again, as he made his way from the settlement by jeep. Tseshuu said, 'The foreigner walks fast. Exactly the speed of a happy camel!'

'Shall I slow down?' I asked.

'No, you must walk as is natural for you and I will go the pace I want.' He added that I mustn't worry about catering for him. 'I will eat Mongol food and you eat camel food!'

We spoke little, Tseshuu gliding along on his camel, me walking. We ate some of Ermek's donated chocolate as we walked. I noticed that Tseshuu, unlike Ermek, Kermit and everyone else, doesn't litter. If caught out, nowhere at all to put a wrapper, he neatly tucks it away under a stone, carefully folding and refolding it until it's out of sight.

On we went, Tseshuu giving the occasional whack with his stick, when his camel indulged himself too excessively on a bush. Tseshuu has a refined travelling system: a canister of cold tea around his camel's front hump, along with a little cotton bag full of mutton cooked up by his wife. We all have such systems – you have no freedom out here unless your life is regimented. Thus I carry my pouch with compass and torch around my waist; UV cream in my left pocket, alarm clock (plastic, for light weight) in my right, loo paper (for nose bleeds) in the back. Nothing else – it would restrict leg movement.

It was a cool day, and I kept my thick Mongol jacket on through the afternoon. Winter is coming, but no one can tell when. By mid-October, I can expect at times 0 degrees by day and minus 10 at night, plus the wind-chill. Even that I can survive without a tent. But in November, when I mustn't be out here, daytime temperatures will sometimes drop to minus 20. It's a thought which will help me keep up my 50 kilometres per day.

A black fox, floating over the sand. The stars shining out, long before the sun goes down.

We stopped at last light, after doing 40 kilometres with no break. We are between two craggy hills, pitching camp beside a sand hummock to slow the wind. At last I could see inside the two mysterious sacks carried by Tseshuu. In the first, a large heavy casserole dish, devoted to brewing tea. Packed into it, a cup, ladle and lid, each separated by a layer of cloth padding. In the second sack, a thick felt del for sleeping under and a felt strip for sleeping on.

Though Tseshuu was slow in his old age, around the camp he was always somehow ahead of me. While I was sorting my luggage, he was already gathering firewood. While I was battling with my stove, he was warming tea. It was all to do with economy of effort. Every move seemed timed, each action calculated. His system extends even to the camels: each was placed at a particular woody saxaul shrub which will suit our departure tomorrow – the first camel that we'll load is the nearest to us. By ergonomics, efficiency of time and space, a pensioner can cope out here.

In summary, I have great respect for Tseshuu, this person shaped by man and desert. EXCEPT FOR HIS SNORING! It's now midnight. To my left, a terrible honking, like a wild boar having a nightmare. Only because the Mongolians have such respect for age have I been able to restrain my boot. I lie under a full moon in such agony I want to howl like a wolf.

Onward, and the skin of my left foot is coming away, but I've got used to there being some pain or other down there and Tseshuu noticed my limp before I did. I'm pleased with our pace – we have done another 45 kilometres. But I will have to keep this up – in fact, travel a little faster still.

15th September

We are sleeping in the shelter of a thick bush – the empty sky suggests it'll be cold which means another sleepless night is ahead of me. How is it possible not to sleep, with the amount of exercise I do a day? Tseshuu's snoring, that's how. Yet I suppose I've been looking for someone like this throughout my journey, someone to teach me along the way. There is no machismo here, none of Kermit's dallyings and drinkings. Nothing to prove to me, nothing to prove to Mongolia. He pays tribute to the ways of his forefathers, their *ovoos*, their lunar calendars, the time-honoured rituals which fasten the Mongolians to the land, but is also able if necessary to free himself from them. He knows the land for what it is. He is not in awe; he does not need Almas, the Abominable Snowman.

Next morning, over a hill range. Tseshuu was a bit vague about the crossing point. 'Somewhere ...' he said, looking out from his camel perch, seeming to sweep the entire northern hemisphere with his stick. I braced myself to spend the rest of the morning walking about looking for the ger of his friend the camel owner – which is exactly what we did.

Around midday, we came to a couple of gers and were directed to Tseshuu's friend by a wrinkled-up old lady atop a giant camel. She steered it carefully, like a little old lady driving a Morris Minor. We came to a wind-blackened man sitting in front of a ger. Tseshuu dismounted and I realised this was the camel owner. We were here.

He wears a corduroy del and a hat like an oven cloth. He blinks with moley eyes and is almost infuriatingly quietly spoken. Tseshuu sat down with the camel owner as he got on with his job, making a wood lattice frame for a ger's sides. The camel owner from time to time murmured about the camel leather binding he was using, 'not as strong as cow skin,' he kept saying. 'Why do the young always give me camel skin to use? So ignorant.'

The two old-timers consoled each other, as they do the world over – the youth of today. Tseshuu got round to the subject of buying camels and, as promised, the man does have three good camels for sale. Only three, and they'll have to be rounded up, so I can't see them until tomorrow, the day I really ought to be leaving. Not ideal.

The camels were waiting, sitting outside the ger soon after dawn. I looked them over with Tseshuu. 'The strongest,' he said, circling round the first. 'He is noisy just now but might settle down. Probably he doesn't like strangers, and likes a quiet home life.' Well he's not going to get that, I thought. Tseshuu opened up the next camel's mouth, examining the teeth. 'Perhaps the youngest camel. He's a calm one and'– he pointed to his humps, which tilted over – 'perhaps the weakest.' The third camel, Tseshuu said, will respond to kindness only. He is very proud, rather tetchy, and needs to be asked, not told. 'In conclusion,' I thought, 'I have a home-loving camel, a weak camel and an over-sensitive camel.'

The financial side was concluded quickly, the reins handed over according to all the correct Mongol practices but without ceremony, as if I was just being handed the keys and paperwork of a new car. The owner was in a hurry, as if winter would arrive any moment.

The old men packed the camels for me, moving as fluently as twins, seasoned Gobi men knowing when to tuck, when to weave the leather ropes. In all the months I'd travelled, I'd never seen such work. Here were men with nothing to prove anymore, schooled by the desert, not the steppe – there're no gers out here to fall back on. The ropes were tightened, the ropes lay still. These two men had no strength to walk any distance, but the baggage was held tightly in place, as if by steel.

I got the camels to their feet and Tseshuu put the silk sashes on each of my new team mates. He said goodbye, yanking my head towards his and turning it to left and right to plant a kiss on each cheek. '*Minii duu*,' he said. My nephew. I was so touched by this man, still a stranger but such a force. '*Minii akh*.' My uncle, I said.

I was loaded with *aaruul* as a goodbye present and the owner led me away – I thought to show me the right direction but in fact to show me off to his neighbours. I escaped from them only half sober, walking off into the desert with camels I did not know.

chapter twelve

THROUGH AMBER LIGHT

A deed is not glorious until it is finished.

Genghis Khan to his sons on his deathbed, about completing the job in hand
— the conquest of the world, August 1227

A very sub-zero night. I borrowed the camels' saddle blankets to sleep under, stitching them together with the wire normally used to seal the water container lids. They are composed of felt 5 centimetres thick and are very heavy. As it is, I narrowly escaped frost-bite to my face.

It's 8 a.m., and the camels are not eating, as they should be, but stand around looking west, back home. They follow the lead of the strongest camel, the home-loving one which I paid rather a lot for. He may be strong but he is a little careless when he walks and I call him Rip-Off. The other two camels act together and must have known each other for years. The large, 'over-sensitive' one is, as Tseshuu said, tetchy – in fact I already call him 'Tetch'. The other, with the tilting humps, is his side-kick; he is impressionable. Impressionable as regards other camels, that is, not humans.

So, 50 kilometres a day for a month. No good me going on about it, but it's a pace the Mongolians are staggered by and it's worth asking why. They estimate 30 kilometres as a day's walk, though they ride and don't travel more than a few days. The answer lies in camels' feet: they'll wear down. Simply put, the camels won't make it all the way there, not according to Mongol rules. But even if it hadn't been for the winter I'd have had to keep to my pace – the distances between wells are too big and even the camels would dry up. My tactic: to take one more camel than the two I need. If I can get to the halfway point, in some two weeks, I'll be out of the hard gravels and this sparse vegetation, some of which is ecologically classified as desert steppe, and able to follow a narrow

18th September

Left: *Having words with Tetch after Rip-Off had left us. Camels feel security in numbers and with Rip-Off having deserted us, the remaining two needed constant reassurance.*

THROUGH AMBER LIGHT

sand band, the pure desert of the eastern Gobi, which is kinder on camel pads. It'll take me to my target, the Trans-Siberian Railway and the settlement of Zamin Üüd – literally, Frontier Door, or Gateway – where the railway leaves Mongolia and continues south through Inner Mongolia, held by China.

19th September

Two shepherds, guiding a flock of goats and sheep across the hill, were up ahead. They got off their horses and sat down directly in my path, awaiting my arrival there in half an hour's time. They'd waited so long – their flocks had abandoned them – I couldn't just walk past. So we sat and they asked all the usual things – where I was going to, where from, how old – the questions which fix you in time and space – and wasn't I afraid of wolves and where was my gun?

Soon I explained that I had to keep going. They didn't really understand that either. How could I be happy to leave behind what is that most essential ingredient in Mongolian life, company? But at least by the time I'd gone they'd answered one question to their own satisfaction, because as I was gathering up my camels I heard one shepherd say to the other, 'You're right after all, he's Korean.'

20th Septmber

A red fox at dawn, its tail floating, puffed up by the cold. Today, the caravan worked perfectly. Four days since I left Tseshuu, and it has taken me all that while to get up to steam, and the pace I need to get through the Gobi. I do not enjoy the solitude, I am gregarious by nature, but I am like an athlete on a racetrack: this is the task I am engaged in and it is time to put aside other things. There is a reward for this, an uninterrupted experience of the amber light, lark sounds, and the soothing horizon lines. Every day I see a gallery of colour, the red and gilt of autumn.

Sometimes, Rip-Off talks to me, communicating in warbles. Sadly, Tetch only opens his mouth to vomit at me. Tourists call it 'spitting', but oh how I pray it was just good clean spit. It's bile from the stomach. Tilt has begun copying Tetch, as he does in all things – first the snarl when I interrupt his grazing at the end of the tea break, wrinkling up his face and staring at me, then the full treatment.

I'm starting to lose track of days, but the space dimension seems more in flux than time out here. I savour the desert, moment by moment, but I cannot fix myself in this landscape – the brown and red monotones which unfurl at me from the mirage, the skies of endless blues. Sometimes I feel like I'm in space, floating. My life line is to my camels, but they follow wherever I go.

This morning I was moved to tears. It started with a strange noise, a throbbing, a whirring: I stopped. This was a new sound to me in the Gobi, and it was coming from above rather than around me. The sky was patterned like embroidery by a huge flight of geese. They were honking gently, but the noise I'd first heard was that of the wind being beaten by their rhythmic wings. It was a beautiful array of life to see in a desert, and one not defined as I was by the rock and sand but arranged according to their own birdy procedure. Of course it was as poignant a sight as it was magnificent because these birds were migrating, perhaps over the Himalayas to India. They were vacating the premises. Other animals – the Gobi jerboa and the optimistic-looking dwarf hamster I saw this morning – are stuck here in the Gobi, and must be bedding down. Slowly, us surface dwellers are getting fewer and fewer in numbers.

Grasses are yellowing and tearing, burnt by the icy wind. They are getting more and more useless to shelter behind when I make camp. As a measure of how quickly the day cools: in the evening, once I've unloaded the camels, hobbled them and let them graze, I put on my undershirt and replace my thick day shirt. But by the time I have done that, it's cooled so much it's time to put on a woolly fleece and then a jumper. Then it's time for my moleskin jacket. Then my Mongol jacket. I build the bags into a wall against the wind, lay out my bedding in the shelter and begin boiling water for pasta and a packet of soup – a twelve-minute slot in which to write this diary. Soon it's dark and it's time to worry that the camels are wandering out of range of my torch. To help me spot them they are by this stage each sporting a white sheet. When the camels start showing signs of settling down for the night, I undo their hobbles, bring them back to the camp, re-hobble them, sit them down, strap up one front leg each – that is, bent at the knee so it can't be used – then tie the camels to each other. If they do escape, it'll be a very challenging three-legged race.

So far, the only snow that I've seen is on hilltops. Yet I'm playing with the Gobi – never a good idea. I am tempting fate and fate has not been kind to me elsewhere in Mongolia. I worry about this and knock arguments back and forth in my head until the stronger argument wins. There is danger in this and sometimes only a disruption somewhere in the camel train snaps me out of it. I recognise that I must stick rigidly to routine to keep my thoughts disciplined.

Day after day, I am getting there. Thank Heaven, thank the Earth, for Tseshuu. How would I be managing now without him? I arrange the camels as he did, bush by bush, and pack as he would, tea cup and

Overleaf:
An untested team: camels will not follow a leader into desert unless he has proved himself Top Camel. Worse, unlike horses, camels stand a good chance of surviving the desert alone, and so will, even after a month's journeying together, abandon their prospective leader if it seems the wisest option.

pot. There was something of Laurens van der Post in him, maybe just the serenity of old age, maybe just a strength of knowing yourself. They both had a conviction and humility that comes of having negotiated a way through life, the good and bad that they have known, and left behind them along the wayside. Old men, at home in the desert, making haste slowly.

21st September

A thick collar of ice in the water containers, but I slept warmly despite not having the use of my woolly hat. Yesterday evening Tetch vomited on it, and there was no warmth available to dry it out in time for the night. By 11 p.m. it was already frozen into a chunk of cardboard.

I got up as usual at first light and set the camels free to graze while I packed camp. As has become the custom, Rip-Off immediately began heading back the way we came, shuffling to the west like an escaped convict. Occasionally, he paused, but only to see if the other camels were going to join him.

Thankfully, he just doesn't seem to have leadership qualities. Tetch and Tilt are more interested in eating, though they do also drift slowly homeward, as if in sympathy. Today I ignored Rip-Off's march home and went on boiling water for my muesli, and preparing the bags for loading up. When I looked, I found that Rip-Off had covered 2 kilometres towards his goal. I was furious: bang went my 9 a.m. start. I collected him, then marched into the rising sun, back to the camp. This little incident is enough to prevent me walking my 50 kilometres today. There are simply no spare minutes of daylight in which to make up time. I only stop twice in the day; two breaks of half an hour in which the camels get valuable grazing and I rehydrate myself with tea.

Later: When I did get away, it was into a flat, flat plain of sand, which broke into dunes with leaden rock extruding from them. I wound through these lands, avoiding the loose sand of fresh dunes and sticking to the firmer, older dunes, where pioneer plants were trying to recover ground, as if asserting the rights of the living. I stopped for a grazing break, and found Tilt was no longer with me. Had to return 3 kilometres, but found him grazing peacefully, as if waiting for his master – by that I mean Tetch. I still need three camels: two to carry, one as a spare. A close run thing.

I came out of the hill, now worried about water. None of the camels have drunk for three days, and I have only two days of water left for myself. Cut north, looking for spring-line settlements along the range. Sure enough, a sprinkling of gers. A young man outside one, fixing an extremely long-suffering camel to the front of a cart. The man looked up, seeing me, and even by the time I was near he was still speechless. He kept looking beyond me, wondering what else was coming his way. I wished him well, enquired about his family and livestock, explained that I was British.

He looked at me blankly.

'Can I use your well?'

Utter blankness. Not even attempting to question who or what I was – just those blank eyes, as if I was an alien beyond human comprehension. I led my caravan off to the well and he recovered himself in time to catch me up and help me operate it. The well had a counterlever mechanism: a rubber bucket crafted from a lorry inner tube on one end of a pole and a counterweight boulder strapped to the other. As I went on my way, he thrust into my hands 2 kilos of *aaruul*. I took them, expressing profuse gratitude, though I still haven't touched the last lot.

Badly behind with my mileage, I walked until almost last light. I made camp in gravelly gentle hills, letting the camels graze, as usual, until they began to sit down to sleep. At 10 p.m. they were settling down and I walked off to bring them closer to the camp, using my torch to pick out their white sheets from the darkness. I bent to unhobble them, each in turn, and then gathered their reins to lead them back. I looked back through the blackness to my camp and I couldn't see it. Only two minutes away, but where in all this dark? There was some starlight and I made myself stand stock still. The biggest piece of information I had to go on was that I would have taken between fifty and seventy paces from the camp. Behind me was the north star and that supported my feeling that I was pointing in the direction of the camp, south. I felt for the camels' legs, and hobbled them again. Using the animals as a reference point, I walked off south, keeping them in eyesight, but this gave me very little range and so I decided to risk moving them to where I guessed the camp was, marching the camels fifty paces. Still no camp. This was getting serious. I was wearing several layers of clothes, but the night temperature would drop to minus 5, even minus 10. I worked hard, making transects back and forward. Nothing, yet it must be right here, around my feet.

The moon. I remembered that it would be up in two hours – only a half moon but it might just give me enough light to see the camp. I took off the saddle blankets from the camels and made an emergency shelter with them, parking the camels so that they were tightly positioned either side, blocking off the wind and giving me their warmth.

I lay watching the low hill, waiting for the moon. First, a hazy light, that slowly strengthened. I waited, shivering uncontrollably by the time the moon itself, a bent silver disc, cleared the horizon. But the light wasn't enough! I had to wait until it lifted above the smear of low clouds. Then it was clear and I could get up and walk with a new confidence – the camels showing up like lone boulders on the plain. But now the moon was too bright! Coming through the dry air right in my face, it was dazzling. I had to walk towards it, and then turn back and look around. And there: I could see my camp at last, only twenty paces away.

Suppose there had been no moon? Perhaps by nestling with the camels, I might have got by, OR perhaps not. Whatever, it was a bad mistake, not to have flagged my camp as I do the camels. This must not happen again.

27th September

A terrible argument with Tetch this morning. He would not let me put on his luggage, and vomited and vomited, ejecting all the morning's grazing. I had to strap up his legs to keep him from jumping up to throw off the saddle. It made him even more annoyed. We were exhausted by the end and furious with each other. He bellowed, I bellowed. Then I remembered that Tseshuu had said I should ask, not tell him what to do. It seemed a bit of a cheek – who was running this expedition? But I took off Tetch's ropes entirely, calmed him and there was no trouble at all after that.

Onward east, through goat-denuded rolling hills which told me there's a ger somewhere near, or was. This is much of the magic of the northern, more inhabited, Gobi – you never know if you are going to die in the dust, or find beyond the next hill a herd of goats and a family to welcome you. The green goatlands rose and fell like sea swell, quietening towards the end of the day into a level expanse – the lull after a storm, a sea textured by an infinity of pebbles. Then, just as the sun slipped from sight, the horizons all around seemed to flare. The skyline was festooned with purple dust.

The days are getting noticeably shorter, now; I can only walk for nine hours a day, and even at 5.4 kilometres an hour that's barely up to my 50 kilometres a day. I'm halfway – some two weeks to go – but the camels are tiring. Psychologically, I cannot afford to think forward, to the end. The way to deal with such large quantities of time is to break them down, not to think beyond the next tea break. It's like climbing a fireman's ladder. To look down to the ground below is too much, but if you focus on the next rung you will get down.

I like Rip-Off because he seems to talk to me, but he is becoming a danger. He will not give up on his escape bids. He doesn't eat and worse, the others stop grazing to think about following him. The shorter days mean the camels now get not four but three hours grazing, and my own two tea breaks have been cut to fifteen minutes.

There is no moon now and the stars shine out like ice crystals, so animated they seem to be eyes that are watching.

Above: *I had abandoned the second pack saddle and all excess food. Only young Tilt was now able to carry luggage.*

28th September

The night was cold; it's still below freezing now and and we're about to leave. I left the evening's cooking pot to soak, forgetting that it would be frozen by morning. There are no stones around to break up the ice, and I can't recycle the water for tonight's cooking, or even do anything with it. No time to wait around for it to thaw either, so I've packed the pot onto Tetch's baggage, still complete with its ice block. In the middle of it my spoon is stuck fast as if by superglue.

The camels are unhappy to be on the move and in a foul mood. They are so far from home now and are plainly worried. Their eyes flick to the west, needing no prompting from Rip-Off, though his influence is there and he is getting desperate. As for their physical condition, my calculation has always been that if I can get them this far, then they will make it, but the sands are patchy, as yet. Their feet may have to last another week.

LATER: Continued across the plain, autumn shadows so long, horizon so low. Water from my cooking-pot ice block, dripped down Tetch's tummy. A niggling feeling: no evidence of humans or even camels here. Where will be my next water? I carry 30 litres, consuming 5 litres a day in the cool, in the warm 6, in hot 7.

I have stopped now: my compass is misbehaving. This is as disconcerting for me as coming across a spirit might be for a Mongolian. The compass is my guide, as the crow is for Tsend on her journey through the spirit world. It's now in a spin, unable to tell north from south. My only explanation is that there's a deposit of iron ore below me distracting my needle. I will continue east-north-east for a while, using the sun for reference. But this is disconcerting, as if the elements themselves – the bedrock on which we mortals stand – are no longer obeying the physical laws. I feel that next the sun might drop out of the sky.

LATER: I kept an eye on the sun as it slipped along low, nudging the hills as it made its way. My compass did recover and we walked again until sundown.

Rip-Off possibly a bit lame, favouring his front right foot. This would be early to lose a camel, but I always knew it was on the cards. Through a valley softly quilted in Gobi feathergrass. The corpse of a long-eared hedgehog. It had been trodden on by a stray wild ass – very bad luck.

It looks like I'll have to work through a nest of low hills and I'm anxious for water. I've decided to leave my intended route and head 10 kilometres out of my way, south to a military well. It had better be there!

I'm about to leave, and I've been examining Rip-Off's foot. He is fine – for the moment at least, but his pads are wearing through rapidly.

LATER: The military well was there sure enough and not exactly sitting there secretively. I saw it an hour before I got there – a wooden structure built like a hut over the well itself, to protect it from the ravages of any stray herdsmen. As I walked nearer, the camels perked up, recognising I was heading to a human object, therefore probably a water source. And at last, I stood beside it: a first-class, military well, just as promised. I led the camels round to the door – to find there was a padlock on it. I turned around and walked away. 'Sorry camels!' It was another 15 kilometres or so before I intercepted my route again. I do wish the army had mentioned the padlock.

Onward, rather anxious, and then a very great stroke of luck. In a plain otherwise void (it seemed) of higher life forms, I saw a ger far ahead, right on my path. Finally, I was nearing it. An old woman in a scarf was milking her camels, one leg raised up to rest on the other, supporting the bucket. Seeing me she alerted her family and a crowd assembled by the ger door. They stood staring as I made the usual greetings. The old woman – short and rather frightening – was definitely in charge here. She summoned a cup of cold tea for me. A sallow, tall youth stood silent behind her, trying to fathom who or what I was.

'My camels haven't had water for four days,' I explained. 'Could I use your well?'

'That's strange,' the old woman said to her family, her eyes fixed on me. 'It's almost as if this foreigner can speak our language. It's almost as if he's saying "My camels haven't had water for four days. Could I use your well?"!!'

I tried again. 'Could you direct me to the well?'

'Do you see what I mean?' the old biddy said to her son. 'That almost sounded like: "Could you direct me to the well." I wonder what this strange man is really trying to say. Perhaps he's tired. We should give him another cup of tea…'

It took some time, but we did establish that we were all speaking the same language. There was a well 4 kilometres away, but no path to it. The youth agreed to lead me there. He rounded up a few horses to bring them along for a drink as well.

Once there, my camels barged through the sheep, I topped up my water containers and then was away, resisting offers to stay the night. I feel indifference, even suspicion and hostility to people I meet. I have my own ship, and all my loyalties and energies are directed to keeping it afloat. But then I stopped, turned round and went back. If there's one thing I should have learnt from the Mongolians, it's that they take advantage of opportunities presented by each other – they rest in the gers they encounter, they glean information. Besides, I can't shut out my species, become a camel. I've caught enough of their bad habits as it is – I've found myself slowly lifting my head from time to time, as I eat my muesli, like a camel raising his head from pasture to contemplate the lie of the land.

Back at the well, I learnt that there's no-one living for 100 kilometres, maybe 200, maybe more, along this line east. It's up to me and my military wells – padlocks and all …

Above: *Tilt, eying
my water supply.
For six weeks, the
time it took to cross
the Gobi alone,
every moment of
daylight was taken
up with duties –
packing camp and
loading camels in
itself took 1½ hours
– with no time left
over for mistakes.
The final month had
to be completed at
50 kilometres
(30 miles) a day to
stand a chance of
avoiding the
Mongol winter.*

I walked on and noticed I've picked up another of the camels' ways. I have almost no bladder control. I have become utterly used to going to the loo whenever it suits me: I'm losing the social disciplines that help define a human.

A resentful snake in the path – almost a metre in length, two fingers' width, but with an adder's laziness. It wouldn't get out of the way and struck viciously when I leant towards it. Its marbled skin reminded me of the boas I've seen in the Amazon and my immediate thought was that it was a Tatar sand boa, but surely it was too plain angry? Again, I miss company to discuss these things.

Walked on until dark, looking for grazing in the low hills. Camel food is often sparse nowadays – sometimes it seems hardly worth scouting around for it as we approach tea-break time. Nearby, a small herd of wild asses on the mud of a dried-up pool. They hardly cared about us. No human could be here, they seemed to think. I can expect to see no one for a week or so. Ahead, in a day or two if I've got my navigation right, an end to the desert steppe, and into the sand belt which will act like a soft corridor for the camels. So far, their feet are holding out, but every day I check them each in turn, and all twelve feet are already in worse condition than a Mongolian lorry tyre.

Out of the blue: the freezing breath of winter. Is this the end of my journey, all I've worked to achieve for a year? I had the first warning in the night. Cloud moved over us: an oppressive blanket in a country that celebrates its relationship with the clear sky. I watched the stars go out, one at a time. Snuffed out, it seemed, and my hope of continuing though the Gobi possibly snuffed out with them. The snow came at first light. First the weather was not that cold – the snow clouds kept out the night freeze. The snow hardly settled and the camels carried on grazing. Then a shift in wind, and the temperatures were plummeting: minus 5, minus 6, minus 8 … The camels sat down, waiting for the weather to go away, but I cannot wait. This might be the same in a week's time. This might be just the beginning.

I stirred the camels and though they protested, they eventually agreed to be loaded up. We were on the move very late – I couldn't tie knots with my gloves on and my fingers were almost useless without. We walked steadily, a bitter wind from the north, Siberia way. The snow came in small pellets, which stung and sometimes bit. Then came a very strong wind. The ice pellets had nowhere to settle other than behind scrub plants where they stacked up, protected like drifts of sand. The horizon was lost in whiteness. I could no longer navigate between hills, but stumbled into them, losing more and more time. But maybe, somewhere in the wind, one of Tsend's crows was watching out for me, because in the late afternoon, as I hunkered down behind dunes with a cup of tea, the temperature showed signs of lifting.

Now it's evening, and the temperature is of course falling again. It's presently 5 below. Tonight could be bad indeed.

Pure desert from now. Cool, but I'll survive. Looks like we're fine. And I've now entered the narrow sand belt which, if the military are right, stretches right through to my journey's end. Rip-Off's right foot, still a worry. More conscious than ever about water, I top up whenever there's a chance. Yesterday, I diverted from my route to follow a promising-looking camel trail. Sure enough, it led to a spring and an old well.

There was a crowd of camels already there. They couldn't reach down into the well, and they'd ruined the spring by trampling it with their feet. They stood sucking miserably at the mud. I filled my water containers by lowering them by rope into the well, letting my camels take it in turns to drink from them. Then the other camels crashed in, pushing us all out of the way and knocking over the containers. So in the end they didn't get any well water either. We were on our way in an hour. I had the feeling of a motorist, driving away from a motorway service station, tank filled with petrol. We'll be fine for a few days.

We are now well into the sand belt. But too late, Rip-Off is limping along – that front right foot. He cannot carry luggage and his foot won't get better. The blunt truth is, I have two usable camels now and I cannot have passengers – especially ones which slow me down. He has always been desperate to get away. He sees no future in us. He no longer eats. He looks forlornly west, towards home, and furthermore keeps willing the others to escape. As yet, the others are not put off, but eat on, ravenously, but I must find a herd of camels with which to deposit Rip-Off. I may have called in at the 'motorway service station', but with Rip-Off out of action, I feel like a driver on a long journey with no spare tyre.

I am writing this while camped on a hill crest in the sands, the tracks of night mice friendly in the last, low light.

3rd October From this hill, I can see that it is a totally uninhabited region. There is no guarantee at all of water. I should either veer north or south. Either way, I'll be along a hill base, the most likely place for gers. I'll veer north, hoping against hope. I still have three days of water for myself. Winter hangs over me like a sword of Damocles. I spend my time looking at the sky, feeling for the wind, wondering when the next blast from the north will be. I can no longer put my finger to the breeze to test it – my fingers are too leathery.

I dropped from my camp down into a plain, the sort of pan you might use to attempt a world land-speed record. There are hills to either side – red, crinkled. Old, settled-down sands. No camel herd for Rip-Off, no animals that I can see at all. I am wary of such views – I remember the view I showed Jigjik 2, the panorama of Death Valley that made him mutiny. It was no worse than this.

Still no gers visible. From such a hill as this I should be able to see one 10 or even 15 kilometres away. Sand, very hard going for me, very easy for the camels. Now it's twilight, and I'm watching the camels, making sure Rip-Off allows the others to graze. A camel herd moved right through here as I made camp. Rip-Off desperately tried to follow, stumbling along wearing his hobbles. I brought him back. Personally, I don't mind one bit saying goodbye to him. However, the herd was in a bad way and I'd be unkind not to find better companions for him. What's more, having the third camel with me reassures the others – their herd instinct.

ONWARD EAST-NORTH-EAST: I've grown disillusioned with military wells – those padlocks – and I have to take whatever opportunities come along. As there was a water source marked on my (ever optimistic) map, I headed that way. I navigated myself by compass to the site, and sure enough spotted a stone shelter. Once there, I looked around, the camels sniffing hopefully at the human vestiges: vodka bottles, the inevitable child's shoe, a heap of freshly stolen telegraph wire. No water. We walked on, curving behind a red hill. There was water somewhere near, but we couldn't potter around for days searching.

Two *argali* mountain sheep, bounded away, as we swerved through untidy hillocks, following a narrow, sand-floored valley of lone poplars. No water, but rich, long grasses. Somewhere up ahead, judging by the tracks, a lone camel. We made our way along the dry river bed – a troublesome experience, as it seemed every snake in the gully had decided to have one last sunbathe before the winter. Many were Central Asian vipers, reluctant to budge out of the way.

I rounded a bend and found the stray camel whose tracks I'd seen. He was peering down at us, from a hillock, a large healthy male, a suitable companion for Rip-Off. I rapidly scribbled a note for whoever might find him, and tied it to his halter. '*NADAD ENE TEMEE KHEREGGUI*,' I wrote. 'I don't need this camel.' It was like preparing to abandon a bear at Paddington Station. But there were no fond goodbyes, no poignant farewells. Rip-Off didn't give me the chance. As soon as I'd undone the lead rope, he was off, taking huge strides to catch up with his new camel friend, who was retreating hastily round the corner with a worried look on his face.

I never really got to know Rip-Off. None the less, I have a feeling of loss, that the team is being weakened, gradually, by this land where man doesn't belong.

WINTER: a feeling of imminence in the air – in the mornings, that is, when I walk for an hour before I can take my gloves off. Then begins a striptease, as the temperature approaches the 30s again.

By chance we came upon a small, goat-stripped zone of desert – a family has recently been here. I walked around, seeing what clues I could gather, and turned to find Tetch and Tilt marching off, abandoning me complete with luggage. They did it in unison, as if they had nodded to each other, agreed a plan, and put it into action. So much disloyalty, after so long. But why now? They feel the loss of Rip-Off and of course this place smells of domestic life, of something they've left. They know that in ten minutes from now they will be continuing once more into the uncertainties of the desert.

We walked on into dry hills. While Tetch and Tilt got on with their grazing, I looked around for dinosaur remains. Some of the best-preserved skeletons ever found are from around here. I remember some remains bearing down on me in the museum in Ulaanbaatar. They date from the Cretaceous and were extinct with the rest well before India moved north into the Asian continent 50 million years ago, creating the Himalayas, which cut off southern Asia's monsoon and brought about the aridity, the Gobi. Yet the fossilised remains were so complete, you got the feeling they were hunting trophies. It seemed a shame that someone hadn't just left them to roam the plains.

I have given up seeking out military wells, but this evening there were greater plovers, and later a flock of sandgrouse working through the short grasses for seeds. I'm sure there must be open water. The map is not helpful: according to it, I should presently be neck deep in a lagoon.

Night-time: Now, the camels tied up beside me. Tetch is calmer than he used to be; we no longer have set-piece battles. He curls his lip at me when I approach to gather him from grazing, but rarely vomits, and instead utters a short squawk of protest, then gentle, reassuring sounds. He is not quite a gentleman but I am fond of him – he has stuck by me.

6th October

I sighted the lake, ahead in a shallow valley. The camels had been pulling, wanting to get at that water, but they were less enthusiastic by the time I got to the edge – the lake was muddy, stirred by wind. Yet they must drink. I waited and waited, letting them try it. This could be the last water they'll see until the end of the journey – only five days or so to go now.

Have I made it? I seem to have forgotten why I originally wanted to do this journey. I only know that this was once my dream, and that it is a more worthwhile dream for having been so hard to attain. And that I must not fail for the sake of Tsend, on the borders with Siberia, Dundoi in the west, the Kazakh girl with the weak voice and the strong heart, Tseshuu, and the hundreds of names in the little red book who helped me from Siberia to the Gobi.

It's cold, but the stars continue to amaze me, as if showering down a light of liquid silver. I lie among humpy sands, sheltered by the luggage bags, listening to the clicking of reed stems. Sometimes a scratching – jerboas. I imagine these kangaroo-tailed rodents bounding through the night. It's said they can leap 3 metres.

A SERIOUS BLOW: Tetch, the stronger of the two camels, is favouring his front left foot. Tomorrow he will not be able to carry baggage. It is all up to Tilt. He is an enthusiastic young camel with a ravenous appetite. He's copied Tetch in all things, including vomiting, but like the other habits he's acquired he's better at it.

Last night, it touched minus 15, at a guess. I poured boiling water onto the muesli and it had frozen over by the time I'd eaten to the bottom of the bowl.

I tipped out all but four days of food supply and abandoned Tetch's pack saddle. Now all I seem to be carrying is BBC equipment and all my litter.

A small salt lake, like a frozen rink. A skeleton of a camel juts out of it, like dinosaur remains fastened into a sedimentary rock. I can now smell victory. Tilt is bearing up, coping well with the load. Tetch has regained his appetite and is appreciating the freedom of movement. He is still trying to turn me back – and so near the end. An assiduous time keeper, he comes up alongside at 11 a.m., to remind me it's tea-break time. I sit and eat Mars bars, even though I have no appetite. I want only to see the end – I want to know that I have not been tricked. That the Gobi has let me through. With a track record like mine, it is understandable, I think: T.C. dead, a dog dead, three horses eaten by flies, three horses eaten by humans ...

To within spitting distance of Zamin Üüd and the Trans-Siberian Railway. 'Nothing can stop me now' – I enjoy saying it, daring the malicious spirits which killed T.C., Ulaan, the chestnut and The Beast – but I know I won't believe my journey is over, until I place my feet on the hard iron of that railway track.

At dusk, lights from Zamin Üüd. Also lights from the other side of the frontier, Erenhot in Inner Mongolia, China. There is a weird dark space in between – no man's land.

I gathered the camels up, already sad – the world I have created with them is about to be broken.

I came before too long to a fence. One of the few I had seen in all my five months travelling, it had been broken down, trampled by livestock. As I followed it along towards the town, the official border crossing point, it became more serious. It was joined by a second fence. Then electrical wiring. Behind it all, on the Chinese side, the ground had been freshly harrowed to show up any human footprints. Nice idea but all these devices – the first fence, the second fence, the electric wiring – were lying broken, twisted, abused. The culprits – cows – sat around dopily between the fences and others were infiltrating beyond. Like true Mongolians, these cow nomads would not be stopped by that territorial, divisive thing of us foreign people, us settled people: the fence.

Zamin Üüd was rearing from the haze, but even the blind would have known they were getting near – the sound of litter scattered in the wind, plastic bags rattling on the border fence. Then, at last, the railway line, like a worn-out snake in the dust.

Well, this was the end. I walked faster and the camels walked faster, almost overtaking me – the sight of gers on the edge of town. Closer and closer to the railway line, my target, where I'd stand and know I had completed my objective, despite everything. But as I approached, the Trans-Siberian was less and less like a worn-out snake. The railway seemed more and more modernised, organised and – I stared, unable to believe – fenced off! Thwarted by barbed wire, ten paces from the end of my journey, and by the only viable stock fence I'd encountered within a country three times the size of France.

Suddenly rather tired, I tied the bemused camels to a telegraph pole, crawled under the wire, and walked up the ballast to the line. Now what? All I'd dreamed of for so long had finished: six months planning, then three months riding towards the Gobi, a month and a half alone in the wilderness. I hadn't dared think through to this point – when it would all be over. Now I was faced with a town, with humans en masse. None of the hospitality extended by the ger here – only people like me, outsiders' with ambitions and dreams: a thousand Kermits, hanging around the bars, sampling the future.

I sat down, right there by the barbed wire fence and made myself a stiff coffee. Then I walked towards the urban mess, kicking through the litter. Perhaps the ger owners on the edge of town would take me in. I braced myself for impact, the town looming larger and larger, louder and louder. A lone figure emerged, shimmering in the rising hot air and dust. He was coming my way, into the desert. And no horse, no camels. He wouldn't last long out here. Did this man know what he was doing? Light flashed from the man's face. The sun had caught his spectacles. They were blue. Ermek …

Ermek was walking out into the desert to find me – with no water, no protection. Now he'd recognised me through the haze as well, and was waving with his maps.

'I have found you!' he said.

'I have found YOU,' I said. I needed rescuing from my town world, but he needed rescuing from the desert.

We began talking at each other. There was so much to say. 'Winter has arrived in Ulaanbaatar!' Ermek said. 'I couldn't sit around there, looking at the frozen rivers. I was getting worried! So I caught the train out here and then I hired a jeep to try and find you, and then got out into the desert and then was arrested by the army – no permit!' He'd spent four hours in jail before they'd believed his connection with me – the strange Englishman that the KGB said was harmless. And Kermit?

'I searched the clubs before I left. Nowhere to be found. But they say he has a new girl friend.'

We walked the camels through Zamin Üüd. The town had been torn to pieces by flying sand and wind. There were dunes between the older buildings, tiles picked off by the wind, windows frosted by sand blasting, green paint seared as if by blowtorch. Other houses had been taken by the Gobi almost altogether, the remains like beach flotsam. Everyone seemed to be repairing their homes, preparing for the winter.

I was still babbling to Ermek, unused to controlling my stream of thoughts into conversation. I told him of the military wells with the padlocks on, how I'd rid myself of Rip-Off. Plans for the future. We agreed to go south by train through Inner Mongolia and see the Great Wall built to keep the Mongols at bay. It would be a fitting end to the journey.

On we went, safely in Ermek's hands. Tetch and Tilt stared at a concrete camel standing outside the police station. Children were dismantling someone's window to peddle for pocket money. Dogs stared at us, then retreated. We made our way to the hotel that lay beside the railway line, walking right beside the track, where carriages were being shunted into sidings. The camels were, like me, agog. How would I have coped with all this alone? I was so, so grateful to Ermek.

We squeezed the camels through the gate in the hotel's fence, unloaded luggage with the help of some street children, then walked the camels to the town pump. Ermek paid for 100 litres worth of water. 'That'll be enough,' he said. It wasn't. The camels drank and drank, then drank some more. They walked, rather bloated, off to the telephone office with me. Ermek put a call through to Ulaanbaatar to tell his wife to get her relatives up here on the next train – I've told Ermek they can have the camels, if they give them a good home. It was now my turn on the phone. I called the UK and, still standing in my desert boots, I told Katie, standing in her wellies in the garden, that I was safe, and coming home.

Left: *New arrivals at Zamin Üüd. All three of us (Tetch right, Tilt left) felt shell-shocked even by a sleepy frontier town after the tranquillity of the desert.*

Below: *Unloading at the Trans-Siberian Railway. The journey was over, not a moment too soon. Winter was arriving and Ulaanbaatar already reported frozen solid.*

No sleep – the still air, the warmth, my legs itching to walk. Outside, the 'humphing' of camels and the footsteps of the old railway man, whose job it is to guard Tetch and Tilt from thieves through the night.

This morning, we gave the camels to the street boys to look after for the day. Their leader has no shoes, but wears adult slippers, tied on with string. He has nothing else, not even access to water for washing off the dust from his eyes. 'Rasputin,' he calls me – I have a ragged beard and mad eyes from watching the desert horizon. The boys brought the camels back, faithfully, at dusk and ran away without asking for money. 'Bye, bye Rasputin.'

I loaded the camels for the last time and they helped carry the bags to the station platform. The train lay there waiting, green and with a yellow band, like a snake, the dust of the Gobi on it. The camels were unloaded and then I had to whisk them away – the customs officers, terrifying women in grey uniform, were getting the neat, dry camel droppings on their smart shoes.

My goodbye to the camels was brief. I should have been practised, but it was as if I'd said so many goodbyes to animals that I'd run out of fresh words. Or perhaps a piece of the Mongolian way of life and death has rubbed off on me: what was important was simply to acknowledge that these camels had stuck by me, had played their part. For my part, I had got them through, and now they would never have to do such a journey again – unless Tetch decides tomorrow that they should both turn around and walk all the way back home.

On the way back to the train, we came across the leader of the street boys in a corner of the station, sitting going through my rubbish bag. 'Why did you run off?' Ermek said. 'We were offering you useful money for looking after the camels.'

'I am happy with this,' the boy said, stirring the litter. He is resurrecting a ripped bag of mine. He wants it for lugging around the bottles he finds in rubbish heaps.

We walked off to board the train. 'When the boy said he was happy,' Ermek said, 'I wanted to cry. He was happy with litter.'

Ermek and I boarded the train, and we looked out of the window at the retreating town. The camels were gazing around them, still as wide eyed as me.

We couldn't take a train south, for reasons I couldn't comprehend. We had to go up to Ulaanbaatar, then back down again, and onward over the Chinese border. I didn't mind, it was a joy to be carried and see the Gobi slip by. Away I was carried to Ulaanbaatar, locked up with ice, the winter already well set in, then back down again, through Zamin Üüd in the night and over the border into Inner Mongolia.

As daylight spread over the plains, Ermek undid the blinds and stretched out on his top bunk to catch a first view of China. 'EVERY bit of ground is used …' Dry hills, golden and green poplar leaves shivering in the autumn gusts. Hay in clumps, spread on tile roofs, leaning on mud walls. After four months of walking through a land of nomads, everything I saw seemed fixed, tied down, even the station masters standing to attention as we flashed by. Maize, onions, cabbage in vivid lines, oxen-leading peasants, it was the same – all seemed fixed, trapped.

I watched through the window, with Ermek and his wife – come to see Beijing as well – I suddenly felt I understood a little more about this man who has haunted me on my journey, and haunted modern Mongolia, on its journey into the outside world – why Genghis Khan slaughtered peasants without compunction. To a nomad, these were a people who were grinding away in the dust; they were owned by it, as were the Islamic and European peoples he destroyed further west. The Chinese were the largest agrarian nation on the planet, but to a nomad they were, like us, no better than sheep. 'Do you only drink water and eat grass, like an animal?' Mongolians ask, if they are accusing someone of being lazy, skinny and generally worthless. To nomads, who exalted in their wandering existence, were masters of the horse and camel, and passed freely over the land, unbowed by it, this was a slavish life. Here, the dirt was the master. So Genghis's procedure was that priests were spared, craftsmen put to good use as slaves and the rest cut down.

'Benee!' Ermek's wife had spotted the Great Wall; it lay clamped over the barren hillscape – angular, bold as electric pylons. It was as magnificent as people always say, a great wonder of the world. But to me, having travelled from Siberia to the Gobi to get here, that mighty wall was a tribute not to China, but the Mongols. Such a giant structure just to keep out those pesky northern horsemen!

The irony is, the felt tent homes of Mongolia all along offered an extraordinary system of democracy and hospitality – the fundamentals of civilisation. The Mongolians allowed me to be part of that civilisation. They made me welcome in their gers, just like any passing herder, gradually giving me modern-day Mongolian heroes to replace Genghis Khan, then building me to the stage when I could accomplish something special to me, a crossing of the great Gobi Desert alone.

A Short History of
MONGOLIA

Mongolia is an arid, land-locked country about the size of Western Europe, but with only two-and-a-half million people living in it, about half of them living as nomads in felt tents. Still known to many as 'Outer Mongolia' (Inner Mongolia is the southern portion, now incorporated into China), this region is one of the highest countries in the world with an average altitude of 1500 metres. It is cut off from that world by the Altai Range in the West, Siberia to the north, and the Gobi Desert to the south.

No one knows where the first Mongols came from, who they were, or even the linguistic origin of their name. Their language is classified under the Altaic group, which includes the Manchu-Tungusic and Turkic languages, and shows strains of Old Korean and possibly even Old Japanese.

One thing is certain, the Mongols were one of many northern Asian, nomadic factions who often intermarried and formed new allegiancies. Mongols would have gone by other names, often names misapplied by baffled early foreign chroniclers. The Mongols were animists – believing in a pantheon of different spirit entities, a relationship with the spirit world guided by a shaman. We know that until the ninth century what we think of as Mongolia was dominated by the Uighurs, a Turkic people whose script the Mongols were to adopt as their own. The Uighurs' defeat by the Kyrgyz (who, with the Uighurs, now live in Xinjiang Province in north China) created an opportunity for the Khitan confederation of tribes (probably dominated by Mongol peoples) to move

Left: The motor vehicle has usurped the horse as the primary means of transport in perhaps every country except Mongolia. At races such as this, Mongolians can still claim to be among the best equestrians in the world, and display their mounts with obvious pride. Jockeys are often younger than their horses.

in to the region in the tenth century. From this point historical sources, for the first time some of them native, report the establishment of the Mongqal clan. Into this clan was born, in the mid 1160s, a certain Temujin, son of Yesugei, a baatar, 'hero' and aristocrat of the steppe. The clan was in a sorry way, having dwindled almost to nothing at the hands of their assorted rivals. According to *The Secret History of the Mongols*, a poetic account of the rise of the Mongol nation composed in 1240, Yesugei was poisoned by a Turkic tribe, the Tatars, and the nine-year-old Temujin fled with his family, eking out a living on the Onon River. Gradually Temujin consolidated his power, forged new alliances and deftly wiped out his clan's age-old rivals, the Tatars – or 'Tartars'. This was a label that the Europeans would later use, in their confusion, to describe the Mongol forces that appeared as if from nowhere. In 1206 a congress of the nomads granted Temujin the title 'Chinggis Khan'. Under Chinggis Khan – 'Oceanic Ruler' or 'Universal King', the nomadic factions north of modern-day China would be united for the first time, with the confederation adopting their leader's clan's name, Mongqal – later fixed as Mongol.

'Genghis Khan', as modern Europeans know him, established his administration by setting out a *yasa*, or set of decrees, many of which formalized rules of conduct and aimed to bring together his disparate people. Genghis Khan adopted the Uighur downward flowing script for his illiterate nation and built a modern, highly drilled army whose disciplined soldiers were promoted through merit. Whether to eliminate any possibility of threat from regional powers, or simply intending to raid the neighbouring settled peoples as bands of the nomadic Mongols had always tended to do, he began extensively to deploy that army on his immediate neighbours. In 1209, with a herding people born to life on horseback and horses honed by the awesome Mongolian winter, he defeated the Tangut kingdom of Hsi-Hsia in north-western China. He then went on to quash the Chin empire of northern China, and in 1218, the Kara-Khitai to the west. The expansion continued when the unfortunate shah of the great muslim empire of Khwarazm, still further west, made the mistake of killing a caravan of Mongol traders. He then compounded the error by executing a Mongol ambassador who had come to seek justice. Though the shah possessed the biggest army anywhere, and had little reason to think this upstart neighbour would dare to challenge him, Genghis mobilized his army again. Moving with extraordinary dexterity, speed and daring and operating from a golden *ger* (or felt tent) that was drawn on wheels – over sand by camels and over rocks by oxen – he applied the same degree of mercy that the shah had accorded his ambassador. Genghis' army demolished the city of Bukhara, as well as the capital, Samarkand – an epicentre of Islamic culture, with a population of 500 000 – together with two dozen other Islamic major towns and cities. Where resistance was offered, entire populations were put to the sword – though priests were often spared and artisans and children packed off as slaves to help build a Mongol civilization. His control established, Genghis sought vengeance on the Tanguts, who had failed to support his campaign, and effectively wiped out the state. By the time of his own death the following year, 1227, Genghis had united Mongolia, conquered Central Asia and subdued the Chin, bequeathing the Mongols an empire more than twice the size of that of Alexander the Great. To Europeans and Asians he was – and still is – the epitome of barbarity. Yet he lived at the time of the crusades, a bloody age even by the standards of our own. By-and-large he spared priests, merchants and those in general not tilling the soil, those whose worth his people, as nomads, could understand. Much of his pitiless reputation stems simply from the shock he inflicted on the sheltered and self-righteous worlds of Christianity and Islam, whose One True God was somehow suddenly allowing them to be overrun by infidels – people without even a fixed town to their name.

After his death, Genghis' body was carried to the heart of Mongolia, his distraught soldiers killing everyone in their path. Whatever his exact burial spot – possibly near Mount Burqan Qaldun at the head of the Onon River, the legendary birthplace of the Mongol nation – it was also said to have been deliberately disguised by the trampling hooves of a thousand horses, and to this day has never been found.

Genghis Khan's even-tempered third son and chosen heir, Ogedei, was elected Great Khan in 1229, and it was he who completely vanquished the Chin empire, launched a campaign against the Sung – further south in modern-day China – and, helped by the loot and the tributes of the newly acquired vassal states, organized Genghis' tent capital Karakorum, in central Mongolia, into a walled city. The great nomadic nation had found it simply wasn't possible to run an empire on horseback. Ambassadors and traders from around the world trafficked to and fro as he ruled from Karakorum, rather too fond of alcohol and the comforts of the capital. He kept control of his empire by means of the *yam*, a network of messenger horse-riders, each of whom were swathed in bells to signal their approach and warn the next post to ready a fresh mount.

From Karakorum, the country's nerve-centre, Ogedei's thoughts were now turning to the area 5000 kilometres away beyond the Islamic world – Europe.

The invading Mongols seemed to come from nowhere. Kingdoms the breadth of Christendom were soon in a state of shock, their heavily armoured knights, designed for the crusades and the confined rules of the Age of Chivalry, were, like the Muslims before them, hopelessly outmanoeuvred by the light and swift, leather-clad horsemen. The Mongol way of life lent itself to warfare. They hunted with a short and powerful composite bow designed to be used on horseback, and were well practised in raiding other tribes. Moving an army, with its accompanying livestock, was no different to moving an everyday campsite. Kiev, the political capital of Russia, was lost to 'clouds of Tartars' in 1240 and refugees flooded west. The Mongols deliberately let them flee to bring fearful reports of the oncoming storm of horse, sword and arrow. Poland and Hungary fell next and the Mongol army was now on the Danube, having eliminated the elite forces of Europe. The Mongols, though according respect to priests and diplomats, had shown scant understanding of the concept of 'mercy' for those who had foolishly offered resistance to their will.

Below: In Mongolia land is free outside towns and croplands. One of the most contentious bills to come the way of the new democratic parliament is one concerning land privatization. Inevitably, people are bound to start erecting fences across the land, like nearly everywhere else in the world.

Every ruler and every settlement up to the Atlantic now lay at the mercy of a country they couldn't even place on the map – in particular, at the mercy of the empire's central, or Golden division. Colours designated the cardinal points of the compass (giving us the Red Sea and Black Sea) and the Golden *horde*, literally 'Central Palace', was led by the brilliant Batu, offspring of Genghis Khan's eldest son. He was ably assisted by Subedei – Genghis' military right-hand man, who'd left a trail of dead Persians, Turks, Georgians, Russians and other hapless peoples in his wake and was perhaps the greatest commander the world has known. The future didn't look good for Europe. Then, much to the amazement of the shattered European armies, as Vienna prepared to be levelled, the Mongols suddenly turned and rode home.

News had arrived from Karakorum that Ogedei had died: the Mongols needed to elect their new Great Khan. The fate of Europe was to be decided in the heart of the Mongolian steppe. For a while, Ogedei's widow reigned as regent and during the jockeying for power Europe was forgotten. Ogedei's son Guyuk – like his father, something of a drunkard – was elected in 1246. He was an unpopular man and only his death, two years later, prevented a civil war. Mongke, grandson of

Above: *Changes are underway. Mongolia is an asset to the US and Japan: positioned beside China and Russia, it is beautifully placed geographically. Maybe, like Switzerland, it can successfully use the Great Powers. Its people's resilient nature and their heritage of self-reliance, are in its favour.*

Genghis and rival to the title, won the election of 1251. An elightened ruler and reformer, he strengthened law and order and encouraged religious debate between Christians, Muslims and Buddhists. However, when they conspired against him he killed many of Ogedei's remaining sons; he wrapped his widow in a carpet and lobbed her into a river to drown. A great general, he also shared the expansionist aims of his father Genghis. Fortunately for Europe, the far West was perhaps considered a doubtful prize and Mongke chose to send his brother Hulegu to tighten control over the Islamic world instead.

Sadly, Baghdad resisted and in 1258 Hulegu sacked the city, sparing only the Christians – once each member of the garrison had been marched out and executed, the remaining population were butchered. Some Persian accounts claimed total losses nearing 2 million. The Caliph and male members of his family were treated to a lavish feast then sewn into another Mongol carpet and trampled to death by horses, while the women and children were marched off into slavery as usual. Islam faced ruin as a political force. However, in 1259, in the same way as Europe before it, the Islamic world was saved by the death of the Khan, Mongke, who had died of dysentery while in southern China fighting the Sung. The following year saw the election of Genghis Khan's broadly educated grandson, Khubilai Khan.

Khubilai had been schooled as a child by both Chinese and Uighurs and had administered northern China from Shangdu, the Xanadu of Samuel Taylor Coleridge. He soon began building Dadu, a lavish new capital in China, in the region of modern-day Beijing. According to Marco Polo, he had assembled a collection of the finest trees in the world – brought to Dadu by elephant. His banqueting hall could serve more than 6000 men, there were pearls from India and more than 1000 cartloads of silk arrived daily at the capital. There were 20 000 prostitutes and from this Marco Polo concluded 'you may infer the number of traders and other visitors who are daily coming and going here.'

Khubilai Khan's foreign policy was an active, though chequered one. In 1279, the Sung empire was at last defeated but an earlier expedition had failed against the Japanese, and in 1281 a second launch against them was caught by a *kamikaze*, a typhoon or 'divine wind'. Most of his 150 000-strong army were drowned or killed.

Nevertheless, by the time of Khubilai Khan's death in 1294, he had unified China, and developed an extraordinarily complex structure of government. His administration included, for example, tax policies to encourage peasant farmers – his census revealed that his grandfather's genocidal policies had reduced their number from some forty million to below nine million. In two generations, the Mongols had changed from destroyers of the settled world to restorers of it.

Khubilai Khan's empire stretched from Korea to the Danube, but he was the last great Mongol ruler: control of the different khanates, the portions of his empire, was already slipping away. In 1368 the Mongols were driven out of China by the Ming army. The Mongols reverted to clan warfare and although Altan Khan (1507–83) again briefly united most of Mongolia, introducing Buddhism as the state religion and also worrying the Chinese enough to make them build the Great Wall, disunity and civil war followed his death. By 1732 Mongolia had been taken over by one of their traditional enemies, the Manchus, whose Qing dynasty ruled over both the Chinese and Mongolians with increasing brutality. When the Qing dynasty collapsed in 1911, the Mongolians quickly declared independence, establishing a theocratic government under a Bogd Khan, or Holy King. The Russians had already taken some of the north of Mongolia (in the Lake Baikal region), and China some of the south (Inner Mongolia), but both countries were aware of Mongolia's value as a buffer against the other. In the Treaty of Kyakhta, signed by Mongolia, Russia and China on 25 May 1915, Mongolia was accorded a high degree of autonomy.

Only four years later, in 1919, taking advantage of the chaos of the Russian Revolution, a Chinese force entered Mongolia. In February 1921, retreating White Russian forces expelled the Chinese, but they proved to be an army of occupation and Mongolian nationalists soon sided with the advancing Bolsheviks. By the summer, a joint Mongolian and Bolshevik force had captured the modern capital, Ulan Bator (nowadays spelt Ulaanbaatar) and on 11 July that year, the People's Government of Mongolia was declared, under the Mongol force commander Damdin Sükhbaatar. Socialism had done the impossible – pulled off a revolution in a country with no social classes, where among the herders there was no proletariate to free from chains.

Mongolia's independence was further eroded when, in 1924, the Bogd Khan died and the communists tightened their grip on power by proclaiming the country the 'Mongolian People's Republic'. Following Lenin's death, his successor Stalin appointed a puppet ruler, Choibalsan. By the thirties Mongolia, like Russia, was undergoing a sequence of bloody purges. Private enterprise was virtually outlawed, livestock was collectivized, monks shot by the hundreds and books which each nomadic family kept, recording their family tree, were burned. By the end of the decade, as many as 30 000 Mongolians had vanished, presumed executed.

Soviet control continued through the Second World War– during which Japan attempted an invasion – and on after the deaths of Choibalsan and then Stalin in the early fifties, under the comparatively liberal Tsedenbal. Only with the crumbling of the Soviet Union, and the easing of relations with China, did things change. Gorbachev retired Tsedenbal in 1984 and two years later his replacement, the reformist Batmonkh, was beginning to implement a programme of decentralization and economic liberalization. Soviet troops began a slow withdrawal. Then, in March 1990, pro-democracy demonstrations erupted en masse in front of the parliament building in Sükhbaatar Square. Batmonkh was forced to resign and the government forced into holding multiparty elections that July. However, much to the bewilderment of the outside world, the Mongolians did what no member of the Soviet Block had done and actually voted the communists back in. In reality Mongolia, the world's second oldest communist country, had been culturally eclipsed by the Russians, and was reliant on the infrastructure, schools and hospitals of the Soviet era – which had given them a literacy rate of 98%, a rate far beyond that of the United States. The plethora of democratic parties had promised 'democracy' but that had meant harsh reforms and uncertainty and an end to the innumerable local collectives (*negdels*) to which every herdsman and herd belonged.

Nevertheless, in order to get themselves elected, the communists had been forced to promise freedom of speech and free enterprise. Mongolia now underwent massive change, as the hitherto protected Mongolians (the population is composed of 85% Khalkh Mongols, and the only other large ethnic minority, the Kazakhs, are 6% of the total) had to cope with the brutality of a market economy. The urban élite, educated in the Soviet Union, prospered under the new trade opportunities while pensioners, teachers and all those still dependent on state support, did not. Nor was the country rid of the ministerial bureaucracy of the old days. On 30 June 1996, a coalition of young democrats won a majority in the Mongolian parliament, the Ikh Khural. After seventy years, the communists were out of power.

As I set about preparing my expedition through Mongolia, the Mongolian Democratic Coalition was still winkling out the last of the Old Guard. Mongolia's literacy had fallen, but only to an estimated 95%,

Buddhism was undergoing a huge resurgence and Mongolians were showing themselves to be extraordinarily adaptable to free market principles. However, though coal was mined extensively, petroleum potential being explored and sheep and goat skins, cashmere, molybdenum and copper exported, less than one per cent of land was cultivated. The temperature extremes and dry climate made most agriculture impossible. Fortunately, some would say, with the proximity of China (either a threat to Japan and the West, or the greatest market opportunity yet seen), Mongolia was again seen as a useful client state. Capitalists poured money and their culture into the country. A philosophy of respect for the land, inherent in their nomadic system and shamanic and Buddhist tradition, was now being challenged by notions of 'development' and 'progress'. The baseball hat was de rigueur and some urban young even entertained hopes of Mongolia becoming a new Hong Kong. The Mongolians had access once again to the world stage, but this time without their Genghis Khan.

Select BIBLIOGRAPHY

The extent of English material on Mongolia is extremely limited. The following publications were those I found the most thought provoking:

AVERY, MARTHA *Women of Mongolia,*
Avery Press, 1996

Sensitive portraits from across the country, illuminating the joy and anguish of the everyday.

BAWDEN, C.R. *The Modern History of Mongolia.*
Kegan Paul International Ltd., 1989.

Much has happened since – not least during – the year following publication but it remains a standard text.

BECKER, JASPER *The Lost Country: Mongolia Revealed,* Hodder & Stoughton, 1992

Travelogue rich in historical anecdote.

BERGER, PATRICIA AND TSE BARTHOLOMEW, TERESE *Mongolia: The Legacy of Chinggis Khan,* Thames and Hudson, 1995.

Elegant, illustrated and authoratative book, designed for an exhibition at the Asian Art Museum of San Francisco. Draws on the history and culture of past Mongolia but always manages to be alert to what is vital in the present day.

BRUUN, OLE AND ODGAARD, OLE, (EDS.) *Mongolia in Transition: Old Patterns, New Challenges,* Curson Press Ltd., 1996.

A range of concise information for those seeking to understand the bewildering changes underway.

CHAPMAN ANDREWS, ROY *The New Conquest of Central Asia,* American Museum of Natural History, 1932.

One of the most accessible of the many accounts available by the American palaeontologist and adventurer whose journeys into the Gobi in the 1920s unearthed some of the most important dinosaur remains this century.

COURTAULD, GEORGE *Travels of a Fat Bulldog,* Constable, 1995.

Dairies of a Queen's Messenger, whose diplomatic forrays occasionally took him through Mongolia. He gives energy and lustre even to the ordinary.

FINCH, CHRIS, (ED.) *Mongolia's Wild Heritage,* Mongolian Ministry for Nature and the Environment, Avery Press, 1996.

Authoratative digest of the key elements of Mongolia's environment and natural history, concluding with a sorry list of endangered species, many of which are now only found in Mongolia.

GERMERAAD, PIETER W. AND ENEBISCH, ZANDANGIN *The Mongolian Landscape Tradition: A Key to Progress,* published by the authors, 1996.

Though obscure, what seems to me to be one of the most insightful publications on the role of Mongol customs in the preservation of the land. Under the Mongol nomadic system, land was carefully maintained as was the capacity for sustaining livestock. 'Today, however, rural land use in Mongolia becomes more and more a process based on the application of alien (mostly Russian and Western) planning approaches under the banner of 'progress' and modernisation.

MARSHALL, ROBERT *Storm from the East: From Genghis Khan to Khubilai Khan.* BBC Books, 1993.

A fine, gripping round-up of the Mongolian saga of emergence.

GOLDSTEIN, MELVYN C. AND BEALL, CYNTHIA M. *The Changing World of Mongolia's Nomads,* The Guidebook Company Ltd.,1994.

Incisive on the everyday dilemmas of a changing rural Mongolia. This account, illustrated in colour, is by anthropologists studying herding life.

HEISSIG, WALTHER AND DUMAS, DOMINIQUE *The Mongols,* Pinguin-Verlag, 1995.

Available at museums in Ulaanbaatar, this is a catalogue designed to accompany a German exhibition and serves as a useful conpendium of the traditional cultural items and ingredients of Mongol life.

MAN, JOHN *Gobi: Tracking the Desert,* Weidenfeld & Nicolson, 1997.

Travels to investigate the Gobi written with thoroughness and thoughtfulness.

POLO, MARCO *The Travels,* translated by Ronald Latham, Penguin Books, 1958.

Classic, often allegedly eye-witness, account.

MIDDLETON, NICK *The Last Disco in Outer Mongolia,* Sinclair Stevenson, 1992.

Chatty account of wanderings as the communists were still clinging on to power.

RATCHNEVSKY, PAUL *Genghis Khan: His Life and Legacy,* Basil Blackwell Ltd., 1991.
Articulate examination of the life of Genghis – 'corpses paved his road to power'.

SEVERIN, TIM *In Search of Genghis Khan,* Hutchinson, 1991.

Travelogue by an accomplished horseman, particularly interesting for the changes underway at that time, just after the fall of communist rule, and his often underlying exasperation at Mongol horsemanship.

TSULTEM, N. *Mongolian Sculpture,* State Publishing House, 1989.

One of a series of fine, glossy hardbacks, this one notable for dealing with the early stone carvings dotted across Mongolia – in the Altai the characters are often depicted with knives and tobacco pouches. Earlier engravings feature deer, from which many people, including the Mongols, believe they were descended.

YUNDEN, YA, ZORIG, G. AND ERDENE, CH *This is Mongolia,* undated.

Advice for the perplexed visitor. Written in broken English and in the days of the Mongolian People's Republic, but has the merit of having at least been written by Mongolians.

ANON, *Program of Land Protection and Rational Land Use Policy for Mongolia's Lake Hovsgol-Selenge River Watershed,* Mongolian Ministry of Nature and the Environment, 1994.

An illustrated document detailing issues pertinent to the Khövsgöl area, but also threatened environmental degradation throughout Mongolia.

ANON, translated by Francis Woodman Cleaves, *The Secret History of the Mongols,* Harvard University Press, 1982.

Part poetry, part history, the medieval tale of the rise of Genghis and Mongolia from the steppe.

ACKNOWLEDGEMENTS

This book owes its existence to the government of Mongolia which allowed me to wander freely and alone with my cameras in places which were remote and often militarily sensitive. Also to the four hundred or so nomadic Mongolian families who, without exception, unquestioningly welcomed me into their homes.

It's an account, like *The Skeleton Coast*, from my diaries: there's no place for 'artistic licence'; the reader gets a depiction of Mongolia as I found it, or as I think I found it, as I went along. To provide a context, at the back of this book, there is a brief history of the country.

Ten per cent of my income from this book will go towards a variety of projects aimed at helping the street children of Mongolia off the streets and back to their families, this through the Christina Noble Foundation. Anyone who is interested in this cause might like to contact the foundation at 10 Gt George Street, London SW1 3AE.

I am indebted to those four hundred families, but also many others:

The vital role of Tleikhan Ermek and Rasaal Khurmit, will, I hope, be obvious from the text. Less obvious will be my gratitude to Nara Gombo who I bumped into in West London when I was first thinking of travelling to Mongolia. Nara diligently and patiently taught me the rudiments of Mongolian before passing me on to S. Obilig, 'Ogi', my only contact out in Mongolia. Ogi helped me feel at home in Ulaanbaatar, enabling me to begin establishing a long, long, chain of contacts which would see me into the project – and out on the other side.

The chain began with Wilfred McKie, Sergelen, Tsolomon and Hartsanhu in the office at the World Bank Transport Rehabilitation Project. Wilfred provided me with a wealth of emotional and practical support as I built up an expedition base in Ulaanbaatar. He found me Chimeg, who helped steer me around the capital in the first weeks, and Ermek, who propped me up during the second recce and was my bastion and link man through the expedition proper. Meanwhile, a battery of teachers worked tirelessly on my lametable Mongolian – Davaasuren, my second teacher, Chimeg my third, Sergalen my fourth, Ganchimeg my fifth and Sarandulan my sixth.

Damdiny Gansukh in the Ministry of External Relations, and Ts. Jambaldorj at the London Embassy, helped champion the idea of the expedition to the Mongolian government. Mr Avirmed allowed me through the Gobi National Park, but also lent me much time and thought. I would particularly like to express my appreciation to John and Shan Durham and the staff of The British Embassy – Kevin and Jane Brind and Sue and Tony Bird – who offered not only a continual stream of support but also access to their precious emergency food depot. John Durhan took an extraordinary interest in me and my camel and horse colleagues, also supporting me in an initial idea of travelling on right to the Great Wall. Catherine Doro, Geof Viner, Kate and Terbish at Nomads, Vicky Bartholomew of Camel Trophy, all gave their thoughts and expertise.

The zoologist Elizabeth Hofer gave me a string of her own contacts, and was the first to tell me about Tom McCathy and Priscilla Allen, both old hands in Mongolia and working on the Snow Leopard Project at the time – they accepted me as though an old friend. A long chat about Mongolian culture with G. Boshigt served me throughout, enabling me to see a bit beyond the obvious in contemporary Mongolia. Boldbaatar Sodnam, from the Gobi Corporation, took time to introduce me to industrial Mongolia; David Pearson, many from VSO and also Lois and David Lambert became greatly valued friends. Back in Britain between recces, Penny Aikenhead and the vet Mick Ponting thoroughly educated and enthused me about the Mongol horse.

Jo Sexton willed me on throughout, organising dispatches of sunglasses, riding trousers, even muesli to keep me going. Photographer Adrian Arbib as usual leant all available energy to the project. Diana Maclean gave me deeply valued moral support, while Estien McKenzie steadfastly fended off all non-Mongolian correspondance and beaurocrasy while I was out of contact. Claire Hermione Dean and the people at Hi-Tec bolstered me with encouragement and resupplies of boots and shoes. I'd also like to thank those at John Smedley, whose longjohns, as promised, kept out the frost.

The editor, Anna Ottewill, with all her usual skill and expertise, guided me along and brought this book to fruition; David Cottingham lent me his patience and judgement to help me weed through the hundreds of both Adrian's and my own photographs. My thanks also to Isobel Gillan for her flair in designing the book, to Olive Pearson for her work on the map, and to Bill Games for his research and proofreading work.

The television side of the project owed its existence to Mark Thompson and the Community Programmes Unit under Giles Oakley. Bob Long, the Executive Producer, guided the idea along, and stood by me, back in Britain, as he had before in the Amazon and Namib. Salim Salam, my producer, propped me up, and went on to make sense and beauty from my hundreds of hours of often dodgy video diaries, conjuring from them a very true protrayal of the journey and, I hope, the country. I would also like to thank Bhavesh Hindocha and Andy Collins for their skill and input, Ruhi Hamid, Carole Gilligan and Fiona Kenneth for their special encouragement, Sue Brewer for her constant assistance and Akiko Ono for her insight and perspective. In this series, as with *Skeleton Coast*, the editor Guy Tetzner has made something special in its intregrity and honesty.

INDEX

Page numbers in *italic* refer to illustrations

Abominable Snowman 169, 179, 181, 187, 211
Achit, Lake 126
Adrian (photographer) 75, 76, 84, 92, 95, 168
Altai mountains 28, 39, 41, 63, 96, 100, 123, *154*, 171, 239
  hün chuluu (stone men) *38*
  Near Dayan Nuur *30–1*
Altan Khan 245
Amgalan (shepherd boy) 165, 166
armies, Mongol 127, 150–1, 152, 153, 240–1, 242
asses, wild 172, 190, 226
Avirmed, Mr (Head of the Gobi National Park) 59–60, 62, 97, 108, 166, 184, 187, 189

Baatar (driver) 29, 32, 46
baby care 42
Bactrian camels *40*, 101, *102–3*,
Bakbold (brother of driver) 29
Bankhar (dog) 100–1, 105, 109
Batmonkh (Soviet leader of Mongolia) 246
Batu (Mongol prince) 151, 243
Bayan-Ölgii aimag 125
Bayantooroi 181
Black Death 8, 152
Bogd Khan 245
Bold (driver) 29, 32, 34, 36, 46
bubonic plague 8, 152
Buddhism *62*, 245, 247

Erdene Zuu temple complex 73
Bukhara 25, 241

camels 17–18, 156–7, 205
  abandoning their leader 200–2, 204–8, 217
  assessment by the vet 108
  Bactrian 40, 101, *102–3*
  Bastion *159*, 165, 172, 174, *179*, 188, 189, *191*, 191–203 *passim* , 208–9
  Bert *159*, 165, 166, 172, 174, *179*, 188–91 *passim*, *191*, 192, 197, 200–3 *passim* , 208–9
  buying 64–8, *74*, *75*, 108, 158–61, *159*, 212–13
  in the Desert Steppe *161*, *162*
  Freddie 68, 69, 97, 98, 100, 106, 108, 112–13, 117, 124, *127*, 128, 132, 133, 140, 144, 145, 205
  and Genghis Khan 40
  in the Gobi Desert 40, 101, 172, 173–4, *175*, *179*, 180, 187–237 *passim 218–19*
  'homesick' 60, 62, 96–7, 98, 106, 145
  Jigjik 117, 119, 122, 125, 128, 132, 140, 144, *159*, *175*, *186*, *191*
  Jigjik 2 165, 166–8, 172, 173–4, 188, 191–203 *passim* 204–8, 228
  loading 40, 98–100, 117, 119, *170*, 184, 189, 192
  milking 198

No.2 68, 97, 98, 100, 101, 106, 108
  Rip-Off 215, 216, 220, 223, 224, 227, 228, 229
  Tetch *214*, 215, 216, 220, 222, 223, 224, 229–30, 231, 233, *234–5*, 236
  Tilt 216, 220, *223*, *226*, 229–30, 231, 233, *234–5*, 236
  Top Camel (T.C) 65, 68, 69, 70, *74*, 97–8, 98, 100, 101, 106, 108, 112, 116–17, 119, 122–5, *passim*, 129–32 *passim* 144, 145
  treatment of 161–4
  Wart 117, 122–3, 125, 129, 130, 133, 140, 144
  wild camel of the Gobi desert 101
children 34–5, *106*
  horse races 135–7
  in Ulaanbaatar 17, 122
Chinbaatar 116, 119
China
  Great Wall of China 8, 233, 237, 245
  Inner Mongolia 216, 231, 233, 237, 239
  and the Mongol empire 240, 241, 244–5, 245
  Mongol raids on 180–1
  and present-day Mongolia 247
Choibalsan (Soviet leader in Mongolia) 246
Choinjin 184, 187, 188, 190
communist rule in Mongolia 246

consultants, European 20–2, 75
Curse of the Three Gers 84–5, 105, 144

Dalai Lama 73
Dayan Uul 141
Desert Island Discs 24
dogs 60–1, 70, 97, *118*, 119, 197
    Bankhar 100–1, 105, 109
dress of Mongolians 13
Dundoi *38*, 41, *42*, *43*, 43–6, 72, 113, 125, 140, 140–3, 166, 230
Dundoi (Kazakh shepherd) 32

eagles 45
    Little Yellow *42*, 44, 45
Erdene Zuu temple complex 73
Eej Uul (Mother Mountain) 181, 184
Ekhiingol 184, 203
Emon (bar) 20
Enkhjin 64, 65
Enke 48, 52, 79
Ermek 28–9, 32–61 *passim*, 63, 71–2, 75, 79–85 *passim* , 92–3, 96, 140–2, 144, 145, 166, 168, 188, 192, 209
Ermek
    at Bayantooroi 182
    at Ehinhol 203, 204–5, 209, 210
    in Zamin Uüd 232–3, 236
Europe, Mongol invasion of 242–4
European consultants 20–2, 75

food 44–5, 76, 104, 105, 121–2, 128, 142, 149, 151, 155, 158

Gana 55, 85, 86, 88, 89
Ganbat (camel owner) 64, 65, 68

Ganchimeg (teacher) 61
Gandan Khiid monastery *62*
Gansukh, Mr (Ministry of External Relations) 16, 23–4, 27
geese 217
Genghis Khan 9, 13, 21, 25, 36, 72, 104, 168, 215, 240–1, 244
    and camels 40
    death and burial 241
    fear of dogs 119
    and the Mongol army 150–1, 240–1
    and nomadic culture 237
    and the shamans 79
    and Subedai 88, 166, 243
gers (felt tents) 9, *10*, 12, 32, 33, *35*, 80, *99*, 125
    around Ulaanbaatar 14, 61
    construction *98*
    Curse of the Three Gers 84–5, 105, 144
    customs and hospitality 101, 104, *183*, 237
    dismantling 95, *99*
    of Genghis Khan 240–1
    in the Gobi Desert 64, 172, 176, 194–6, 225
    Kazakh 137, *138–9*, 141
    layout 33, 35
    and the Mongol empire 74
    overnight stays 33–7, 92–3, 148–9, 156
goats 95, *142*, 146, *147*
Gobi Desert 11, 13, 17, 25, 32, 63, 88, *154*, 165, 171, *206–7*, 239
    camels *see under* camels
    climate 205, 210
    crossing 187–237
    herdsmen 106
    landscape 63, 68–9
    planning a route 59–60
    snow 227
    and television 194–6

water sources 28, 29, 75, 180, 184, 194, 196, 220–1, 224–5, 227–8, 229
    weddings 176–7, *182–3*
Golden Horde 13, 243
Govi-Altai *aimag* 40, 152
Great Wall of China 8, 233, 237, 245
guanz (roadside café) 157
Guyuk Khan 243

herdsmen 106, *118*
horse races 135–7, *238*
horses 17, 24, 39–40, 45, *107*, 124, 126, 148
    The Beast 77, *78*, 80, 85, 89, 92, 93, 100, 114, 120, 122, 126, 129, 133, *247*
    The Chestnut 126, 128–9, 133, 137, 140
    Burnt Umber 148, 149, 152, 156, 158, 165, *167*, 168, 173, 180, 182, 189
    buying 76–7, 120–1, 146–7
    condition of 97–8
    deaths of 133, 137, 140
    on the Gobi Desert journey 175, 180, 181–2, 193
    grey horse with wonky feat 121, 123, 133, 140, 144, 146
    Hairy H 156, 157, 158, 166, *179*, 182, 189
    and Kermit 77, *78*, 80, 85–6, 89, 93, *94*, 101, 120
    manes 166
    mare's milk 144, 146
    and the Mongol armies 150–1, 153
    and Mongol saddles 62, 63, *171*
    Mongolian attitude to 89, 93, 140
    Packhorse X *150*, 156, 158, 181, 182, 189
    Przewalski 172–3

and reindeer *90–1*
shoeing 123–4, 147
Ulaan *59*, 92, 101, 115, 121,
128, 129–30, 133
Khövsgöl Lake, west of *70–1*,
Khövsgöl mountains 65, *66–7*,
78
Hulegu (Mongol prince) 244
hün chuluu (stone man) 38
Hungary, Mongol invasion of
151, 242
hunting 149–52

ibex 171, 197
Enkhbold (brother of driver)
32, 37, 46
Inner Mongolia 216, 231, 233,
237, 239, 245
Islam, and the Mongol empire
244

Janibeg Khan 152
Japan, and Mongolia *243*
jerboas 230

Karakorum 72, 73, 241–2,
243
Kazakh woman *134*
Kazakh gers 137, *138–9*, 141
Kazakh grandmothers *146*
Kazakhs 32, 130–1, 140, *143*,
246
Dundoi *38*, 41, *42*, *43*,
43–6, 72, 113, 125, 140–2
goats and sheep *142*
grandfather and
grandchildren 148–9
Kermit (Khurmit) 46–7, 48,
49, 53, 55, 56, 60, 61, 92–3,
121–2, 158
at Dundoi's 141, 142
at Songon *sum* 116
at Tsaagan Nuur 80, 84
birthday 164–5

and camels 64–5, 68, 72, *74*,
75, 97, 98, 100, 108, 113,
117, 124, 131–2, 159–60,
201
and the Curse of the Three
Gers 105, 144
and the desert 119–20
'equipment requirements'
61, 63
and the Gobi Desert
journey 69–72, 168, 169,
171–2, 173, 174, 175,
177–80, 188
and horse races 136–7
and horses 77, *78*, 80, 85–6,
89, 93, *94*, 97–8, 101, 120,
126, 129–30, 146, 148,
149, *150*, 152, 155, 156,
157
in Khövsgöl aimag 104
motorbike accident 108–9
in Ölgii 135, 145, 146
and *ovoos* (roadside
shrines) 113, 157
Khitan confederation of tribes
239–40
Khovd aimag 41
Khovd river 126, 127, 128,
130
Khövsgöl aimag 104
Khubilai Khan 53, 72–3, *74*,
244–5
Khwarazm (Muslim empire)
240–1
Kyakhta, Treaty of (1915)
245
Kyrgyz 239

Lamaism 53, 73
land privatization 242,
242
literacy rate in Mongolia
246–7
Little Yellow (golden eagle)
42, 44, 45
log cabins (moveable) 41

McCarthy, Tom 181
McKie, Wilfred 27, 28, 29, 180
Mad White Giant (Allen) 24, 27
Manchu dynasty 245
Marco Polo 153, 165, 178, 244
market economy in Mongolia
246, 247
marmot hunting 149–52
Marshall, Robert, *Storm from
the East* 11
medieval Mongol armies 127,
150–1, 152, 153, 242
Mendee 195–6
Moguls 8
monasteries, Buddhist *62*, 62
Mongke Khan 73, 244
Mongol armies 127, 150–1,
152, 153, 242
Mongol culture 124–5, 184–5
Mongol empire 73–4, 241–5
Mongol saddles 62, 63, *170*,
171
Mongolian Democratic
Coalition 247
Mongolian language 15–16,
25, 239
Mongqal clan 240
Mörön river *94*, 95
mosquito zone 152–3, 155–8
Möst *sum* 159, 161
Munke 48, 49, 52, 53, 55–6, 79,
80, 81, *82*, 82
Murat 128, 130, 131, 146
music 21
herdsmen in the Gobi
desert 106

Naadam (annual holiday)
131
Nara (Mongolian student) 11,
25, 27
Naranbulag *sum* 123
Near Dayan Nuur *30–1*
nomadic culture 41, 74, 95,
114–15, 119, 237
and the Russians 114, *114*

Ogedei Khan 72, 73, 241–2,
    243
Ogi 11, 13–15, 16, 17
Ölgii 96, 98, 122, 126, 127–8,
    130, 144–6
ovoos (roadside shrines) *26*, 53,
    113, 132, 157

Pearson, David 23
poisoning 101–4
population of Mongolia
    109
Przewalski horses 172–3

Ratchnevsky, Paul 79
reindeer *47*, 47, 49, 89, *90–1*
    herders in Siberia 89
rickets 76
Rubruck, William of 73–4
Russia
    Mongol invasion of 242
    Soviet control of Mongolia
    245–6

saddles, Mongol 62, 63, *170*
    171
Sainbayar 48, 53
Samarkand 241
Second World War 246
Sergelen 180
Serikgul (daughter of Dundoi)
    141
shamans 53–5, *54* 79, 80–2,
    82–3
    see also Tsend
Shamarowal (Jockey No. 66)
    136–7

Siberian border 28, 29, 88–92,
    239
snakes 187, 189–90, 226, 229
snow leopards 181
Songon *sum* 116
Soviet control of Mongolia
    245–6
spring 64, 76
Stalin, Joseph 52, 73, 246
Subedei (Mongol military
    leader) 88, 166, 243
Sükhbaatar, Damdin 245
summer 109, *110–11*
sums 32

Takhiin Tal 172
Tatars (Tartars) 240
tea (Mongol) 35, 39, 151 *151*
television 17
    in the Gobi Desert 194–6
Temujin (later Genghis Khan)
    104, 240
Tengger (sky god) 33
Tengis river 86
tents 79, *174*
    see also gers
Trans-Siberian Railway 209,
    216, 231, 232, 233, *235*, 236–7
Tsaagan Nuur 47–57, 79
    tents *50–1*, 80, 86, *87*
Tsaatan *86, 87*
Tsedenbal (Soviet leader of
    Mongolia) 246
Tsend (shaman) 48, 52–7
    passim 54, 72, 77, 79, 80–5,
    82, 83 109, 140, 156, 166, 230
Tseshuu *198–9*, 204–5, 208–9,
    210–13, 215, 217–20, 222,
    230

Tsetserleg *sum* 106–8

Ugantsetseg *47*, 49, 52, 53, *54*,
    55, 79
Uighur people 239
Ulaanbaatar 13–14, *15*, 59,
    61–2, 72, 245
    and nomadic culture
    74
United States, and Mongolia
    243

van der Post, Laurens 24, 25,
    27, 72, 220
VSO workers 22, 23

weddings, in the Gobi Desert
    176–7, *182–3*
William of Rubruck 73–4
winter *18*
    survival strategies 32
wolves 180–1, 193
women
    Kazakh *134, 146*
    milking goats 146, *147*
world politics, Mongolia and
    243, 247

yaks *34*, 92
Yesugei (father of Genghis
    Khan) 104, 240

Zamin Uüd 216, 231, 232–6,
    234–5